THE SCALABILITY COEFFICIENT

TREVOR HALL

Steward House Publishers
Port Orchard, Washington, U.S.A.

Visit the Steward House website at www.stewardhouse.com

STEWARD HOUSE and the Steward House logo are registered trademarks of Steward House Publishers, LLC.

The Scalability Coefficient

Chief Executive Officer, Steward House
Sharalyn Shafer (sharalyn@stewardhouse.com)

Editor-in-Chief, Steward House
J. Gryphon Shafer (gryphon@stewardhouse.com)

Cover Art and Design
Chris Kennedy (chris@stewardhouse.com)

Manufactured in the United States of America.

ISBN-13: 978-1-937097-09-7

US $27.95

To my best friend, my beautiful bride. You've never stopped believing in me and always stand next to me. Thank you for your love, patience, and strength in all the crazy things we do together.

To my children, who remind me every day how powerful curiosity and imagination can be. I hope this book can be an example of why you should never sheathe those weapons.

I love the three of you with all of my everything. And for everything you are to me, this book is yours.

Introduction

Businesses operate on a complex network of information and decisions. Good, bad, made, or unmade; the heartbeat of every organization pulses decisions, pushing information like blood. They need one another to survive. Politics, assumptions, gut reactions, and leaps of faith are all drivers behind these decisions in every business. Although power, hunger, and faith are all part of the human spirit, they can be a detriment to the success of any business or unit therein. The larger the organization, the more each these attributes are magnified. Growth will increase the complex nature of each of these interactions, but we must never forget complexity must be embraced in every organization, big or small; growing or shrinking. To avoid irrational decisions making takes planning and forethought. You must be able to consider every affected element in your environment before making decisions in order to make a sound decision. You must be able to make quick and precise decisions at the same time; not all decisions can take a month's worth of analysis to perfect your answer. How can anyone be successful at making sound, logical, and factual decisions; considering all affected complexities and components quickly?

The Scalability Coefficient's goal is to outline a new paradigm of business analysis. By taking an engineering-centric approach to the break-down and organization of any business, this book will show you how to reconstruct your thoughts into a logical masterpiece that will help you determine how to make changes in any given situation. The method will demonstrate a path to understanding how to digest the intricacies of your business and how they relate. From determining which employees are best suited for a given project, to which projects the company should even consider, to if the company is organized correctly to absorb the projects it plans to take on. The actions taken will remove the abstraction between the direct business operations, creating higher visibility. It is with any level of abstraction that the details of its operations become vague, information becomes incomplete, and assumptions begin to patch in. This is where the strength of decision making begins it's decent into an eventual breakdown. Visibility is half of the goal here, the other is how to effectively organize your operations so you can fully understand them, remember them, and act on them; potentially changing them. To have a complete information is our primal focus. But complete information is impossible in any fluid, complex business - every business. It's the organization of the visibility that provides its memory, the memory providing a path to quick, intelligent, and precise decision making based off facts gained from the truths of your functioning business.

What This Book Is

The Scalability Coefficient will demonstrate the application of this concept through the means of a fictitious company that should resonate to any reader. Intellicorp Inc. will demonstrate how easily a small company can dissolve into dysfunction by blending their needs and wants with inefficiencies, incompetence, and brilliance. You will get to know this company, its people, its products, its goals, and its failures. The book then breaks this company down into its smallest logical parts. It then evaluate these parts, their meanings, and their relationships to then assemble them into small, independent, and logical equations that will summarize the particular component. This is the Scalability Coefficient for that component. Continuing this process, you will begin to see the relationship between each component as the book creates a broader Scalability Coefficients that fits the entire organization, comprised of the Coefficients of its subordinates. The goal of this process will not be to memorize math functions or to copy and paste the specific equations into your organization. Rather, you will learn:

Organizations Are Complex

At any scale, companies, organizations, teams; are all complex. This complexity should be embraced and leveraged, not discouraged.

Understanding Your Business

It is easy to lose sight of how your business works when looking from the outside in. It's also easy to lose sight of what your business goals are when looking from the inside out. This book will teach you that you that decision makers must do both.

Decisions Based off Fact

Provable facts are the catalyst to the best decisions. This book will teach you how to separate fact from fiction, removing the ability to make assumptions while collating each facet into a function which will explain your critical business components.

Effective Memory Management

It's one thing to dissect and evaluate the smallest intricacies of your business. It's a another to remember everything when it comes to decision time. The book will direct you in a level of thinking that combines reiteration, alternative creation, and explanation.

Effectively, by reviewing evaluations respective of one another and formulating them with a new way of thinking, you remember the main points of each focus and interaction.

The Pattern of Thought

Making concrete, trustworthy, and factual decisions is a product born from forethought. Thinking and forethought are attributes of a strong leader, which come naturally to some and not to others. When followed, this book's methods will lead you down a path of critical thinking that will become your second nature as you continue to use it.

What This Book is Not

The Scalability Coefficient will demonstrate a new method of thought and practice to aid in decision making, but it is not and never will be a replacement for your existing methods of decision making. This is key to remember. The audience this book is aimed towards are already decision makers, are to become decision makers, or who want to become decision makers. Whatever title best suits any individual, it must be acknowledged that decision making is a cognitive part of the human experience. The instincts, knowledge, experience, and other un-attributable and assumptive traits of your decision making up to this point in your life should still be part of your decision making process. The Scalability Coefficient's intent is to expand your ability to make decisions, and help refine them to become consistent and sharp. Decisions are building blocks, where each one builds from the one before it. But life and business can sometimes feel like you're balancing ten spinning plates at a sprint. That environment isn't conducive for a thorough examination of all the variables at play. In this situation, or when you have time to sit and consider all your options, your businesses Scalability Coefficient will only help you to find what is best for your business at the time of execution. Knowing and applying the principles of the Scalability Coefficient will be your new tool when you have the time to ponder larger decisions, where the memory of past applications through reiterations will provide you a new toolset for when time is crunched and key decisions need to be made now. It is a new tool you can use to help create the building blocks of decisions you will take up your career's ladder.

Section 1
The Beginning

The quintessential goal of every leader and decision maker is to understand their organization. The ultimate definition of where every company, big or small, wants to be "right now". It is near impossible to get to this ultimate destination. The few who can get there become the target of others generation after generation. For those who are still fighting to become that company, many attempts are made; few with success. And although (buzz) words change and paradigms shift, trends in decision-making always remain the same. Older companies want to be young again, remembering when they could bring product to market in a week rather than a month or longer. New companies want to be big, delivering products efficiently and intelligently while expanding their product horizon to differentiate their income. Throughout each of these organizational progressions is a transition; a step down or up, but a transition nevertheless. A primary goal of any business is to find the efficiencies that have been lost in growth and to capture the ones that are apparent so they are not lost. The ultimate question becomes: how do we take these steps and how do we prevent the steps all together in order to define or redefine ourselves.

Every organization has nearly the same goal and ideas of how to get there. The forgotten concept is they do not always have the same road to get there. Changing the software development life cycle of an organization may benefit efficiency, but will it maximize it? How do you know? Why would one web-based company work well under an agile development philosophy where another company exact in structure and nature would not? Why would change seating arrangements of critical employees to a project work well with one project and not another? It is rarely about the paradigm or thought process of a team or organization. The success or failure of either is a direct function of the attributes that compose the makeup of the product, the project(s) and the team. Not to say an agile philosophy will not succeed in most organizations. To the contrary, it is that the organization must be prepared to undertake this paradigm. Your organization is not a mold of every business concept and design.

The goal of this book is to remind decision makers of all the attributes of their organization and how they work together. I am to instruct the dissection of any organization into its logical and modular pieces. This disassembly will demonstrate how to articulate how your business works in order to make informed decisions on its behalf. You will learn to digress from theories, assumptions, and personal philosophies to take a look at the real facts, leading you to real, logical, and explainable decisions.

What to Expect

My hope for this book is to demonstrate a new, different way of applying critical thought to your organization. My demonstrations should prove you that your organization is complex and you need to think that way. It doesn't matter if you're a century old company that has hundreds of product lines or a new start up that has one. If you and your buddy are not in your garage being paid by donated Mt. Dew cans - your organization is complex and you need to embrace that fact. The more you can accept the complexity, the easier it is to understand it and make logical, qualified, and justified decisions with respect to the complexity. I am going to suggest a precise, and new way to think. Rather than thinking of what level of engineers to put on a project, for example, think of what *kind* of engineer you want on a project.

What is the quantifiable difference between the different levels of engineers you have as resources versus the ones you have available? How would each difference impact the project based off the known? It is not about taking the subjective attributes of the project respective of the people you have fit, but the factual evidence behind them; a designed and logical approach to making sound business decisions and what to do with them. Do you like SCRUM over some other development philosophy? That's great, but you need to position your organization so it can absorb this philosophy as efficiently as possible. You must take the attributes of that particular agile team and position your team's attributes so they fit. Otherwise, it is like fitting a square peg in a hole that doesn't exist. Even if you have engineers who know how to make holes, it won't be the best fit.

Goals and Things to Remember

The bulk of the content of this writing is an example of a thought process I suggest you take. Although you should not spend your next few weeks taking the literal equations I outline herein and apply them to your organization (although you can and still be better off than if you didn't). Instead, think of your organization as a combination of small particles that can be arranged to fit your needs and how to evaluate each particle as an independent contributor to your goals. Where I do want you to absorb the concepts and algorithms from the outlined examples and customize them to your specific business.

Every action has a reaction. Not, necessarily, an equal or opposite reaction but a reaction all the same. You should expect linear (or less) time patterns with growth and development. Each relative and similar change should not take longer than the last (with exceptions). You can dissect your organization down to measurable components that can be applied to mathematical algorithms that are suitable to your organization.

A Coefficient of Complexity

We must remember in business that very few things are simple. We can add labels to products, calling them "beta" or "hacky" but that alone will never make anything simple. The minute you leave your garage and stop paying yourself in empty aluminum cans is the very minute most things in your business become far more complicated then the day your original idea was born. We want to keep everything simple - keeping things simple implies things will get done fast. Yet when speaking to a business, particularly one that thrives from software-related products, the realm of simplicity quickly falls off the table altogether. What I've found in most organizations that like to "keep things simple" in terms of design and implementation is they don't really mean it. Leaders try to solve for the least common denominator of design to get a product out the door but forget they may have been dealing with prime numbers all along and there's no reduction in complexity from the beginning. Some say that the application of simplicity is really the distribution of complexity, which implies complexity, is like energy: it can be neither created nor destroyed. In fact, to define simplicity is a very complex matter. In the grand scheme of things, the concentration on simplification isn't ever the true desire of leaders. Is giving yourself a "beta" tag or asking your team to "just hack it together" to keep things simple really what you want? When you release a sub-par product and customers fall from it like flies or call and complain about something not working - is it suddenly the biggest priority of the team? I would be willing to bet the answer is yes. This means you do care about what your customers want and that is not a piece of crap with a bow on top. It is the simplicity that you are looking for or is it the time and efficiency gains that come from the perceived goal of a simple design?

Memorial Complexity

I am reminded of a Memorial Day celebration that took place in Honolulu, Hawai'i in the early summer of 2009. I remember this event less because of the dramatic speeches or symbolic references to the near by Pearl Harbor, but much more to the "behind the scenes" coverage the local news station had on the event. The coverage was a specific report on how the coordination of the United States Air Force took place in order to get to-the-second perfection of a traditional, symbolic Air Force fly-by after the mayor's speech to the attendees at the Punch Bowl. The Air Force's coordination efforts were far away from anything simplistic, to say the least. What I found more interesting was the mayor's speech. At eight minutes in length, it was a well-prepared speech that received good critical acclaim from all of the attendees. An eight-minute speech is a simple task for someone whose career is based on public presence and presentation. Simple in theory, yes, but in reality: absolutely not. The speech was originally scheduled to take approximately eight minutes. As with many organized events of this nature, there were scheduled activities on either side of his notation, each with seconds or minutes of variability in their entertainment. Each one compounding on one another could be a matter of a few seconds to a minute or more of time shaved or added to the allotted time the mayor had to speak. This is commonplace for people in his position. This practice is only a matter of taking the variations into consideration when writing the speech to have different cutoff times to ensure the climax of the presentation takes place in the time that is left. The added complexity of the Air Force's fly-over, however, played an interesting part in this eventual schedule alteration. If the mayor strayed, even by a few seconds, from his scheduled stop time, he would effect the dramatic demonstrative conclusion displayed by the Air Force, causing them to either slow down or force a re-approach. Both events would cause a major disruption in the local air space, colliding with Honolulu's International Airport. An improper adjustment of his speech would therefore ripple down not only to the flying conclusion of the ceremony, but also travelers to the Island along with impacts back to other coastal airports that are the hubs to the local flight paths. In other words, assuming the entire ceremony was perfect in timing from start to finish, the mayor would be given eight minutes to speak. Over or under by any range of seconds would impact people as far away as 3,000 miles. This simple eight-minute speech was nothing simple at all, weighted with cause and effect that the mayor needs to know and plan for before he takes the podium.

It must not be forgotten that complexity is inherit in any business. The thing people forget is that it is OK to have complexity. I suggest that you harness the complexity by understanding the intricacies of your business in order to gain efficiencies from it. If you hide your complexities in a cloak of simplicity, you will never be able to gain from them and therefore lose time and money. Not only do I suggest you embrace the complexities that surround you, but will try to prove that measuring each of them individually will allow you to reposition what you have dynamically to best suit what you plan to do next. For example, if you like the vision of creating a "hacky" environment that allows for developers to smash different little pieces of product out the door in a small measure of time - that's great. In fact, for the right business model, I think it's a brilliant idea. The truth is that to do this - to make simple mini-products and throw as many against the wall as possible to see what sticks - is a very complex process. But again: complex is not bad or scary - it's just complex. So you must approach these organizational-wide decisions with a mind that has organized your complexity in order to ensure you arrive to the most well informed decision. Building a system that is "hacky" can be fine. You must, however, have a system in place that allows your products to be reliably built with infinite hacks. And that is the hard part.

The question then becomes, "How?" What can be done to evaluate an entity in order to determine how to gain efficiencies from it?

It's certainly not about changing paradigms or development philosophies within the organization (although I'm not suggesting doing so is bad - change is good) as each is a complex matter. It's about breaking your organization into smaller particles and evaluating the measurable characteristics of each element in order to come to. The sum of these characteristics, *The Scalability Coefficient*, will present you a usable metric, which you can then use to make or change decisions with. By evaluating the complexities of your dynamic organization, you can make the best decisions into how to take it where you want to go next.

A Warm Welcome

Drawing examples of exactly what I mean by all of this: let's assume you are a technical leader and have worked with the larger part of your organization to introduce a more agile methodology into your development life cycle. For this example, let's also assume that the adoption of an iterative incremental framework for managing complex work is adopted to support the agile methodology. In doing so, you and your product managers realize you are comprised of two exclusive teams of developers who work on two independent software systems; each team consisting of one Senior and one Junior Engineer. The future will bring a number of two projects, including the team integrating these two systems. From the surface, this all seems easy enough; a small engineering staff with two independent pieces of software, each team presumably the expert of either respectively. At the surface, yes. Yet there is so much more to take into consideration. How do the Junior Developers grow over time? Does more experience in the team give people with lesser experience more to work with over the course of larger projects? What happens if the teams to combine their products? Does the cross-functionality grow the complexity as a whole? If so, by how much? Is it a function of Metcalfe's law or less of an exponential network effect? How do you take future projects into consideration when half of your new, joined team has minimal experience with the opposing portion of the application? What happens if multiple projects hold requirements respective of the latter portion of the newly joined application? How do you form your teams? Will cross team member's work well with one another? Would it be a positive investment to re-write the entire application all together, or would the return take too long to be feasible? How do you evaluate whether or not the gained efficiencies from a new system will come to fruition in a reasonable amount of time? What could be done in the same period of spent time to do or come to another conclusion? Do the two Senior and Junior Engineers equate to the same level when now compared against their respective counterparts? What if each of the Senior Engineers has twenty years of experience? What if, for one of those Engineers, ten of those years were with the same company; the last five of which with the same team? What do the difference between these two people with the same tenure of career experience bring to the team and to new projects in the future?

These amongst countless other tedious yet similar questions are the ones that should be asked over and over again when determining the assembly of the general and efficient structure you need to develop and deliver your products to the best of your ability.

You can see that from the surface, a very simple project can easily become something far more complex. As I will continue to reiterate throughout this writing: this is okay. Pretending everything is simple is just as ignorant as making something overly complex. There is a middle ground to well-educated decisions that could make or break your business, and through my suggestions I'm assured you can find that happy medium. By dissolving your organization into desolate and independent attributes, we will be able to analyze each of them in order to draw decisive conclusions of what can be done to gain efficiencies throughout the whole of them all or as individual parts. I will further explain to you how each of these measurements can be reused and manipulated in order to find the solutions you are looking for. Whether you are trying to find a good paradigm fit or you are trying to fit your organization into a paradigm, I will explain the different attributes that you must look at in order to come to a reasonable solution in how to evolve your organization.

The dissection of your organization is the catalyst you will use to come to independent and specific Scalability Coefficients. Before we begin with this, I will explain what this term means.

Scalability

In 2000, André B. Bondi noted, "scalability is a desirable property of a system, a network, or a process, which indicates its ability to either handle growing amounts of work in a graceful manner, or to be readily enlarged," which I would agree is the partial definition of what scalability means in a full technical organization. I say this with a level of ambiguity, as I believe this definition - as with so many others - only takes the physical pieces of a developed product into consideration. While I do think this is a critical piece that should be considered when evaluating scalability in the scope of any organization, it should be generalized a bit to encapsulate the entire organization. "How well a particular solution fits a problem as the scope of that problem increases" is a much better definition by Theo Schlossnagle, as it does a better job of explaining the same concept while taking more into consideration. A team must scale with the product they are developing, which must scale to its customer-base gracefully as it grows and shrinks. In terms of our earlier example, how will the new bond between the applications fare with the current and projected user and consumer base? How will the team's work with one another and how will their experiences with the opposing pieces of software impact the development of their respective products? If the Senior Developer, for example, was only a Senior Developer on one product, then his role doesn't really scale into the new team. If that same Senior Engineer is 50% less efficient in writing code in half of the new application, then something or someone must be there to replace the other lost 25% of his lost productivity assuming all projects are equal and spread evenly across the two halves. That 25% loss can become very costly not only in terms of product delivery, but in morale and other social impacts that are difficult to measure. The same consideration should be put to the new application itself. Does the new integration steal 25% performance from the old business cases they independently solved as they are attempting to solve the new one(s)? This could be a substantial loss if it is a direct reflection of new hardware purchased and the hardware is inherently expensive.

The point is, scalability isn't just about what your server's load average is. It's about how your organization fits into change; from an organizational, product delivery and personnel management perspective.

To define the scalability of an organization is well beyond the scope of this book, however. The point of this writing is that every organization is rigidly different in so many ways that I couldn't begin to hand out cookie cutters of how to define them. There are, however, ways to evaluate them, which I hope to help with.

Coefficient

In mathematics, a coefficient is a constant multiplicative factor of a certain object. A coefficient is a constant, as pi is always 3.14159265[...]. Always. Our coefficients are constants as well, though I like to consider them a constant multiplicative for a constant state of time and can allow for change within this dimension.

Regardless of the definition, in terms of this book, the coefficient is the constant multiplicative that can be assigned to an evaluated sub-particle of your organization and can be used in evaluations of change to determine if the alterations are best for the situation you are in. I will demonstrate how to assign people in your organization (in a technical setting for the scope of this book) their coefficient in a number of different situations. As I will explain in much richer detail later, individuals can have numerous coefficients depending on the environment. In the context of a team, a project or as an individual; each will take into consideration a different set of attributes, each contributing to the contextual coefficient of that organization's sub-particle.

Scalability Coefficient

The combination of the two terms is where I find the best application of the description. The essence of what most decision makers are hunting for is the maximization of the output respective of the input over the course of time. You want to produce more and better products over the course of time than your competitors in an attempt to make money. This is a truth you will have to always carry with you throughout this reading; remember this if nothing else. From the goals we all have, we can extrapolate two ideas. The first of the two being:

The maximization of the output with respect to their input.

This is nothing more than one of many definitions for efficiency. You want your input to be less than or equal to your output. Pure or 100% efficiency is when your input is equal to your output. Adding little and producing a lot is the goal of everyone - beyond pure efficiency if and whenever possible the second idea is:

Gain efficiency over the course of the companies existence.

This is scalability in a nutshell - the ability to sustain the gained efficiencies gracefully over the course of time and changes.

The combination of these two ideas formulates a number of different concepts to evaluate throughout this writing. Where can we gain efficiencies? How do we measure our current state so that we can control our decisions? How do we predict future states?

What attributes can we take into consideration and which ones do we ignore when finding efficiencies? All, and more, are questions I will help you answer throughout the progression of this book.

This book isn't simply intended to show you how to measure efficiency, but how to modularize it to the point where you can use the information and thought processes you will gain from this reading and apply it to countless past, present and future decisions. Where the teachings herein will demonstrate how to make true, educated decisions and how to change your organization to better itself. You will learn how to build your organization so that it can sustain effective efficiencies over the course of time and endowing the confidence in your decisions by harnessing one of the few static principals of every business: math. You will learn how to convert the attributes of your organization into hard numbers that can be readily evaluated. The Scalability Coefficient is a concept you can measure your organization with. That measurement is your organization's specific Scalability Coefficient for that point in time. That number will be the ultimate summation of your organization, accounting for every aspect of your critical operations. With change or adjustment to any particular component, your coefficient can change too. It will demonstrate how simple changes can cause exponential, logarithmic, or linear growth (or declination) in your Coefficient, where the closer you can get to 0, the better (where 0 suggests you are doing nothing; the absolute most efficient thing to do). More than a single number, the implementations of how to obtain the number is where the learning is. The Scalability Coefficient is nothing more than a guide to help ensure you are making wise decisions, not the gospel of how to succeed.

What to Expect

The nature of how to evaluate your specific Scalability Coefficient is a largely complex matter. The best analysis that can be done is built from a thorough analysis of your company and your organization, which should span from the construction of the organization to the micro-attributes that make it. I will navigate you though numerous situations of you and I working together as a pair of consultants for Intellicorp, a fictitious company that will task us with numerous goals and assignments. We will work through each of them through a process of evaluation of the situation and application of our specific Scalability Coefficient. The intent of this exercise is to show the levels of critical thinking that are necessary when making complex decisions for your complex business. The point to remember throughout is that this will be an example narration. This is not your company, any company you've ever worked for, nor any company you will ever work for in the future. This comes from the perspective of two contractors trying to learn a company and apply the Scalability Coefficient. Although this is not an example of your real world, the examples will be relevant, the theorems precise, and the points clear. You can work with our situational analysis and integrate it into any environment. You can take from this the thought process and general philosophy I have taken to demonstrate what can be an extremely powerful decision making tool that can be wildly successful if you take the time to carefully analyze your company, apply my philosophies and have a good enough memory to keep track of the different pieces of your responsibility.

The Buildup

As mentioned earlier, the analysis we will derive throughout the entirety of the writing will be based off the following fictitious example narration. Although it is your prerogative to skip over this, leaping directly into the meat of our problem solving, I don't recommend it. The narrative will take you through a high-level interrogation with the teams at Intellicorp which will prove to be the foundation of the analysis at the heart of this book. Choose your own adventure.

SC, Inc.

You and I have had quite a career together. We first met in college as strangers holding the legs of a stranger vertically over the luminous glow of the moon shine glimmering off of the aluminum shell of a dented keg. Finding humor in the otherwise awkward situation we were in, a quick chat opened up just how similar we have been. We learned we were dorm roommates for the past two years. Through the pony wall of pizza boxes and the maze of cabling, monitors and other standard geekery we interestingly never crossed paths even though we shared a bunk. It was nice to meet you and I'm certain you had said likewise. It wasn't shortly thereafter when we started working together closer with some of the local companies throughout the greater Seattle area. Mostly small businesses, some large; doing the only thing we knew how to do - pretend to know everything about computers, software and technology and get paid for it. Through the final years of our undergrad, desperately trying to keep our head above water by keeping our clients happy while maintaining our rigidly high-standard of mediocre grades, we found ourselves becoming more confused and frustrated with the decisions that were being made around us. We found an amazing level of consistency with critical decision-making that resembled a listless bear hunting for fish in a dry lake just before hibernation time. No thought or foresight was applied respective of the environment or the decisions being made therein. The companies were always taken back of how the company could never meet their goals or come to sound decisions. At the time, what did it matter - we got paid by the hour. Without it, we would have to revert back to the pitchers from the leftovers of the previous night's tap rather than the high-class variety of mass-produced American lagers. We soon graduated against our will and without a penny to our name yet with a small handful of happy clients; all to our surprise. It was with our observations and our diminishing education that we started paving our muddied, golden road and founded SC, Inc.

It's been 20 years now and if nothing else, we have flourished. We have hired on a number of new consultants, have worked with some of the largest companies in the world and continue to have an extremely satisfied customer base. Best of all, over the years we have been able to specifically decipher what exactly it was that most of the companies that had come before had lacked in their foresight. With those and other experiences, we have been able to build a general algorithm that when applied to an organization with surgically precise analysis were able to demonstrate how to make better and well informed decisions. We called this the Scalability Coefficient. It had become our eternal torch of infinite fame (in a small planet only known by a few). That small, make-believe world was just enough to keep a roof over our heads and we were satisfied. Yet, it is with this that we can continue to work with clients, helping them with their specific organization problems.

Our most recent consult was for a medium-sized company based out of Downtown Seattle name Intellicorp. Their primary revenue-generating product was an intelligently marketed online question-and-answer portal. A simple idea where if someone were to have a question, they could post it to their site and have a community of specialized contributors would answer back in a timely fashion. Their market differentiator was their patent-pending system of applying sourced data to the questions and augmenting the answers with relevant research topics. Patent yes, bot no. It is what they used to gain notoriety in the blogosphere, nods by some of the top media agencies and swarms of investors knocking at their door. Still, a little known company that had a commonly fought problem: their revenues were in the red, product was taking longer and longer to release, profits were non-existent, investors were becoming upset and the relevant content market differentiating bot that was intended to make them rich and famous had yet to get off the ground in terms of development. They knew something had to change, but they did not know what. They knew they had a million ideas they wanted to throw against the wall, but every time they tried to do so things oozed on slower than molasses in wintertime. They contacted us.

Foggy Mountain Breakdown

Our first meeting was with little prior knowledge about the company's situation. The receptionist gestured towards a single room, walled with glass and shaded with pulled blinds. The only light to the room was from the partially exposed windows facing the outside, the sunbeams glistening off the dust in the air. We sat on opposing sides of the table hoping to hear about how another company eroded into the same situation as so many others. Three men faced us on the opposing end of the rectangular, wobbly table; each without introduction or credentials nodded as if to suggest a welcome. The dark room and three expectant, cold, unwelcoming men made us both feel out of place in our tee shirts and shorts. It's our expertise they sought not our wardrobes. The yet introduced man at the head of the table leaned comfortably back in his chair, brushing his hands through what was left of his comb-over. After a large sigh of discontent, he started to spill his guts. First came his name and his title: Charlie McFey, Executive Vice President of Enterprising Technology. He threw an ocean of information our way with no less than a piece of Styrofoam as a life preserver. Our experiences with this very situation, to our benefit, have gifted us the ability to understand and summarize what our needs were. The organization isn't too large with three development teams, each managing between one and four network applications of one flavor or another, each with between three and six engineers of varying skill and expertise. Although the teams seem to have great rapport and morale, the product cycle had become longer than what seemed reasonable. For a stable, new company existing for three years, things were moving at a snail's pace compared to the way things used to be. It was not that the gentlemen sitting before us were naive in thinking growth did not create complexity, but more that they could not explain how it could have changed so much. It seemed quite dramatic. We were debriefed, at that point, in their vision and goals. They were going to work with the product teams in finding a new development methodology. The current, somewhat organic method was simply not working any more. With declining revenues, they were facing layoffs, which everyone feared. They needed help. They didn't need help with finding a development philosophy as much, but to find where all their time has been going. This is where our expertise starts to shine. They didn't know where things would take us afterwards as with layoffs, contractors come first and the investors are getting itchy to cut costs. Our marching orders were given.

Web Application Team

The first step of our process was simple: we had to learn what the composition of the teams truly was. A vague definition of numbers and general skill sets were useless when taken out of context. The first team we came to was the "web team", an intelligent team consisting of two and four Software and Web developers, respectively; all managed by Chet Smith who was more of a working manager than a team leader - but was full of useful advice. When we brought the team together to try and learn more, we found ourselves in good company. The awkward geek humor oozed from the enchanting laughter around the room, well into the first quarter of our half-day meeting. Although it seemed as though no control was had with the welcoming party, it didn't take long for the team to settle to a whisper while the room's concentration re-directed to Chet as he began to speak. He explained in further detail the history of the team, including the legacy of the applications they managed. The front-end web application was the primary application they managed, still in its first revision and being stripped of its original code from the "founder days" (as the endeared term told the most of that story). The second of their applications originated as their page cache tier when surges of traffic were taking the rather unstable site down at the time. Although it was intended to act as a stopgap until the time a "better solution" could be developed, it now acted as a central caching tier for the entire company. Each time the team spoke of "C", the name coined for their caching tier, laughter filled the half the room and groans filled the other. It was apparent the application that received little attention or little was still an integral piece of the organization's architecture. Along with jovial conversations about archaic applications, a trend of realization also came about revolving around the reality that the two applications were in a lot of ways the most critical to the success of the organization. A blissful wave of pride rippled through the team each time this became apparent. With all of this arose the roles each of the members played. Chet was indeed their leader and rightly so given his position, but most of the pecking order was otherwise linear. Judging from conversational contribution alone, it was apparent the two software developers had far more experience with the intricacies of the applications they worked with, which was later quite suggestive of the tenure the pair had with the company relative to that of their web developer counterparts. Nothing much more came from the rest of the meeting as it drew to a close, with the exception of a few more jokes orbiting their beloved applications and executive members of the board. Chet, however, decided to stick around through the remainder of our free lunch to discuss some of the interpersonal and social elements of his team, which we were quite interested in. The remainder of our time was mostly about the living history of the company, the team, and the application set.

Strider Johnson was the first development hire for the company which at the time was nothing more than a slender startup and a lean bankroll startup; coupled with nothing more than an idea, a web site and the beginnings of a prototypical demonstration of what the idea would look like if someone were to develop it. Fresh out of college with a Bachelors in Computer Science, Strider was more than eager to put in his time to see an exciting startup through its paces, applying all the great things he had learned through the finest education the local community colleges and remote universities had to offer. For six months, he was able to evolve the prototype into the original vision of the company, powered by caffeine and raw intelligence while in his proverbial development vacuum. The release of the founder's evolution of a product by Strider was the catalyst for the companies series B funding which immediately brought on the capital to hire Arwen and Erwin Little, two brothers out of Western Kansas and the launching pad of the jestering from the meeting before. The duo had crusaded as a pair of under-qualified developers across the small business circle which somehow led them to Charlie, who had yet started with the company. He knew the founder through some network of randomness before. Through this relationship, they found themselves with an offer letter to start full-time with Intellicorp. Knowing the lack-luster technical climate that was available from the small-business circuit of Western Kansas, they packed up their Atari and mountainous wolf tee-shirts and headed to the Pacific Northwest. Arwen's experience led him more to be more helpful to Strider than anything else, where Erwin's passion had always been in more of the user-interface side of things, becoming the companies first resident, full-time web developer. The trio never really became that great of friends, but were able to drive the product even further, to the point where the company was starting to see some growth; slow, steady growth. Over the course of the few years that followed is when Chet, Perl Wall and Grace Hopset were hired on as the hiring manager, and web developers respectively (both in terms of order and position). Through the years, and to our dismay, the team had not seen a trickle of turn over, neither internally nor externally through standard attrition (an interesting point we certainly took note of). The silence of inter-office instant messaging was the pungent queue to the stench of geek that swarmed this bunch, but the content that illuminated from the rectangle that comprised the web-tier applications team was an interesting one.

When Chet had completed his tranquil voyage into the description of his beloved subordinates, he seemed less divulging when it came to the description of the applications themselves. We were not only able to strangle read-only access out of him, but we were also able to get some of the more general details out of him as well. This did suggest that to the contrary to the "working manager" statement he made earlier, he mostly works on shielding his team from inane banter of corporate politics. The conversation didn't yield us without any fruit, as the things we did learn were to be quite useful. The Quality Assurance team, although regarded amongst the rest of the development teams and conveniently left out of Charlie's original description of the organization, was far too small to undertake the large amount of testing that was required for the entire organization. A small percentage of new development would be passed through the QA department (if any) for a given project. Over the course of time, the application undertook a level of versioning that would take place behind the primary proxy. The intent was that a small percentage of the visitors to the site would experience some of the new features for a project and in theory expose issues and requirement misses along the way - acting as a guinea pig for the project as it were. The versioning system was nothing more than stand-alone installations of new code in one or more of their web-servers in their server cluster, yet it was a way to enjoy the benefits of skipping a QA phase while exposing the vulnerabilities of the same practice to small batches of random users at a time. The cluster that entertained the multiple versions of the web-tier was, fortunately - and for some definition of fortune - bound to a few constants. First, only one version could run on a particular server. There are five web application servers in the cluster and therefore only five versions that could run concurrently. This also implied traffic to the application could only reliably be split into fifths of the full traffic load, else the undue expense of overloading the rest of the servers would overshadow any success or failure of the version in test at the time. As is the case most of the time, budgets are always tight and the concept of virtualization lost in the clouds somewhere never let the team grow their clustered application hardware past the complete minimum of what they needed to run the site with only a single version. The web application, as we found out before, was still in its first revision of its original architecture. Things have been added and removed over time, but the underlying core of what embodied it was still a direct product of the founder's original work in conjunction with Strider's vacuum coding efforts when he first began just six months after its original creation.

The cache tier, which had been mentioned and ridiculed over, was a different story all together. As was mentioned before, the birth of "C" was intended to be no more than a stopgap measure to prevent the sudden popularity of the site made by a plethora of blogging and news aggregation sites. Simple in its design and implementation, "C" was nothing more than a distributed memory bucket suited to store compiled HTML pages for quick return through an initial proxy. The celebration over its success appeared to be its demise, as it was never planned to make it past the second version of the web-tier when the maturity of the organization "grew up". As with most great ideas, the execution didn't happen quite as planned. Life happened first and neither the priority nor funding was given to create the second major version of the web-tier. As life usually decides to make its own course and follow the path of success, so did the rest of the organization's blossoming software counterparts: the search and the information collation teams, both of which we were promised to visit with in the days that followed. The simplicity and reliability of "C", coupled with the cost that had already been taken in its development, spelled enough success for the perpendicular teams that needed a fast, reliable memory bank for somewhat static data that was reused often. Just as ecstatic as the team was to never see "C" die, they eagerly anticipated its solidification as the newly founded teams started to use its features without much more than a crashing server as notice. It was the beginning to what would become the glue that held most of the company together and the Rogaine that would be applied to the hair losing developers that maintained it, all at the same time.

I'm Feeling Lucky

With a new day came a new team to sit and chat with the search team, the smallest team in the organization, with two developers and nobody to manage the lot. They were a simple service organization that somehow maintained operations by feeding off of a bug queue sorted by age and priority, both of which were managed by the external teams. If someone needed to search something that didn't exist, they would file a bug. Sometime thereafter, it would show up with email notification from the bug. Sometimes, it wouldn't. By definition of the pair, it was the forgotten team of overwhelming necessity. Their transparency was so fluid it became their cloak. The benefits of a black box enveloped them as they staggered into the meeting a half hour late, barely contributing too much of anything. We had brought obvious attention to them and they didn't like it. And they had no problems with making it apparent with direct body language and other passive aggressive gestures.

Exemelle (we only know her first name) seemed to have come out of nowhere to start the search division nearly a year and a half prior to our meeting. She spent a lot of time avoiding her origin with the company, although her lust of search melted from her personality. From her recollection, which spanned back to the dawn of the search tier, the project started as the need for the site to gain unique data sources grew. She was tasked with finding different methods of accessing new data sources and pipelining them into a single interface that the web product could use. Although the concept seemed sound, it was the beginning and end of the direction she would receive. With this lack of direction came innovation to the point of destruction. From the original direction, and her dedicated hours of research on the topic, she came to the conclusion that the best solution for the job was to build on top of the open source search and indexing platform, Lucine. Out of the box, the open source engine was customized. It was customized to the point where an upgrade was as close impossible as anyone ever wants to travel, slowly evolving the search engine into less of a community supported application into a proprietary show box of data organization and retrieval. Even to this point of her tenure with the team, there wasn't a client to consume the non-existent data. This quickly changed with the rising of the data. It was then that the organic definition of the team would be created. Exemelle brought on Bugzilla, an open source bug and issue categorization and tracking system, originally to keep track of all the work that was pending up in her personally prioritized queue. It was when the data team came into fruition when she realized she would have to cater more to their needs than her superficial ones. It would be their data after all that her system would be searching, so it was only logical her focus changed. It wasn't intentional to begin with, but every interaction she had with the new team, the retort was the same "file a bug and prioritize it". She gave the team permissions in Bugzilla to manage their own specific queue, which she always promised would be worked on in order of priority and age and descending order respectively. To her content and hard work, this method satisfied the new team. It was when then web team came into the picture that the demand for her work outgrew her ability to get it done. Like ants following one another, she asked of the web team the same as she did for the data team: "file a bug and prioritize it" for all requests of her time, which they did religiously and to the point where they stopped asking and immediately filed the bug. "Persistence is great that way" Exemelle chuckled as she fed her stringy, black hair back behind her ear away from her face. Not much time had passed before her bug queue was starting to grow out of control and well beyond her means. Without a manager, she spoke with Chet to see what she could do about getting another person on board. As good fortune had fallen her way before, a young college graduate out of the University of Washington had just started on Chet's team yet was turning out to be a little too junior for the projects that were coming down the pike. He seemed like a natural fit for the now-growing search team and Exemelle enjoyed his company and fresh attitude.

James Cartwright sat directly across from me and started to smile as the nostalgia of the year passed washed over his memory. When he started, his job was nothing more than familiarizing himself with what was going on by fulfilling the requests in either respective bug queue. From his knowledge with the web platform as he had just transitioned from, he worked mostly on their queue. As the obscene learning curve finally settled to more of a plateau, the team did well in fighting off the randomness their system provided with good work that six months later led to the joining of the data team and the web team via their highly customized version of Lucine. To this day, their system continued to work well enough to hear little if any complaints from either of the independent teams. Their queues continued to grow over time. Yet their adopted methodology was quick to work against them as each independent development team continued to fill the backlog with issues of the utmost urgency.

Information Super Highway

The data team was one of the last pure technical teams we met with over the course of the first week of our contract. Of each of the three teams we had worked with up into that point, they were the newest and certainly the snarkiest and most cynical of the bunch. Each team member was brought on near the time the group was first formed about a year prior The three of them filed into the room, sitting down with one seat separating each another along the faux oak table. It had seemed that wind had been caught of our team-wide meetings and perhaps questions and assumptions of our presence were making their way around the office. That or the group was simply a unique bunch that had a vendetta against anyone new they came across. We were no exception to whatever level of judgment they were giving us and it was obvious we were outnumbered. With a few quick introductory questions, surrounding the information we already knew after working with the search team, we learned that the manager of the group: John Overheimer. John was the one who intended to keep control over the conversation. Certainly we had no objections to this stance as our quest was to seek information rather than to pass judgment - as long as he satisfied our goals of learning of the composition of his team. He was quick to point out his qualifications, spanning from his undergraduate education through his masters and all the positions he held in between, emphasizing on his executive experiences. Each were laid with meticulous detail and an overdone verbosity while a smirk filled his face while he slid his five page resume across the table, stopping out of our reach and forcing us to stand and pick it up. Flipping the pages through my fingers like a blackjack dealer finding his way to the joker at the end, I made note of the first position he took as a data-mining technician for a company I can't remember from 1992. All of this was interesting enough, but it seemed to be more in the tone of maintaining his superiority complex rather than helping us with our mission. Much of this passed and to our content, yet after enough it was time to learn more about the team and technology he managed than himself.

Percy Greentrain sat to the right of John and was the first introduced. He was their sole data analyst and coordinator whose responsibilities were as wide and ambiguous as his title. His primary job was to maintain the different data streams into and within the company. Their primary and most volatile data source was their proprietary store of user question and answer information. It was up to Percy to evaluate the quality of the data to see how it could be improved upon. Working closely with the search team to ensure it was being indexed well and even closer with the web team to ensure it was coming to them in the most managed state possible. He spoke with striking accuracy in answering each question with noticeable efficiency and elegant pronunciation embodied with an emotionless and static tone. Somehow through his robotic disposition, his sharp wit made him just likable enough to consider him more of an ally than a foe. This was a genuine and refreshing feeling as the growing undertone of our presence was becoming quite the opposite. As we dug more into his daily contributions to the company, we found him to be the underpin of everything the company was successfully doing nothing about. The data that was intended to be the backbone of the invisible answer-linking robot was his intended and primary focus. It was up to him to forge partnerships with data vendors, evaluate open and proprietary data feeds and decide whether or not there is a benefit to using them and if so, what would need to take place to integrate the feeds into their searchable data tier. Each of the tasks he faced were well suited for him through the positions he had held for the five years prior with a very similar online entity with similar data necessities, he explained. As there was nothing to use the data he was supposed to be finding and sorting, his focus slowly faded into his reality: fighting the fires that come with an open input stream from a moderately popular web site. It was his research that spawned the relentless barrage of new bugs from his department into the search tier, whose architecture and design became more or less dictated by these requests. Thwarting attempts at soliciting entrepreneurs, 1337 hax0r (and not so elite) attempts with next to impossible data validation. All of this while sustaining the best method of storing the data into a logical, maintainable, searchable, and indexed structure; prepared to be consumed by the still absent answer-bot. This as the foundation, referenced by the only standing intellectual asset of the companies now meager existence: their patent. It seems as though taking away the software that drives their consumers in and out of the product, the business logic rests on the shoulders of a single, highly intelligent, satirical and new friend of ours. As soon as we pieced this together from his vague descriptions of his position, he ran off to continue his never-ending quest of good data control.

John next introduced Stan Keyhang undermined by lowering his tone by an octave. It was clear that Stan was new, still trying to learn his chops amongst the ranks of the other two. His short, spiky hair which seemed as wet as the second he left the shower, his oily face smothering the countless freckles congregating across his nose. Stan pulled off the "new kid" look with perfection. His plain tee shirt, tattered khaki shorts holstering his left leg as it fully crossed his right, exposing his worn Nike running shoes. His presence stunk of a new college graduate that has yet to receive enough paychecks to get a new wardrobe. It seems he wouldn't get enough paychecks for a couple more years either. He was nice enough, though. Stan didn't seem to realize his position and loved that he could be tasked with so many things at once. He was the laborer behind Percy's endless work. When Percy would be tasked with the evaluation of a new data set or feed, which happened less and less frequently as time wore on, the data was eventually handed over to Stan. It was then his job to convert the stream into something that could be better read by a human rather than a computer. Translating compressed, fixed-width content into a standard web-based interface backed by the database of his choice at the time was his job. For Stan, this had yet to become the mindless work that it was destined to become, which was partially a product of John's directionlessness. This meant that if Stan wanted to use the Ruby programming language over Java for one source, C for another and Perl for yet another - he could (and did). If he wanted to use an RDBMS, Excel or a document-based database for each of the destinations - he could (and did). In fact, if there were a dire urgency to get the results to Percy in any immediate amount of time (which could always be adjusted by 20% or so given Percy's already hectic workload), he would even have the flexibility to pad his new and evolving resume by researching and implementing technologies he knew little about. As long as Percy was able to read the data in a consistent manner and fit the simple requirements of format and layout Percy defined, he could take any road he wanted to get him there (and he did). This did transform Stan into an above average analytical mind for his relative position and age yet almost to the point of overconfidence. He finally took the strategy of bragging about the fact that he had used Perl, Ruby, PHP, ASP.Net, C, C# and Java as languages to pipe data into MySQL, PostgreSQL, SQLite, Berkeley DB and S3 (that one comes off his own dime) in near as many projects. Two of the databases are even partially being used by the search team with a new project they are working on. This last statement took John a little back, but his directionless management style with Stan prevented him from making any snap-judgments and said nothing after his eyes closed to normal height as he leaned back in his chair.

We asked John to stay once we were done interrogating Stan. Stan left with grace, handing us a business card of John's with his own name scribbled in black ink like a hurried doctor's prescription under the transparent jigsaw pattern that was intended to disguise the original owner. The incorrect title still existed. We were curious to know how many people thought Stan was the manager of the data group. Of the entire bunch up to this point, he was the only one kind enough to extend a hand in his departure and offer his contact information if there were any more questions we had. Surely there would be and he almost seemed to ache with anticipation that he could be our portal into the rest of the technical organization as he finished with a statement of clarity to remind us he knew everyone and everything in the organization given his knowledge and position. John's head nearly spun around as Stan pulled his hand away from the generous shaking seeming to suggest he didn't agree. As the door gently closed behind Stan, John's full attention was again to us rather than the iPhone he then stashed away in his pocket. He leaned forward just enough to place both elbows on the table, leaning, separating us as if opening himself up to further questioning about he and his team - something we weren't planning on doing. Our remaining inquiries were nothing more than to reiterate and confirm what we heard from his team to ensure our information was accurate. Not to say we would never be back to chat with him or his team, just not now; not this early. Through the day and a half of meetings with his team, it seemed that through a lush valley of information regarding what his team did every day, only a desert of sand and cacti were the fruits they bore. They had no quality assurance or issue or bug tracking. They were much more of a cult than a group working together, blind and in a vacuum towards an undefined yet unified goal. Most issues, if not managed directly by Percy would float up to John who may go as far as documenting them in a shared Excel Spreadsheet. And although Percy evaluated a lot of things, the better part of his day was spent reading the incoming data from the site and making sure it didn't bend the curve of reality too much. Yet, for the things that he did have to evaluate, he would mostly shove off onto Stan who would do nothing more than play around with a new piece of technology until the output looked to be close or exactly to the defined specifications.

Quality is in the Bag

The second week started with a meeting of the much anticipated quality assurance team. The three person team was early enough to meet our arrival as they were all huddled around the table at the far end of the room gathering various over-ripened fruits and watered down coffee from the company sponsored "continental breakfast". By this time you would have though we would have learned to stop at a coffee shop before we came in - it was Seattle after all. Filing in behind, it was noticeable that we would start with the man sitting closest to the door as he seemed to be the lesser of the annoyed by our early morning meeting. At least we were courteous enough to let the coffee sink in before we rattled the rest of the bunch too much. It was either the trench coat of pre-coffee meetings or the reviews we had received off of the previous three teams meetings with us, but the animosity towards us seemed to be stowed at a minimum this morning, which was a nice way to lead the week. Caleb Alan stood up before we considered addressing anyone, forcing his welcoming hand out to be shook while introducing himself to us. His tall, slender build made his un-tucked, collared polo shirt hang from him like the drapes in our seedy hotel room. Yet his smile made it clear that he was ready enough to tell us what were interested in and anything else we may inquire about. He sat down introducing Addie Lane and Therese Jean sitting directly to his left respectively. A slight of sarcasm rolled off his tongue as he introduced them as "the companies last line of defense before making the rest of the team look like idiots". The two must have found this endearing as they both chuckled under their breath, swallowing their unappetizing fruit. Caleb then moved to introduce a missing team member, Bill Votex, mentioning he should be joining them all soon, but his normal arrival is three hours from then and the likelihood of his promptness was quite unlikely. Duly noted.

Therese and Addie obviously spent a lot of time together as they finished one another's statements with laughs while their hands moved in near-perfect synchronicity as if they were sisters. It was like watching a low-scoring synchronized swimming pair at the Olympics from a team who had never swam before. Impressed, you still felt a little sorry for the two. Though their banter was entertaining in this regard, the speed of which they flew through the details of their job was a staggering reflection their life at work. Including only the teams we had met with at that point, which didn't fully define their scope of responsibility, they were in charge of testing all non-automated bugs and features as they were landing on the last days of the development cycle. Without saying, although it was said a lot, this was the general understanding of software quality assurance across the entire company - engineering and elsewhere: they are always forgotten and never given enough resources to complete what they need to do while deemed as a necessity when something bad happens, throwing mud in the company's face. Still, the meager duo did their best to work together to try and knock the "big things" out as they came down the pike. The entire process seemed like utter chaos, yet was understood by the web team (and likely others) and only gave them the most critical pieces to test. When we brought up the web team's partitioned version control, the sound deadened as if a funeral procession had entered the room, headlights on and all. Caleb stepped in to point out this was the first time anyone had realized his team was never going to get the support they needed and built features to work around it. It knocked the wind out of his blossoming team's sails, losing two great testers through it and never regaining the budget to replace them. It was the beginning of the redefinition of their team. The definition marked them as an inadequately necessary expense and had to keep on with minimal tow. The web team never mentioned this struggle of power they took to eventual victory. They knew their role and pretended they were satisfied with the situation as long as we didn't mention the project again. Through the pain of dragging their open sores of a memory through the salt plains of Nevada, we learned all that we really cared about - what they did and how they did it. It was indeed a layer of chaos encased with by a blanket of confusion and polyester that kept them going, but they did keep going. Caleb paid attention to what was going on with each of the development and data teams. By either talking to the managers directly, keeping tabs on the local bug/task queue the search team maintained or through other methods. He would conduct his own legwork to find the work his team was responsible for. Albeit a gross, inefficient method to operate under, it was better than having the blind lead him into a dark alley by forgetting his team even existed. His approach was an evolution of his time spent with the company and finding the best combinations to make sure he and his team wasn't to their neck in hot water most of the time. He was rather successful with it. Once he knew what his team was going to work on, he would work with the still absent Votex. He would first determine if the work could or should be automated or if the work could be extended into automated tests that were already automated. If Votex and Caleb had determined the work to be manual, which most of it turned out to be, Caleb would then toss it to Therese, and Addie, letting them fish out the details of who would and how to work on it. Work on two tasks, verifying other's work when they were complete. An evolutionary approach again. They would let Caleb know when it was complete. Caleb would then, in turn, let the responsible development team know of the completion and verification. The other team, in most cases, still ignored the fact that the QA team was evaluating their software. This always caused a rift as not only would the development team, at times, release software before the validation would be complete, but if a bug was found after a release, QA would become the immediate scapegoat. A great relationship, indeed. Yet, the QA team took this with stride and worked quicker on the more important tasks (the portions of the product that people saw the most) in order to beat the release schedule that hadn't been communicated to them. It was a bacon wrapped mushroom of morale devastation: delicious but eventually killing you. Now it was our job to help if we could (or if we though it needed it, it may not). If nothing else, it seemed as though the proverbial twins in stranger's clothing were the most eager to have us working with them. The desperation of this fact spilled on the table each time they leaned onto the partitioning table stating "We're so glad you're here." or something of the like. We would always remind them we will look into the best thing to do for the company, which may or may or may not have an impact on the relationships with other teams. We were always ambiguous like that, as it was never that easy to conduct fly by the seat of your pants analysis like that - particularly with a company we know little about and have only been working with for a short few weeks.

Votex, what we called him at that point, sauntered into the room as Caleb dismissed Therese and Addie and started into more detail on his own position. Used to the interruption Votex brought with his casual tardiness, Caleb stopped his statement on a dime and waved to Bill stating only "Votex", bowing his head. As he turned a chair to the position of his liking, Bill moved in front of it, adjusting his Disneyland sweatshirt underneath the tassel-laced brown leather jacket. As he sat, he drew a small pad of paper from his breast pocket which had a perfectly proportioned ballpoint pen fit inside the black spiral holding the tattered pad together. He rubbed his weary eye with his right hand while he scratched the top of his bald head, moving his hand to his jaw, contrasting they day's missed shave. The bitterness that drew across his face as he guzzled the first two Dixie cups of cold, watered down coffee was soon replaced with a much more cooperative man heading the table where we all sat at. The indications of his position were quickly confirmed. Without title, salary or responsibility, he considered himself the lead of the team and Caleb did nothing to suggest otherwise. He took the position in stride, undertaking the self-imposed responsibility with it as the team officially had no lead. A team with no funding gets little for promotions along with a lack of new hires. He has evolved his role in being the glue between Caleb, Terese and Addie; leaving Caleb more time to be the go-between with the rest of the company and the QA team. It was a dynamic that seemed to work well as they both chuckled and exchanged glances, describing the relationship they had built. Along with the self-promoted responsibility of managing the work fed from Caleb to the rest of the team, he was primarily and officially in the development, maintenance, and regression of automated tests that validate the different pieces of software that are in - or will eventually hit - the production site and services. This, he says, is one of the most difficult parts of the job. Existing features, bug fixes, improvements and advancements usually do not tend to fall victim to the last-minute production pull and are easy to evaluate. The more complicated are the new products or features that were in development a short period of time and seem to have been all but forgotten by their product backer as they transition to the "new feature of the week". These are the items that are removed from a release, usually by the web team, as they are the most intimate with the product. A reasonable assumption to make, some would say, but quite hard to schedule throughout the development cycle. Over time, the patterns seemed to be clear enough where Votex seemed pretty confident in the decisions he had made and Caleb had no suggestion to the contrary. Although the dynamic of the team was a matter of concern to us as all, we were mostly interested in what took their time on a day-to-day basis. Once we exposed this as our drive, Votex seemed to lower a bit from his saddle of self-imposed leader and draw us to the realization that the most of his work was the continued maintenance of the ever-growing suite of automated tests. The tests, from his description, were an elegant dance between individual tests encapsulated within a very proprietary scheduling and invocation system which Caleb birthed and maintained until Votex joined the team. Taking as much as possible into account, given the tight timetables they routinely worked under, his tests spanned from verifications of bugs to full regression suites for particular portions of the site. He was the first to admit the coverage was minimal, but it was there and what was there was good. He seemed somewhat ashamed that he had to pawn off as much as he did on his two female counterparts. Though he shrugged it off as he tried to do the most with the time available and that he just never had enough. He moved into a light overview of the system he and Caleb had built. The feature he seemed to enjoy the most was the system's intelligence in determining what to run, and when, and the fact that the tests were language-agnostic as long as they were executable. Although the majority of the work was pretty straightforward, he admitted this was because the systems were getting more and more involved and therefore hard to write tests against in the time he would be given. His eventual resolution was to shift the rising complexity to Therese and Addie. Missing the conversation from earlier, he began pointing fingers at the web team's versioning system and the brilliant complexity that came with it. It seems that with each version deprecation, the sun setting never takes place in actuality. This means that when a version goes out of existence, either to fade the main-line product or to get a testing version into the main-line, the old version will remain, throwing some interesting quirks into the way they automate their tests. Through months of research into this, they had found that it was a function of how they tested the code rather than how people would interact with the code. Caleb and Bill nodded at one another when they agreed to the fact that it was a dire tragedy that the way they tested did not match the way the application was used, but this was their reality. They barely had enough time to test what they needed to, how in the world would they ever find the time or resources to fix and test bugs in their own system? He concluded the description of his average day with the best summary he could come up with: three languages, twenty-five versions to manage; ten of which were automated and three of which were currently live. It was all he could do to keep those up, running, maintained and running again. He then fell into a slurry of apologies to the now-absent ladies who picked up the remainder of the work he could not have computers do for them.

As any selfless leader would want, he stayed in the room when he finished (after Caleb had suggested he didn't), stating he was interested to hear more about what Caleb did on a day-to-day basis. An annoying and eventual power struggle was sure to come of this, but that was beyond our concern. The remainder of our meeting with the two went pretty smoothly and quickly as the first three members of Caleb's team did a good job of describing their day-to-day. "Running around like a frustrated chicken with my head cut off as short as the shotgun tied to my back" was Caleb's personal job description. In more than one way, his job was to make sure QA was in the face of everyone to keep them all relevant in the eyes of everyone they affected while reminding them how necessary they were. A thankless job filled of defense, but one that he happily took on.

The Wonderful Wizard of Oz

It was no sooner that we left the bubbly empire of Human Resources that we entered the vacuum of confusion that our next stop would be. We wandered down the halls to each 90-degree turn, etched by the shape of the building, lit by the sun light from the ten-foot floor-to-ceiling windows. The light seemed to shine from the neighboring buildings at each turn we made, throbbing the temperature from mild to chilled as we would pass under cooled vents of air. It was about the time we came full circle to the interior meeting room we had just left before we ran into Charlie again, his satchel over his shoulder, an indication it was his time to leave for the day. Slowing his pace as our eyes demonstrated the need for a question, we asked what teams were left to interview. With QA out of the way, we were a bit unsure of where to turn next. We launched into a list of what teams and short descriptions of whom we had met with when Charlie's slight shrug indicated we were done. The question of "who maintains the hardware?" almost seemed too obvious to ignore as Charlie hit his temple with his palm: "The SA's, yes." The best indication of a good Systems Administration staff is when you never remember they exist. This also means they do a good job of staying out of the way, which means systems' uptimes are high, which is what people want - whether or not they ever say so. Even if they tell stories to the contrary, high availability is almost always the true desire when the dove's cage is opened. With our calendars free at this point, it was soon thereafter we realized this wasn't the first time the team was forgotten. When Charlie's finger directed us to their general location, he was off and so were we. We took an about-face and back-tracked the line we had taken to get to where we were by about one hundred paces to what we could only assume was the indisputable stomping grounds of people who had to deal plenty with failing hardware. Hard drive platters tendered to the walls in shapes of factorials, a design of Christmas lights decorating the borders, complementing the Cat-5 cabling who's origin was a large spool at shin-height as you entered the trio of cubes. Peeking into each cube, a voice came from behind a stacked pyramid of empty Talking Rain aluminum cans "Ooh! Watch it, they're not gummed together yet." was said as a slender gentleman slid his chair back from the desk, his eye glasses tinting as he looked up at us from behind his monument of aluminum.

"Just put those back together today." he said with a victorious grin.

Impressed with the four-foot spectacle of wasted labor, we stepped back telling him our interests in finding the Systems Administrators of the company, clarifying between Help Desk (which we were not interested in for this work) and Production support.

"You found it." he said, tossing his palms above his ears. "What's up?"

We tried to be as gentle as possible in explaining to him our intent and position with the company, and also our job we were working on - interviewing the independent teams of the tech staff headed up by Mr. McFey and how his team was somehow missed. Not only was he not surprised to finally see us, as he had heard "so much about" us, but he was not taken all that back by the forgetfulness of his peers in scheduling his time to take with us. Noticing the singularity of his speech, we asked if his team had already been dismissed for the day. His smile turned flat as he said, "I'm it. Honestly, it doesn't take much to keep the lights on here."

Satisfied, we stole two of the chairs from the empty cubes that surrounded, Charlie laughing at the time he took to build his castle of silver and white that he would have plenty of time to chat with us before the day's end. "Jason Watcifer". His name was blurted as he stood while we sat, as if to greet his significant other to a meal. Taking a seat, and with little provocation, he started into the description of his job: keeping the lights on.

With a one-man team, he described, it was hard to keep up with everything. "I've been doing this forever." he started to divulge.

"The last two companies I've worked for seemed to have put me in the same position. Hang out by myself and don't let anything break. Its sort've become my specialty." Jason continued.

This was echoed in the resume we filtered through in the massive seizure of personnel information we were able to negotiate from Human Resources with Charlie's nod and a few menacing signatures.

It was his job to make sure everything ran when it was supposed to, which was just about every piece of software in the Production house. This included the operating systems that powered the development and production environments, the custom software that ran on them, the databases the data team needed, the two code repositories the different teams used (CVS for the web team and Subversion for the search team - QA and the data team used neither), the databases and indexes, the Lucine engine, and the versioning proxies amongst everything else. Each piece in duplicate, at minimum, as everyone had a development environment. Some portions with added redundancy as, for example, the web team had ten cloned Production boxes. Through the years he had come up with some more intelligent ways of keeping his job sane. Release scripts to help with the distributed software helped with the web team's deployments and management, and local installations of customized monitors were also useful to help keep tabs on servers and other critical pieces of the architecture to make sure the heart beat of the company was always existent, no matter how faint. He poked at the canned tower as he demonstrated how his work came in waves. Either everything was working or everything wasn't, and it was his job to fix it before it also became his fault. He didn't mind (or so it seemed). It was feast or famine and he preferred both extremes over the middle. Just enough work to nearly make him break and never enough to justify any help above a temporary intern or a misplaced developer on his way out. Between the 50 or more servers he managed, each networked together in one of five independent networks with nearly sixteen independent pieces of custom, proprietary software and countless others that are either paid for or downloaded free off the Internet. It wasn't for the faint of heart. Jason, however, was like the last puzzle piece of an edgeless puzzle sold with five extra pieces - a puzzle you would never expect to find and would never take apart once you did.

The Departed

As Jason twisted his chair back around, concealed by his shrine to the aluminum Gods, we stood to call it a day. With our laptops snugged between our arm and torso, we stopped by the meeting room we had previously adjourned from to gather the rest of our things before we took our memories and notes back to our hotel to get to work. We had the seeds we needed to start analyzing the organization and applying our De facto analysis to begin the delivery of our first assignment. The lobby was a maze of clouded glass walls with abstract indicators of entries and exits like a local Mexican restaurant trying to be cute with their Baño naming conventions. Tapping the "down" arrow to the right of the stainless steel elevator doors, we smiled at one another as I leaned my body weight through my shoulder on the wall accompanied with a sigh. To the building's main lobby, through the cab ride, and into our room, we discussed all the pieces we had in an attempt to confirm we had everything we needed to get working. We knew the teams, or at least we thought we did. We can confirm this with a quick call to Charlie - knowing he's already forgotten to mention two of the teams under his umbrella of organizational hierarchy. We knew the web team. Who they were, what they liked, what they worked on, what they were planning on working on and where they fit in and within themselves. We knew the search team and what drove their work while hiding their existence in a cloak of open source software. We knew the data, QA and systems administration teams; each contributing less to the product yet required enough to make sure one existed. We understood the teams, the people, and the software - at least well enough for a week and half's worth of interviews. We knew enough to get started and make Charlie happy. Let's go.

Bringing It All Together

I will complete all chapters with this section, mainly to summarize what was taught and what should really be learned. I may have said it a few too many times already (and will continue to do so), but this book is not intended for you to use as a guide but more as a suggestive method to change the way you think about your organization, building a tool to use with your existing (or new if you need it) knowledge as one of the strongest tools in your decision making toolbox.

This first chapter has been a narrative, yes; but this is only the introduction. A story that begins as fiction, evolving into a generalized reality you will feel comfortable with as you begin to recognize it as your own. There is a lot to learn in the following chapters, but each subtle helping from the plate I am about to serve has two attributes, both of which I hope you comprehend (but really hope you get at least one). The first is the literal teachings. The memorization of the numbers, and facts, and nothing else. Without any context, I believe these can still be useful, just not powerful. The second course is the contextual situations that we can analyze and this is where the story of Intellicorp is reviewed, studied, constructed and decisions built from. I am not trying to demonstrate these teachings through a fictitious organization that I created, more to create an organization that has a lot of what everyone has and a lot of what they don't. Like I said before, I can't show you every path every spider takes to build its web. What I can show you is a web, how it was made and more thoroughly examine some of the threads and joints so that you can better teach yourself how to build webs. This is mostly how the dynamic of SC, Inc. was built. There is a lot to take here for a small company with an even smaller (for some) technical staff. There are multiple levels of developers, each interacting together in different roles and conditions. There are non-intuitive networks such as the case of the data team's databases being used by the search team - to the surprise of just about everyone. There is dysfunction, friction, calm and ease all wrapped up into a single work place. The larger point is to show how each of these attributes of the individuals, independent teams and the larger organization impact one another and one way (not *the* way) to apply effective and measurable metrics to them. We also take this from the context of two independent contractors coming in and learning about a company over a short period of time. This may or may not be the same situation you are in, but the odds are that you are more likely a W2 employee who has been with the company for six months or more. This should help you after reading this as my examples will draw from the little information we were able to get, whereas you will have much more experience to use in your favor. You can be more specific, use more data and widen the scope of your analysis. More complex, sure, but more accurate as well.

Things to take from the beginning of the story we've covered so far are pretty simple. Think about everything the company is made of that can impact other people, a project of any size, or anything in between. People have an impact on people, development times, schedules and all for a variety of reasons and all in positive or negative ways. Software can also impact literally everything in positive or negative ways. It's all a function of what are you working with, how you analyze it and what you can do to change it to try and make your organization more efficient. Should you re-write an application? Maybe. In any case, I can show you how to help determine that for yourself. How should you change to better fit a new development paradigm? It depends, but I will show you how to dissect your teams so you can best evaluate what to do in order to make the best decisions. Maybe there is nothing to do, maybe there is a lot to do. The right decision is yours to make, but the story I've outlined will help me guide you through the process that can be taken by demonstrating a number of things that can change. Take what is in the story: everything. It's complex, but that's half of the point. Keep in mind my suggestion of your company and it's complexity: it's complex, too. No matter what you, your superiors or anyone else says - it's complex. Being complex is OK as long as you understand and embrace it. Little will reduce complexity, but you can be more efficient with what you have if you are given the right tools. Take with you the people, the tools they use, the software they write, the connections (social and network) they make and the work they do. With this, think about how each element will impact another (and its self). How does a person affect software? How does software affect people? How does software affect software? How do consumers change everything? Or do customers change anything at all? How do you take this information, more importantly; evaluate the information and make intelligent decisions of what steps to take next all in a reasonable time? It may seem too good to be true, but it's not. In fact, I believe you already know how to do it, I have just taken the time to organize some thoughts to better think through the clutter. You're welcome. So take the memory of this story with you as we start the dive into what the Scalability Coefficient is. You will learn and maybe even have a little fun.

The Implementation

Knowing is half the battle. If this is true, then what's the other half? In our case – here, right now - the other half consists of two more halves (yes, I meant to say that). It's the first half of the second half (having fun yet?) we can now concentrate on. Knowing who works with you, what they do and what they do it to are important nuggets to keep close to you. The nuggets aren't of gold, however, until you know what to do with them. It is great to know that Exemelle has been with the company and the same product for a year and a half. Knowing this doesn't tell you what it means and how to make decisions based off of that. When you spread this throughout the rest of your organization, it becomes even more critical you not only understand the metrics that comprise your organization but understanding them to the degree where you can make thoughtful and highly complex decisions quickly. Is Exemelle best suited to lead every project because she has the most tenure with the Search group? I don't know either, which is the point. We need to know.

The Open Sea

We've interviewed, we've listened and we (think we) understand the dynamic of the business. Enough to be satisfied and enough to start working on our own. We've met with each member of each team - not a single absentee. With the week and a half of daunting question and answer sessions with apprehensive geeks, we knew as much as were ever going to for the time we have spent.

The first step of any good analysis is to remember what our goal is. We know, for the short term, our goal is to "find where the time is being wasted", as directed by the VP of everything tech, Mr. McFey. A single sentence to define what we will be doing is less than ideal, but the goal is in there. We need to find out where the company is spending it's time so we can try to make things more efficient. If we even *can* make things more efficient, that is. Interviews can only tell us so much. To start bringing the information we've learned together into our acclaimed strategy, we need to do one thing first and always first: understand what we have to work with. Now we have two ambiguously defined statements to drive our focus. What we do have are a few more things at our disposal: a wealth of information fresh in our minds from our interviews, a lot more information we didn't receive but can hopefully catch as our progress continues, and a solid and proven strategy of business and technology analysis.

Hammer Time

The first step to obtaining the Scalability Coefficient is to break down what you know into its most atomic pieces. For simplicity's sake and for the lack of a better term, I will refer to these simplified atoms as a "particle". Particles are nothing more than the objects that are left over after a full destruction of every piece of the organization. In terms of this book, respective of the story, we have a lot to do here. We are new to a company and know very little of the back-story that makes it up. In your case, with a few exceptions (e.g. it's your first week on the job), you will likely be able to breeze through this portion of the analysis. You may not realize how well you know your organization if you put your mind to it. This is the primary focus of this entire book: think about your organization in a new light so you can make better decisions. Easy. Not that easy for us (at SC, Inc.) - the *extremely* new guys who were hired guns to help fix the devastation caused by a new company evolving into a bigger entity with their eyes closed the entire time.

To explode our knowledge into its respective particles sounds overwhelming. Finding each object in an organization that can make an impact on your decisions (project decisions, hiring decisions, organizational decisions) is a long trail to follow. We don't need to sweat evaluating every particle of every object, however. Just the important particles require their due attention. The important ones will be something specific for this writing, where they should be different for you. This means this particular controlled explosion will not be a copy and paste cookie cutter of your organization, but the same approach can be taken. Remember what you're looking for (where is the time going for us in our context?). Now, by the root definition of what we have been saying, the full explosion of an organization will take everything possible into account. Doing this will give you perfect accuracy in terms of the Scalability Coefficient, but it's not perfect accuracy that we're looking for. We don't want to shoot our arrow in the exact middle of the bull's-eye every time. 90% of time may be sufficient (maybe more, maybe less), as this isn't the only tool you have or should use. Your gut is one tool; your experience is another. This is intended to be nothing more than a new tool. If we were trying to be perfect, the explosion would include the evaluation of things like: each character of code. The letter 'z' is difficult to type for some, for example, so what can be done to make for efficiencies there? What if you generate a style guide that says variable names and static hash keys can only be written with letters from your home row? This starts to knock a bit on the door of a number of topics, which I will get into a bit. First, this is too precise. Not to say there isn't value in looking at the number of characters of code, but more to say it is equally destructive to get lost in a tide of low-level details. The removal of the "z" key amongst other letters outside of the home-row of a keyboard may come off as an efficiency gain (you never have to move your fingers, therefore gain) but you then lose 65% of the alphabet which will have your developers scratching their head thinking of new words to use for their variables. If they decide to use full words at that point, listening and understanding your underlying suggestion of efficiency in the first place. In each of these four examples, you will have created inefficiencies that can overtake the efficiency gains from losing the letter 'z' (and the other 65% of the alphabet that forces you to move your heavy fingers). One must stop and think about useless things like home-row-only named variables. Variable names that make no sense or not listening at all will either give you the same efficiency of coding or worse, which is never your goal. Not to say losing efficiency in one place to make up for it somewhere else isn't possible - it is, you will see; but it's more to the point of being too precise may actually get yourself in trouble, and it's the reason I suggest you don't do it. That said, let's take the time to fully explode what we've learned about Intellicorp and evaluate all the pieces to see whether or not we should take them into consideration. As long as we can build a confidence level that will be sufficient and accurate in order to supplement our other decision making tools we have all been using up until now, we should be happy.

What We Have

Before exploding the organization into its appropriate particles, we have to first recollect what exactly we have to explode, from its highest point. What I mean by this, is the necessity of a detailed organizational unit that describes more than just the people, but nearly every high level component that plays a role in sound decision making. This includes the structure and roles of people, what they work on, whom they work with and any cross team interaction to start. For our exercise, this will be nothing more than depicting a visual representation of the previous chapter which we can then use to help us with our explosive analysis. For yours, it may be totally different. I would suggest that no matter how long you have been in your position, you do not skip this step as it may be one of the more important ones to take.

Furthermore, don't let it be drawn once and left for static destruction. Let it evolve as you remember things instead. This isn't the true organizational structure but more of a map of exactly how your company works. For the example I will demonstrate; take the concept above anything else. The legend, the layout, etc.; take these things with a grain of salt while understanding the outline I'm drawing so that you can do the same with your organization. I ask you keep with this, even if it's etched on a napkin and stowed away in your top drawer, as it's easy to forget the things that make your organization run. In the case of Intellicorp, Jason the Systems Administrator enlightened us to the fact there are two source control systems he maintains and told us which teams used which and which used none. Albeit convoluted and likely not the case for your company, it would be easy to forget one (if not both) of the source control systems as you examine your organization. Yet, these systems play an integral part in your decision-making. Above most things else, I urge you to work with this exercise if for no other reason to remind yourself of your organization specifically.

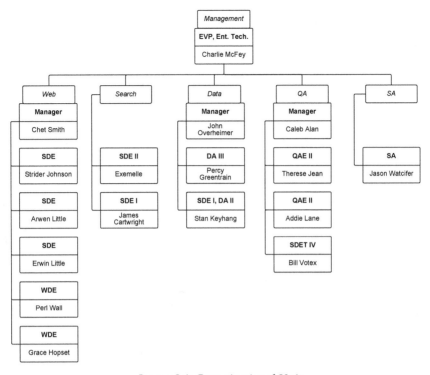

Image 3.1: Organizational Unit

What we have here, from the highest level is five teams all under Charlie McFey, the Vice President of the Technical staff that runs Intellicorp, sixteen total employees, three of which are managers (four if you include Jason) and all cascading to some level under Charlie; your typical organizational unit and the building block for a good analysis of how they all interact.

What They Use

Now this is where a bit of the interesting connections start to get made and we start digging a bit harder into our daily rituals to come up with what everybody uses to conduct their jobs. Even for our example, we don't know everything. We only know what we have been told, which is all but guaranteed to be missing some part of the daily operations of at least one member of the sixteen on staff. It should be noted we don't have perfect information - and nobody does. This is acceptable for at least two reasons. First, we are gauging for relative perfection and good accuracy. Not true perfection, but close. Second, we should let these documents evolve as we remember or find out new things. Say, for example, we didn't learn of the data team's database architectures created for evaluation purposes, which are now being used in a project by the search team. Somewhere, somehow, this is taking time and money which will draw from the total efficiency of your organization. There is a good chance we would have learned about this database later and when we did, we would then adjust our depictions and our analysis to take the new facts into consideration. Change is good, and if I can do my job well, easy.

So what is in here that wasn't here before? The additions that were made were the tools that people use that hold two attributes (that we will consider at least): they are non-proprietary and they help people get their job done. I call these items out specifically for one major reason: non-proprietary tools will impact schedules and your organization, but in a far different manner than proprietary tools. This is because the maintenance of these items are outside of the scope of what you do, which makes a big difference. It is not to say that third party software solutions are free of cost - they never are. Although the examples we will continue with are far less involved in terms of the organization's efficiency, we know there is no active development being done to them internally. That is with an exception, the search team's Lucine installation. Although it continues to technically be a piece of third party software, we remember its original source has been supplemented internally. The fact that it has been modified suggests that not only will there be the management, maintenance and uptime cost and time incurred, but the same in regards to the development staff it consumes to maintain and continue development of the code. We will hit more on this in the latter portions of this diagramming. What we see now is Bugzilla, Subversion, and CVS amongst many other utilities. Although there are some shared attributes between these types of utilities (all different pieces of software in this case) and the software that is written by the staff at Intellicorp, there are differences as well. Some are different to the point where we will have to take them into consideration, where others will have to consider regardless of the differences. You will begin to see a bigger difference between this once we start breaking them down and analyzing them further.

What They Do

In specific terms of Intellicorp, we have this portion of the diagram to illustrate little more than the product they work on: the data, hardware and software (the entirety of the IT staff under Charlie). The impact of the proprietary software should be pretty obvious as we have already drawn its contrast: you have to develop and maintain it. Being this exercise is intended to be a visual road map of your organization to assist you through the analysis and breakdown that will take place, we want to be able to visually represent a difference between the software that is used rather than what is developed and used. There's more work and different work than before and must be called out as such. In all levelheaded honesty, this is also the part of the puzzle that will demonstrate the bigger impact on projects. This is the guts of what gets worked on and will be represented as such with any organization, even in the case of Intellicorp. But just as this will lack proof to be your silver bullet, this could become the section that can be manipulated the most to show where efficiency gains can be obtained. The more you have lost, the more you have to gain. This is a mantra of many elements of life, technology organizations are the same (and any other for that matter).

What They Do and What They Use

Called out earlier and missing from the previous diagram of Intellicorp's proprietary mix is the existence of the modified Lucine installation. In the context of this organization this is important because of one critical reason: the added development of this open source piece of software has an added complex component which we can define and is accompanied by the community that also modifies the code line. This is critical to think about as any modifications to an open source piece of software will have to be patched into future upgrades that happen, as the mainline software won't be aware of any proprietary changes you may have made along the way. This creates a third dimension of complexity, as the combination requires an extra maintenance step and care with any upgrades that take place. This of course can all be avoided by ignoring upgrades but that's akin to riding your childhood tricycle into work when you're 40. You should have upgraded years ago even though you really, really like to ring the little bell and still get giddy thinking of the handlebar streamers flying through the air. It is not commonplace for development organizations to download a fully functional piece of free software only to change it later down the road. In each case I have witnessed, it only leads to stress down the road since added maintenance issues are fourth dimensional vacuums. However, this will demonstrate exactly the point of the considerations you will have to take when giving your organization a full analysis. What is going on exactly? This can become a simple oversight on anyone's part but can also be a drain for time when it comes to the execution time on a project that necessitates the search team (and their black-box development which, something we will get to later). If absolutely nothing else, the knowledge we have gained about this piece of software should show us that it is different than the rest, that it has the potential to slow you down in the long run, and why we need to take it into special consideration.

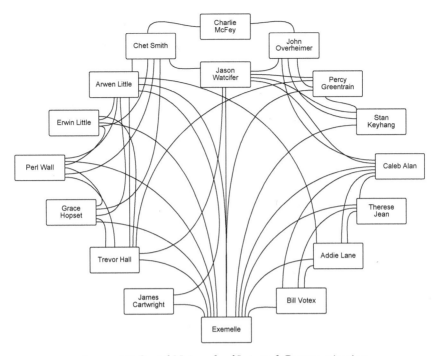

Image 3.2: Social Network of Internal Communication

The true complexity of even a small organization starts to unfold. Once you start looking at the network effect and social interactions of a single group or combination of groups, you begin to find the dynamics of psychology start to wreak havoc on planning. This is yet another dynamic of Intellicorp we cannot deny. Much more depth will go into this as we continue as there is a lot to take into consideration here. People can bring into others many positive and negative characteristics and only some of which can be applied to this approach of analysis. To what extent can you evaluate a learning curve of someone? What would be an impact of having a Senior Developer work on a large project with a Junior one? Where would the Junior Developer be, developmentally, after the project's completion? What about a smaller project with the same two developers? What would this mean to the rest of the organization? We are continuing to build a visual representation of each of the factors we can think of that will impact where you, your team and your organization spend their time. People, I guarantee, is one of these elements. Are you reading this at work? Do you think someone might be reading this book at work? Are you sure that's the absolute best use of your or their time? It is, perhaps. You won't know with a high level of confidence until you think through all the related (and potential unrelated) contingencies.

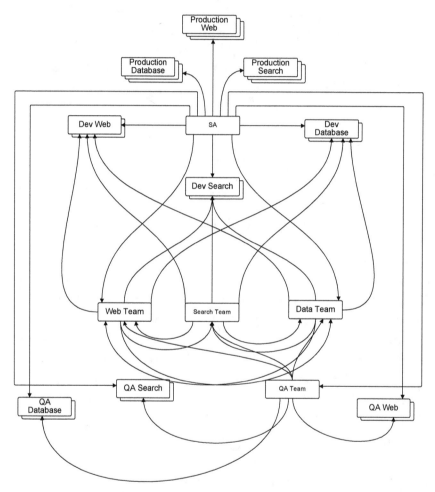

Image 3.3: Internal Computer Network

The great thing about working with technology is that you get to work with computers and computers are nothing more than an evolved electrical circuit: they are reliable as a light switch. If you set a computer in the same room with a bigger, faster computer that has an order of magnitude, more software, and artificial intelligence installed on it, the lesser of the two computers will not learn how to be a bigger, faster, better computer. It will sit there and do what it's told, nothing more. They still have communication with one another, simple as they are, which is an added layer of complexity as you are now learning. You will see in this example, I have included two new points of interest in our growing diagram: internally and externally managed communication networks. I have made the point about things that are developed and maintained within your organization, and those who are developed and maintained by outside communities - no matter of their communities set forth to deliver free software or purchased software. The point here is still the same: you have to worry much less about your connections to MySQL than you do between your web and search platforms, as the latter connection is proprietary technology. Have you ever had to care about whether or not the Inbox on your computer connects to your mail server? If you have built your own proprietary mail server, then I will be willing to bet the answer is a distinct "yes". You see, when you do things yourself (rhetorically speaking), there is a tendency to believe in failure above perfection, whereas with a leased or outsourced activity, people simply expect perfection.

The Final Frontier

With this map of your organization you begin to see just how complex even a simple organization such as Intellicorp can become in short order. This is drawn from a quick debriefing over a short period of time. Imagine what you can illustrate with your deeper reach of resources. A technical staff, sixteen strong and around for a couple of years has the ability to create a network of complex connections, becoming overwhelming with great velocity. We are humans of course, and at least for this example we are working with computers. Our tools and ourselves are complex creatures that can handle this chaos. It is a matter of how we organize the chaos that will give us the most out of our time.

At this point, we have the first building block of managing the Scalability Coefficient of Intellicorp; A visual mapping of each of the connections and objects that can (and will) impact your decision-making. You will be able to make every decision with respect to this map, knowing each of the objects and their decomposed particle's impact on different aspects of the organization through further examination within this book. I will demonstrate the power of an overwhelming analysis that will erode into simple math terms that can be manipulated in short periods of time to make complex decisions with little hesitation. You can then take each microscopic aspect of your organization into consideration when making decisions. Making decisions while taking the impact your issue tracking system will have (assuming you have one as our examples from Intellicorp will) is the basis of the best decisions made. It's easy and common to make decisions without consideration into the pieces that comprise the whole. It is a conditioning exercise to help you remember to look at the entire picture and my job is to teach you how to reliably do that; later, we will learn how to evaluate change. You will understand why Bugzilla matters while the database behind it doesn't, and how they both will impact any project when taken into consideration with "C". They all matter and they each impact one another, and this is the sole reason you should take them each and all into consideration when making decisions.

Particles

Whether or not you decided to follow my recommendation of outlining the impacting interconnections of your organization, the steps that follow will only build on top of it. We will take each of these objects, networks and connections and decompose them into their respective particles. In doing so, we must continue to remember the end goal: we need to build a tool to add to our arsenal and not to worry about being perfect. You will wither into obscurity in the pursuit of perfection, chasing every complex corner, ruining you in the long run. I can assure you that your decision making isn't, hasn't been and will never be perfect, but the bull's-eye of your decision making is in the eye of the beholder. Though knowing any decision making tool's true power is defined by its ability to change, evolve and be moldable, and improved upon every time it's used. Reliability of your decision-making will be seen, but if the tool is used well - with intuition, knowledge, experience, and expertise - you will find yourself in a powerful spot.

We the People

One of the most complex and curious creatures of any organization is the people that make it up. The people that make the ideas, the products and decisions are the one genuine aspect of any organization that is taken with the utmost care and compassion, as they are one of the few things that can make or break any organization. A bad product, failed marketing or any other combination of internal or external factors will make a critical piece of any success or failure. No matter the situation, it is the people who will take you there. Even further and perhaps more obvious than anything is that people are human. Your teams are creatures of their creation; each with individual with minds, personalities, emotions, memory and levels of intelligence. Each of these can, will and should be a critical piece of every decision you make that concerns them. You need to weigh each of your team's attributes with careful consideration and with respect to any alternatives in relation to their environment to make the best and most well informed decision regarding them.

The first thing we will need to do is separate the physical properties of the people you work with from the psychological properties. Of course, both will have different impacts on the decision you will make, but they will impact one another differently and dynamically. It will be up to you of which to include in the decisions you make. The classification of these different properties is critical. Physical properties are those that are evaluable, whereas psychological traits cannot. Take Strider Johnson for example. A young developer who had grown with Intellicorp as their first developer directly out of school. A single, descriptive sentence of a person can tell us just enough to demonstrate the two classifications. We first know he joined Intellicorp as soon as he had graduated college, acting as Intellicorp's first developer. We know a few critical things with this information: he has (at least) three years of total experience and three years of experience with the company. These elements, amongst many others we will see later, are critical. Physical attributes are as factual and can be used without hesitation. I will outline a few more of these along with their importance as we continue. The psychological particles that can be drawn from Strider's descriptive sentence can likely tell us a few more things. Being the first developer of the company, it is likely there is a slight superiority he takes with his co-workers, no matter their relative experience or position in the company. Without knowing Strider, it is hard to say whether or not this is true, but there is the chance. If he doesn't, then he may hold an ear to more experienced developers, learning from the more experienced, who themselves may not be as apt to learn new concepts and patterns as Strider may be. You can begin to see, there are a lot of attributes we can take into careful consideration when making important decisions about anything that would include Strider or his team. However, not a thread of these hold a truth beyond a reasonable doubt. Each of these (and similar) attributes will take a specific and detailed analysis of each person on a team and by a trained psychologist. In terms of general efficiency, this falls as far from efficient as possible. These are volatile attributes that will fall outside of our analysis and within the expertise of the more appropriate authorities. Some can be battled with good hiring practices, a topic we will talk more about in the later portions of this book. We can take into consideration some things as long as they come with some predetermined assumptions. These attributes are universal throughout any organization and can be assumed near-truths if the assumptions are taken into consideration. Each of these attributes and assumptions will be called out specifically as we continue through their analysis. You can start to see why I call out this classification of attributes, regardless. They are completely different yet each will impact your decision-making. Because of this, people are one of the most difficult and important attributes of your organization. You can take as little or as much as you would like into consideration as long as you are aware of the difficulties of pinning down an unarguable, bullet-proof analysis; as with any decision making tool. With that, let's take a further look into these classifications and see what if we can build something bulletproof.

Physical Attributes

Physical attributes as a subset of the particles, representing the attributes which can be physically measured in one manner or another.

Time with a Company

The first physical attribute we will evaluate is in terms of an employee's tenure. A large part of this attribute is nothing more than a general learning curve. All companies have lesser controlled aspects of them, born by questions, conversations, eavesdropping and further networking that come along with being inside the walls of an organization operated by humans. Decision-making is sounder, history is experienced not taught, and knowledge is contained not asked. Tenure with an organization is never bad, in general. It can be argued that a person who has grown stale with a company and is only holding out for some sort of time-based compensation is a drain more than a benefit. I agree to the highest degree with this analysis although it is not your job (nor mine) is to fix your company. It is up to you to suggest ways to make the decisions within it, breeding a more efficient place to work instead, paving the groundwork for repair. If your team is littered with people awaiting for their decade-long vesting schedule, no longer contributing to the company, this is an issue that can be resolved by other means. Assuming there are methods in place to prevent this type of event (along with the many others similar events), tenure is good and something you should take into consideration.

Time Working with a Particular Product

The time with a product is the second property we will evaluate. The tenure with the product holds very many of the same attributes that we considered for the tenure at a company. When you take a specific product (or suite of products) into consideration a different dynamic grows. For example, a person who has been with a company for a decade, yet with a product team for less than a week will continue to suffer a learning curve to his or her new position. They will continue to have the company's perspective in their back pocket, meaning more to a team and project than another person who is as new to the team as they are the company. The rubber begins to burn the road here when working with a product. The product is what sells; it is what funds the checks and keeps the lights on. This is what the company, particularly a tech company, puts to work when they want to make money. This is where the major projects are. With major projects come philosophies, efficiencies, analysis and ... decisions. Any further knowledge a person has with a product will be to the benefit of a company and even more so when the tenure with a company is high. Much as to the tenure with the company, this assumes no rate of diminishing return and is something that will be considered. This theory of diminishing return, however, is much more of a psychological attribute than a physical and we will talk more to it in the later section of this chapter.

Time Working with a Particular Team

The time spent with a team is not much different from the other attributes we have already covered. An employee's time with a team, much like their tenure with the product, should be discussed separately, as its impact has its own unique dimension. The use-case for this is rarer than most others but doesn't mean we should ignore it. The case is either an entire product coming onto an existing team or a new team merging into an existing team. There is going to be a ripple effect respective of the event's impact. As a ripple in water will fade over time, so will this. This type of transition is a case for a company in flux, for the most part, which is not the case at Intellicorp. It seems to be the case with a lot of companies these days and I felt it appropriate to mention regardless. Has your company downsized or merged with a different company? There will be team transitions of one flavor or another in either, or similar events. Maybe the sole remaining member of a "downsized" team was recruited into a team. Their impact on that team will affect the previous, existing team's dynamic in terms of morale, experience and general comradery. These attributes are a function of personal and psychological challenges, but there is also a unit we can measure from this concept which we know will have an impact. To the same degree, we also know that if a larger existing team's product is dropped from the companies repertoire and merged into another team, the dynamic of both teams will change, both on the team and on the personal level; both in physical and psychological terms. Team analysis will come later but if our goal is to break down an organization into its most atomic pieces, a particle of a team is its people and we should look at them as individuals.

Time Working in a Particular Field

We're now getting into more of the obvious places of the physical analysis of individuals. The length of a person's time in a particular field will impact how they perform. Imagine you have a pipe burst in your house and you know you need a plumber to fix it. Would you chose the plumber just out of plumbing school over someone at the same price who has twenty years of experience? Unless the former is a close friend or relative of yours, then I could only imagine the most reasonable choice would be the more experienced plumber to and bout the leaky pipes. We have to also take into consideration the few things that are wrong with analogy. First, the example pointed out the two plumbers came at the same price. This may well be the case if the less experienced of the two didn't know much about his market or trade. However, there is a good chance the younger of the two in the trade has a smaller price tag to match the lack of experience. Keeping the price of the lesser experienced plumber intentionally ambiguous, it could be possible to hire three less expensive plumbers for the price of a single, more experienced plumber. Which is better? Will three people get the job done faster or would one with more experience get the job done quicker? At what point do you start losing efficiencies selecting the cheaper option? If everything with the exception of experience was the same, who would you chose? I can safely guess nobody reading this will say "I don't care". If you do say that, you should care. There is a difference and I will show you what that is.

Number of Companies Worked With

The number of companies a person has worked for is one of the lesser-considered attributes that will still have a substantial impact on an individual. We need to look at everything when evaluating your teams and the people that compose them We need to dig up the dirt, so to speak. Let us evaluate two people, each with ten years of experience. One has worked with three companies and the other only one - right out of college. As we said before, there is a benefit to working with a company for a longer period of time (though we still haven't gotten into diminishing rates of returns yet ether), but there is also something to say about people working at different companies. Experience comes in other dimensions than time, and because of this we need to take them each into consideration. How many times have you heard someone say "I remember from company X, we did it this way ... "? We all know the people that say this but have nothing but horrid ideas that relate in no logical way to the topic at hand. The announcement of past experiences is very rarely a bad thing to do, even if they have no logical connection to the conversation's context. It brings new ideas to the conversation, good or bad. Some of these notations may end up creating trails leading to a great idea and fixing a problem for you. In any event, a second dimension to experience is breadth over time. Different companies have different people and different challenges to overcome and problems to solve. People stay within a trade and their past experiences. These experiences will be born from the same mold, albeit different in some way, shape or form. It is much harder to argue this would be as big of a case with the person who has been working for the same number of years but with only a single company. Most companies tend to stay within a single business and revenue model with a few core products they maintain and continue with. Every company will have problems, challenges and difficulties - each of which a person can grow and learn from. But the context of a different view gives a different perspective on the same problem. This is a characteristic that is valuable and will be considered, even in a minimal context.

I want to take a short stop here to point out some of the evolutions that are already taking place with our (still) early analysis. We haven't gotten past the first level of decomposition and we are already seeing how different evaluable attributes can start to play chords on one another's instruments. I have, in this case, shown how the tenure of a company can play a negative role as well as a positive role in the overall evaluation of a company. We also have to figure out how to demonstrate these differences in mathematical form to form our decision-making machine (so we're clear, you are the machine), beyond the fact of recognizing these differences. You can begin to see the intricate levels of complexity we will need to keep track of and take into consideration as we continue. Imagine when whole entities play roles with one another. If we're looking at people now, what happens when you join those people into a team and join those teams to build a new product? That fuels the fire for a complex situation that is too often glossed over when it never should be.

Number of Promotions Taken

This is another attribute that builds off of others and considers the number of promotions one receives. The concept here is that the number of promotions taken over a period of time respective of the number of positions one has had is a good suggestion into their effectiveness in any given position. It's a valuable portion of a larger equation that will tell us just how a particular person will impact a decision using some of the individual's past as a basis for their success in the future.

I will take this time to pause yet again to bring up another point and trend you may start to see as we travel further into the winding logic of the Scalability Coefficient. You will likely disagree with assumptions, logic and statements I make throughout this book. I hope you do in fact. I want you to take the examples I use with a grain of salt, while the concepts I hope you can forge into the tools you can use. This is the base-line of the book. The intent of your reading this and my goal for you is to start thinking critically about the things around you, preventing assumption-driven decisions dictate your office. There are countless counter examples to using promotions as a basis to gauge success in the future. Maybe the person only worked at a single, very small company and received many promotions as the company grew along with their revenue. A simple case that happens all the time where original staff grow like a balloon filled with air, they stay on the top as the company expands underneath them, changing the surface around them to fit the extra pressure underneath them. In this example, using the promotions would be a discounted measure for success as the only reason they may have received the promotion was due to good luck (although I also believe people in this situation demonstrates good, hard work as well).

We can take a quick step away from this to remember this section is designed to evaluate the things we can physically measure. I will also show you two more concepts as we continue: how to take all these arguments into proper consideration when generating our Coefficient and how to reduce the subjectiveness of the evaluation so there can be no argument at all. It will be impossible for anyone to argue the fact that we made the wrong decisions if we can take as many factual variables into consideration with success when making decisions. Not to say you will always be perceived as being successful 100% of the time - that will never happen. We can try though, can't we? To the original point disagreeing with me is encouraged.

Salary

The almighty dollar. This number is a perfect gauge into the relative worth of a person in a number of ways. People are the highest fixed and/or variable expense an organization has, as the case is with most organizations. This fact also tells us that pay ranges are one of the most researched and critical measurements of the value a person has been assigned. An entire HR staff at your company has designated pay ranges for each position within the company. We can only assume this number was meticulously defined under a combination of experience, market research and other financial guidelines that have defined salary ranges since the dawn of the capitalistic market. It would be ignorant of us to ignore the amount of money someone makes, particularly when judging different people amongst one another in a team setting. The salary of an individual can be used as a benchmark to their effectiveness as well as the general cost as a measure of performance. This is, in fact, another attribute with an impact of an area we examined earlier. Remember how the length of tenure in a field should impact your decision making and how you could hire three lesser experienced plumbers who charged one third the price of a single, more experienced plumber and may be able to get the job done three times faster? This is another attribute in the same equation. Let us say the example was true and you were able to fix your plumbing situation in one third the time as you hired three plumbers for the same price as you could have a single, more expensive and experienced plumber. Regardless of whether or not you think this is even possible, there is still a function of quality that must be taken into consideration. Salary is one attribute that will be able to demonstrate the level of quality if you believe when you pay some one a lot, you expect a lot; when you pay them little, you expect less. Maybe you could get the job done three times faster, but will the pipe break again next week? We can hope not, but we did hire three plumbers who have no less time out of school than what it took to come to your house. Yes, indeed - let's hope that pipe doesn't break again.

Psychological Attributes

Psychological attributes are a subset of the particles, representing attributes which define an individual but each to varying and largely immeasurable degrees respective of the individual.

Time with a Company, Product, and/or Team

As mentioned in earlier sections, there are psychological attributes to take into consideration as well. The first of this laundry list is the diminishing rate of return that comes with time. Perhaps you are familiar with this term from your early undergraduate economics classes. If not, imagine you find a particular candy that gives you goose bumps every time you think about it, excited for the next piece. Every day you sneak one more in your mouth than the day before, each one melting over your tongue like a crisp waterfall of flavor. You savor it for a few minutes as it's incredibly delicious; ensuring each molecule of the enchanting sweetness rolls through your taste buds as a sea of molasses on January. You eat more than the last, every day for ten days. Now that you're eating ten pieces over the tenth day in a row, you're finding the wealth of delight sliding off your skin and onto the floor. When on the eleventh day, the eleventh candy is spat out of your mouth onto the floor and the rest of the bag of what used to be your treasure trove of enticement found its way to your kitchen garbage can. The thought of that candy now makes you sick and you hope to never see it again. That feeling of plateaued excitement followed by raging disgust was the diminishing return of the original, exciting candy. Too much of it made you hate it and never want to see it again. This pattern is also seen within every facet of human activity. Everyone has a threshold that can be broken as his or her enjoyment begins to level off and eventually decline. People will get burned out and start to degrade the team as a whole rather than improve it; no matter if it comes to a company, position, product, team or anything that carries the same tune over time. You will want everyone to climb the hill of diminishing return as it is a catalyst to excitement, engagement and education that can only be gained by the people that make the journey. It is the manager's job to handle the state of diminishing return by either pushing it out in the future or taking care of it when it happens. It will happen, it's just a matter of when.

The point of this discussion was to demonstrate the psychological impact some of these attributes have that should make an impact on your decision-making. These attributes are tough to wade as the evaluation of these attributes are a function that is embedded deep into the psyche of each individual on your and everyone's team; so deep that the individuals may not even know the answer to their own analysis. With that, we can take average consideration into account. Averages will not take the full breadth of your team's psychology into consideration as they are each unique and have their own personalities and thresholds. Another option is to try and dissolve as much of the psychological trait into a physical one that we can measure with a high level of accuracy. The problem with this approach is that we will continue to define the trait within accuracy, as we're doing nothing more than renaming it and attaching a coefficient to a varying measurement that nobody can define in the first place. Being as there is no fact to measure, we should not measure it at all. My recommended approach is to ignore the trait completely. In terms of our coefficient measurement, the most logical approach is to manage the dangers of diminishing return of a job on an individual basis in order to prevent this from having an impact in the first place. This particular attribute is dangerous and imminent and, but avoidable. It is the job of every one's manager to ensure its impact is not as broad as it is devastating. Combined with the fact that it is impossible to measure suggests we don't need to take it into consideration for decision-making, but on another plane of our corporate ritual all together.

We are exposing an area of evaluation and is comprised of your own subjective analysis. The remainder of this book will demonstrate the level of critical thinking respective of each of the attributes that effect your organization - physical and psychological. As I have said all along, I will not outline everything every organization should take into consideration but what I do point out you will hopefully disagree with. The examples are there to prove a point, take the concept away with you. For this case, it is up to you whether or not you agree with my analysis. It is your decision to ignore diminishing rate of returns and make sure your managers understand the dangers of a stale employee and how to prevent the creation of them. It is more than reasonable, however, that your organization is as deep as the Mariana Trench of the West Pacific. It is inevitable that a worn employee will be a common case. If so, then it is up to you to either change your organization to prevent this destructive track from happening, or find a way to measure its impact on your organization. This case is the rarity, as there are far fewer large organizations of this nature than smaller ones that can effectively manage their people (and even large companies do a relatively good job of managing individuals at this level). It is my justification to recommend leaving it out of the equation entirely.

I recommend we don't take the rate of diminishing return into consideration when evaluating time of tenure respective of a company, team, position and the like. I've mentioned before the goal of good decision-making is to make bulletproof decisions that are driven from the fact that you cannot find a reasonable argument against a decision, and therefore must have the right decision with the information you have at the time. Doing this also includes the things you don't include in your decision-making. We are not including the diminishing returns over time (in this case) but we need to call this out and understand why we are not including it. We won't have answers to every question. We will not think of every variation of what to take into consideration. We can, as humans, learn and adapt to just about anything and this is no exception. However, a good and thorough analysis will include each of the things we include and exclude, along with a good thought into why.

Capacity to Learn

How individuals learn is a discrete function of so many things in that person's life and genetics that there is no defined method way we can apply a precise evaluation. The Scalability Coefficient revolves around rigid facts to aid in obtaining the most accurate and indisputable decision, so we cannot pretend to build this with such a variable and unknown source of information such as a individual's psyche. Whether or not we can formulate an equation of its impact doesn't matter as it will impact your organization, as is the case with countless attributes such as a person's learning curve. You want to hire quick and thorough learning minds to reduce the slow and trudging evolution into an experienced and usable team member. When things change; products are added, created or removed; people are shuffled - all will introduce change that will necessitate a re-introduction of the learning process for one or more people. Humans never stop learning. There is a new cave of information that is waiting to be unearthed, even as change vanishes. Memory, being the advancement of learning, is sustained through repetition. Therefore, one's learning curve is simply how many repetitions it takes to move on to the next unknown task of learning. Once is ideal. Yet even when the principal of learning is simplified, there is still the function of determining how many iterations it takes for every learned task when we also know that some people learn differently than others and many tasks are nowhere near alike. What to do?

I believe there are three approaches we can take to evaluate a learning curve, as I outlined with other psychological attributes. The best of these evaluations being a function of your environment: the average of all, find relative physical attributes or just ignore it completely. I believe we can take a different track as there are some physical attributes within learning curves that will guide us through a partially opened window into a person's psyche. If you remember earlier, we talked about different levels of experience and promotional ability when referring to some of the physical attributes of people. Using some of these in varying degrees will shed light into the evolving and uncontrolled spectrum of learning. For example, the most obvious relationship from a physical attribute into a person's learning curve is their promotion history within your company and throughout their experience with other companies. Promotions over time respective of the number of companies they have worked for will tell us about how fast they learn. We can take the nose-diving assumption that your company and all previous employers of the person you are evaluating promote people who are knowledgeable, proven to be experienced and suited for the position. This may not be the case what so whatsoever. However, it is a light we can use to navigate our way through a person's learning curve by means of what they have done in the past. We can then use some of their hard physical traits to further reduce the liability of past companies granting promotions to people needlessly. The employee, for example, has worked at two or more companies. We can use the number of companies over time as a function of how to determine the reliability of the number.

The fewer the companies, the lower the impact of the function and therefore a lesser dent will be made to the Scalability Coefficient of that person, respective of their learning. We will get into the precise formulation later, so get excited. Tenure in their current and past companies, along with the industry as a whole, can play a part in the evaluation as well, much the same as with the number of promotions. We can assume that people who have been working in an industry have a number of things going for them: they have experienced a number of issues before, have learned a number of things over time and have honed their learning into more of an art. We are still evaluating a psychological attribute and so the use of these somewhat abstract details of a person leave much room for error. However, if we combine these with a person's promotional ability relative to their career path with a sliding scale to reduce liability of incorrectness on a personal and functional level, we can achieve what we are looking for while taking only physical attributes into consideration in order to explain a psychological tendency.

Foremost on your mind should be whether or not you trust using any psychological facet. A safe bet is to ignore them completely and let the raw facts navigate the definition of them without directly answering them. It's much easier to say "I didn't take that into account, but my formula did include x, y and z which proves a." This is your decision to make and should be made with careful thought. The concept I am trying to demonstrate with the previous two examples is that you can take a different and custom approach to each one, depending on your comfort ability level. To find any facts within a diminishing rate of return function for a person is next to foolish as there is nothing to grasp, next to hiring a psychologist and rendering each of your staff through years of psychosis to determine what a good evaluation would be. It is much safer and logical, when looking at the learning curve of individuals, to say there are actions they have taken on their road to the present that can help demonstrate their ability to learn. If we have this, we can adjust the impact of this with a small application of practical mathematics. Scaling this to zero is easy - ignore the trait all together. Scaling up will be respective of your understanding of the attributes that play a part into this and how they impact one another as I have already demonstrated in the earlier example.

Everything Else

I hope at this stage, the point is becoming clearer. Psychological traits of humans are complex and unique creatures, making them difficult to quantitate without an advanced psychiatric degree. In the same light, you can think of each of the traits and determine if there is a way to subtly apply metrics to them through the use of physical attributes as we had in the example above. I recommend you stay away from psychological analysis without a thorough knowledge of the general human psyche along with a rich and personal understanding of everyone on your payroll. You should still put some thought into this portion of the analysis for reasons I mention earlier (you can explain to people why you don't take them into consideration). Think of the many other psychological traits we didn't get into. Coming back to the introduction of the web and search teams, you may remember the relationship the Little brothers had with Strider and Exemelle with James Cartwright as a countering argument. For the former, Strider didn't get along with the Little brothers. Could you imagine this will impact your team in any way? Of course it will. Anything less than a great and open relationship between co-workers will be a cause for siloed work, aggravation and elevated levels of competition; to name a few things. How do we define the impact of Strider's contempt? How do we define it respective of other groups of people that don't get along? Is it a suggestion that hiring brothers into the same team is a bad idea? Is it a suggestion that Strider should have an attitude check? Is it enough aggravation to talk this much about? To the counter argument, what will the impact be from Exemelle and James' relationship? They get along well, which is partially the reason James is on her team. Getting along is good. It boosts morale, and supports healthy competition (yes there is a difference between degenerative and healthy competition; one is based in anger when the other is not). In both cases, as good managers, we know there is an impact - positive and negative; there is no question into that. When you apply the level and depth of analysis with this book's approach, the problem becomes more apparent as it becomes laden with varying levels of difference that it's best left to you, as a manager, to deal with. Foster well-working relationships and extinguish the ones that are negative. If you find a team full of A-Type personalities is a bad idea, then change it. The Scalability Coefficient is a tool you can use; you must always remember this. It is a tool that is based off the premise that you can use raw, hard facts to help you along your career path to make important decisions. There is no hard-drawn line of how people will act. It's a difficult line to draw since it is such a big part of every team, it's one of the downfalls of working with humans. The better parts of most important psychological traits are those that can be explained with closely tied physical attributes. Such was the case with defining a learning curve. We didn't interview each person to find a good psychological metric we could use. Rather, we will use their history and experiences as a gauge into how well they learn over time.

The Collective

The fun part starts here. We now can start to take everything we've gone over and begin applying it to generate it to our Scalability Coefficient. To do so, I hope you have already done all of the things I have recommended:

- Learn and understand your team and organization.
- Map out the connections your organization has made.
- Describe and understand the particles you are going to work with.

I will not argue that the first two steps are the most difficult and time consuming of this entire process. However I will redundantly point out that they shouldn't be. You should already know the intimate details of your organization; from the people to the tools they use and everything in between. If this has been an involved and tedious exercise, it means you're learning. It must be remembered that it all matters, and the more you know, the more power you have to be successful. There are the few of you that manage organizations that are so large in scope there is no conceivable way to know everyone and everything. Yet this is not entirely my point. There should not be an employee that can fly under the radar or a tool that a few people use and is barely known about. Each person has at least one manager. One person that is employed to make sure they know who works for them. Maybe you manage managers of varying degrees who, themselves, manage more managers and so on. That is fine as long as you understand that every person and object should be understood and known about at some level. Maybe not you, but your subordinates should. Budgets and recourse are always tight, and reconciling an entire organization can be daunting and perceived as a needless task. In my opinion, if you feel confident that you can get any bit of information about everything from someone in your organization. If you give the three tasks I bulleted above, you will gain the confidence in reaping a detailed description of everything under your control. Only then should you not care. Otherwise, knowledge is power and the more you don't know, the more mistakes you will make. Imagine, if you will, the friendly spider we talked so kindly of earlier in this book. I mentioned I won't be walking you through how to fully construct a perfect spider web and all the chemistry, biology, and engineering principles that go into every joint and strategy known. However, I can show you enough to build your own web. No matter your knowledge of the web, if you don't know that spiders have the ability to excrete sticky and non-sticky lines, the latter for navigating across the web, then you are going to be stuck. Learn what you're working with and don't get stuck.

With the information we have, we can apply the physical attributes we want to concern ourselves with against the technical staff at Intellicorp to start building our case study of sorts. Let's get into it.

As a Team

After interviewing Strider, we know quite a few things about him in very little time. We learned he was the first development hire for the company, fresh out of college and aimed to take over where the founder of the company left off. This one sentence, alone, tells us almost everything we need to know in terms of the physical attributes we are concerning ourselves with for this exercise.

At Company	3 years
With Product	3 years
With Team	3 years
Within Field	3 years
Companies	1
Promotions	3
Salary	$30,000/year
Diminishing RoR	N/A
Learning Curve	TBC

Table 3.4: Physical Attributes

Using this table gives us a very quick glimpse into everything we've been talking about. For the lack of a better acronym, I've indicated Rate of Return (RoR) as N/A as for this example we've decided to completely ignore it and a To Be Computed (TBC) note for Learning Curve. Also, I want to point out that I am starting with an outline of the raw data we know up into this point. Later, we will standardize each of the numerals into terms that are more alike, as anything that is determined off of three years will have some awkward conversions into one year increments, and even more so when everything else we have yet to cover. We will start this later in this chapter and continue to evolve it throughout the book as we learn more. Another good point to remember and one that I will keep poking you with is this first, small table is for example purposes only. There are more attributes you can take into consideration. I recommend you find the ones you feel pertain to your organization the most and find their physical properties within them. Maybe they're exactly like Intellicorp. If so, that's great and let's move on. Maybe you can't think of any right now. That's fine, too. We're not carving this analysis into a tablet of stone. You can change your formula to be more precise at any time. It's an evolving portion of your everyday thinking. To believe you will be perfect on your first attempt, you are either a genius or wrong.

Now the task will be to apply this same tabular breakdown for each of the employee's we have interviewed. Nothing more than a simple reiteration of the same task sixteen times (in the case of Intellicorp). So let's give it a try.

Using the first table as a key reference for the second table:

C	Tenure with the company
P	Tenure with the product
T	Tenure with the team
F	Time working in the field
N	Total number of companies worked for
R	Number of promotions received
S	Salary
Rr	Diminishing rate of return
LC	Learning curve

Table 3.5: Physical Attributes

Name	C	P	T	F	N	R	S	Rr	LC
Strider Johnson	3	3	3	3	1	3	40k	N/A	TBC
Arwen Little	2.5	2.5	2.5		15	0	35k	N/A	TBC
Erwin Little	2.5	2.5	2.5		15	0	30k	N/A	TBC
Chet Smith						0	45k	N/A	TBC
Grace Hopset						1	38k	N/A	TBC
Perl Wall						0	30k	N/A	TBC
Exemelle	1.5	1.5	1.5	5	2	0	35k	N/A	TBC
James Cartwright	1	1	1	1.5	1	1	30k	N/A	TBC
John Overheimer	1	1	1	17	4	8	45k	N/A	TBC
Percy Greentrain	1	1	1	6	2	2	30k	N/A	TBC

Stan Keyhang	1	.5	.5				30k	N/A	TBC
Caleb Alan							45k	N/A	TBC
Addie Lane							25k	N/A	TBC
Therese Jean							25k	N/A	TBC
Bill Votex							35k	N/A	TBC
Jason Watcifer	3	3	3	8	3	1	35k	N/A	TBC

Table 3.6: Individual Physical Attributes

There is nothing simpler for any concept than a two-dimensional table to explain any concept and this is ours. This table, along with the many more we will review, will begin our guide to a successful analysis in determining our Scalability Coefficient. A quick glance at this table reveals one thing that pops out immediately: a good portion of it is blank. It is more than acceptable if you don't have perfect information. Surely having 100% of all the data you need for every bit of analysis you do is preferred. However, you must realize you live in reality. You may not be able to get to the data as quickly as you had hoped, but you still have decisions that need to be made. Remember that this is a process of evolution. Update your knowledge as you continue your analysis. The closer you get to 100%, the more accurate your decision-making will be. On the other hand, maybe missing data is a reason to do things you normally don't do. Even though I say it doesn't matter, the fact that the closer you get to 100% perfect data grows your accuracy screams that it is important. You still won't be 100% accurate all of the time no matter how much you try and want it to happen. There is yet a balance between striving for what is obtainable to get as close to 100% accurate versus going overboard with your analysis. Looking too deep into your attributes becomes overwhelming, but getting the data for the ones you have is not. Take the time, in this example, to meet some of the people you have less information on. In our case, maybe I should reconcile some of the differences with Addie, Caleb and

Therese. Being one of the last groups I interviewed (remember the story you probably didn't read), I forgot to ask some of these critical questions. Or you could take a quicker and more direct stance, as I took for this story, and go to your local HR department to offload resumes and general career stats.

Referring to the original column heading definitions:

C	Tenure with the company
P	Tenure with the product
T	Tenure with the team
F	Time working in the field
N	Total number of companies worked for
R	Number of promotions received
S	Salary
Err	Diminishing rate of return
LC	Learning curve

Table 3.7: Physical Attributes

We then have:

Name	C	P	T	F	N	R	S	Rr	LC
Strider Johnson	3	3	3	3	1	3	40k	N/A	TBC
Arwen Little	2.5	2.5	2.5	7	15	0	35k	N/A	TBC
Erwin Little	2.5	2.5	2.5	7	15	0	30k	N/A	TBC
Chet Smith	2	2	2	5	2	0	45k	N/A	TBC
Grace Hopset	1	1	1	7	3	1	38k	N/A	TBC

Perl Wall	.5	.5	.5	3	2	0	30k	N/A	TBC
Exemelle	1.5	1.5	1.5	5	2	0	35k	N/A	TBC
James Cartwright	1	1	1	1.5	1	1	30k	N/A	TBC
John Overheimer	1	1	1	17	4	8	45k	N/A	TBC
Percy Greentrain	1	1	1	6	2	2	30k	N/A	TBC
Stan Keyhang	1	.5	.5	3	2	0	30k	N/A	TBC
Caleb Alan	2	2	2	10	4	5	45k	N/A	TBC
Addie Lane	1.5	1.5	1.5	8	3	1	25k	N/A	TBC
Therese Jean	1.5	1.5	1.5	5	2	0	25k	N/A	TBC
Bill Votex	2	2	2	10	5	4	35k	N/A	TBC
Jason Watcifer	3	3	3	8	3	1	35k	N/A	TBC

Table 3.8: Completed Individual's Physical Attributes

You remember from the story we had submitted to non-disclosure and received some HR handouts which helped us fill in the holes of our Swiss-cheese-like example, concluding our first task. Although the time it has taken us to get to this part far exceeds the output, this data will become infinitely valuable.

Let's quickly review what we have in front of us before we move on much further. We now have a subset of some important metrics that define each person of our organization, from a conceptual standpoint. They are indisputable facts that each play a logical and independent role, each impacting our decision-making. The latter parts of this example are the most intriguing and will come to fruition later in the book, once we've completed the analysis for the rest of the organizational pieces.

Implementation

We are finally getting to the dirt. We've interviewed, we've mapped, we've planned, we've analyzed and now we finally can implement the Scalability Coefficient and get the rubber to the road. Let's first get a few things out in the open before we dive much deeper into this. First, the implementation will grow more interesting and useful with the more information we have to use with. Remember how different components within a specific particle impact one another? Imagine how inter particle relationships pick on one another. It's not until we've completed each of our implementations when we start to see the power of this style of analysis. It's a necessary evil, but some of the early implementations will do nothing more than make you the master of the obvious. Without them, however, the rest is useless. Each are independent Legos in an iconic structure of the Statue of Liberty.

One of the toughest parts of this approach to organizational analysis is defining relevant functions for the different particles we will want to take into consideration. This is particularly true when you believe that there is no definitive set of functions that everyone can use because every organization is different. The examples we will walk through below will hopefully shed some light on a few things. The first, a nice and generalized approach to obtaining the Scalability Coefficient as I've defined. And the second, some general functions most companies and organizations should be able to use.

Learning Curve

There is no better place to start than with the attribute we considered earlier. This is the first example of how to particulate an examination into a larger Scalability Coefficient.

We start with a table of hard-driven, indisputable facts for every person in our analysis. We can use a few of these facts to design a function, drawing from earlier discussions, that will allow us to take individuals learning curves into consideration. Looking back at our graph (to keep it a slight less overwhelming, we will again only look at Strider for this example), we have a few things that can give us a glimpse into this: time within the field, number of companies they have worked for, and the number of promotions they have received.

Within Field	3 years
Companies	1
Promotions	3

Table 3.9: Snapshot of Strider Johnson

How we will think about these attributes is simple: the number of promotions they have received over time is a good indication into how fast they are able to learn. We can assume with a level of safety that promotions are an indication into the mastery of a position and the preparedness of another; they've learned enough to move on. Much more goes into promotions, but this is certainly one attribute. And most certainly there are plenty of cases where someone may have been hired into a position that was too low for their skill set and was quickly promoted out of it. In fact, I have personally seen this happen quite often. This, along with many other similar examples are to the contrary of my earlier statement, should make you think of whether or not you should be taking this into consideration at all or ,if you do, how you can adjust it to have less or more of an impact on the overall Scalability Coefficient on an individual and/or a group level. It is the latter I will demonstrate.

The first step is to find the average time at each company the employee has worked for. For now, we will include Intellicorp in this.

I will also demonstrate how to give different concessions for Intellicorp and why we would possibly want to.

$$\frac{within field}{companies}$$

Nothing too groundbreaking there. Next, we need to find out the average length of time between each promotion at each company.

$$\frac{within field}{companies} \div promotions$$

We need to pat ourselves on the back next, because we've just figured out a basic way of mathematically demonstrating an individual's learning curve for the first time. A function of the number of promotions a person has received over time with respect to the time they have spent at each company. We will demonstrate this from here on as:

$$learning(w, c, p) = \frac{w}{c} \div p$$

Where:

w = time within field

c = number of companies worked for

p = number of promotions received

I want to point out some of the more obvious holes in this equation before we get into some examples of this. It will be up to you of what approach to use specifically, with this information. First, the equation takes the average amount of time with each company and divides it by the total number of promotions received. Therefore, if someone has worked for ten companies for a total of twenty years and has received a total of ten promotions, all of which were at the last and current company they worked for the past six months - this equation would give them a decent score, demonstrating they have received a promotion once every two years. They went 19 1/2 years between promotions which are probably a good indication that there is something else to consider. Wrong or not, this equation will not show you the justifications behind the lack of promotions. Second, the denominator of the equation, number of promotions received in one's career, is not normalized to the same relative perspective as the numerator. What I mean by this is you are dividing a function based in time by a simple and irrelevant integer. The argument could be that we need to convert the denominator to promotions over time so we can compute the average amount of time over the time between promotions. I would be taken back if there are not more similar holes such as these two, but before I start to explain the first two I want to remind you: it's OK if there are holes. Patch the holes to your comfort level and move on. The goal of this entire exercise is to compute a value for your organization using a long set of these and similar equations, and changing the variables to reduce the number as close as possible to zero. What you will find is all three of these examples will do the same things with varying degrees and rates. It is up to you to decide what suits your organization best. Remember these are examples, not the answer to life.

For the first poke at the original equation, if you have the need to take more specific care into consideration with the example I drew, then I would recommend doing something more along the lines of:

$$\sum_{n=1}^{n} \frac{promotions}{timeatcompany} \div timewithinfield$$

Or using the same notation as earlier

$$learning(w, c, p) = \sum_{n=1}^{n} \frac{p}{c} \div w$$

Certainly this is more exact but also more time consuming to compute for an entire organization. It is more accurate of a measuring device than the original and therefore will give you the best results. If you are comfortable that your company doesn't hire twenty-year veterans in an industry that did not receive a promotion for 97.5% of his career, then you are probably fine with the first equation. If not, maybe the second. Maybe you prefer a third ... go for it. Just remember the point of the exercise and your goal, but go ahead, it is your decision to make.

The next point is a bit more mathematically precocious, and that is why I bring it up. It is a question of where do you want the weights of the values to be? What would be the impact of canonicals each part of the equation into related terms? Let's find out, shall we?

$$\frac{number\,of\,companies}{time\,within\,field} \div \frac{number\,of\,promotions}{time\,within\,field}$$

This is a bit nicer of a change than the former for two reasons: it uses averages which will reduce the computational complexity and its parts in alike terms, which is mathematically sound. Let's keep this for now as we will throw each of our equations through the ringer and decide on one to use. We now have a third method to compute which is:

$$learning(w, c, p) = \frac{c}{w} \div \frac{p}{w}$$

I want to point out two more things you can take into consideration before we start evaluating these for their worth. The first is going back to what we spoke of earlier, in terms of the difference between physical and psychological traits and your trustworthiness of the latter. There are a number of reasons why we should not take learning curves into consideration, most of which revolve around the fact that they are difficult to put into a reliable educational pattern to make sound decisions. There are two methods to combat this. The first is: don't use it at all. I do not recommend this approach, yet is (likely) the simplest. We have also determined that there are quite a few physical attributes we can use to help define this psychological trait, which is why my recommendation doesn't come attached. The second concept is to apply an adjusting weight to the number, reducing its impact on the larger Scalability Coefficient you are looking into. Remembering that the ultimate goal of any decision is to find the total Scalability Coefficient for the situation. The learning curve along with every other independent coefficient is only a part of it. If we shrink the impact of the learning curve to better fit our levels comfortably, respective of how reliable it is, then we can take some of the question out of the formula while still making sure it has an impact on the overall decision. For example, if we take the simpler of the three algorithms:

$$learning(w, c, p) = \frac{w}{c} \div p$$

We can adjust this by using a few methods.

Arbitrary Weight Method

$$learning(w, c, p) \times arbitraryweight$$

This method is by far and beyond the simplest in that it applies a static number to the evaluator, adjusting the outcome in some comfortable term. Any number less than one will automatically adjust the number to a lesser percentage of the original total, where any number greater than one will do the opposite. There are obvious down sides to this method that will also apply to the following method where I will explain them.

Specific arbitrary weight method:

$$\frac{w \times w_a}{c \times c_a} / p \times p_a$$

Where:

w_a = *Arbitrary weight applied to w*

c_a = *Arbitrary weiht applied to c*

p_a = *Arbitrary weight applied to p*

For obvious reasons, this grows the complexity while giving you much more control over the variability of your comfort set. I don't imagine your uneasiness of the equation will change if you offset the time with a company respective to the number of promotions you have received, but the point is here nevertheless: you can adjust things to make them less or more of an impact if you have justifiable reason to do so, and when speaking in terms of psychological particles. You first have to be careful about your weights with a more complex method like this. A reduction weight on the numerator will give a dampening effect. Yet if the same is applied to the denominator, the reverse will happen. I'll skip these math basics for you, but you see the gist.

Although these can be appropriate and acceptable steps to work out the unreliability of basing psychological particles off of physical ones, there are new issues that arise because of our adjustments that should be taken into consideration. First, the entire concept of arbitrary weight is completely flawed. It is a self-imposed number that is used to make you feel better about the outcome of an equation. It has no meaning and was likely drawn by zero conclusions or facts. Although these types of weighting algorithms can be found all over the place and considered well suited for trusted people, I don't agree. In business, the path of least resistance is usually the one taken. I've done it, I've seen some of the best decision-makers and leaders in my industry do it.

It happens and that's fine; we're human after all. Nevertheless, the point of this decision-making strategy throughout this book is to avoid the path of least resistance, meaning you should do one of two things: if you are to the point where you want to adjust a psychological particle or trait, just take it out of the equation. If not, then don't. The minute you start allowing yourself to apply arbitrary numbers, you will always to get the answer you were hoping for. It's the easiest thing to do, so why not? In other words, yes, you can adjust your figures as we had with earlier demonstrations, and that is why they were included. But now that you have realized the full context of its impact, I would suggest that you don't include them. The second issue is that if you ignore the fallacies with the arbitrary weight method, this still takes nothing into consideration respective of the rest of the organization. If you remember, I mentioned earlier that the Scalability Coefficient is a number that can be applied to anything in your organization. It can be big, it can be small - it does not matter. However, knowing this, if the overall Coefficient of the scope of your decision is big, then you must take that into account when adjusting a small particle within it so that it makes the adjusted and appropriate impact you want it to. If it's small, you will have to take this into higher consideration. The point of this exercise is to drive the number as close to zero as possible, no matter its original size. Where if it starts at, say, 10 then a learning(w,c,p) adjustment to 1 would still be 10% of the entire Coefficient. Whereto the former point, if it starts at 1,000, an adjustment to 1 would be an impact of 0.1% - a big difference (some would venture to say two orders of magnitude or so). Taking this full circle brings me to my third and less revealing approach below.

Global Adjustment Method

This method is much less to discuss at this point because we can't figure it out yet. We have to wait until everything is taken into consideration and all the Coefficients have all been equated. It is not until you sum the Coefficients for your decision-making scope that you can truly find an appropriate adjustment method, whether it be a weight or otherwise. At that point, it's far less arbitrary of a weight which can be reassuring as well. It's a relative adjustment to say we only want to take some-odd percentage into consideration because of reasons x, y, and z (which we explained in gruesome detail earlier). The idea of applying weights is still flawed. Yet this takes some of the self-imposed randomness out of it and gives the numbers a little more context. Not enough to take away my recommendations from earlier, but enough to maybe help you think independently.

Other Notable Adjustments

Adjustments and considerations can be taken, not to change the impact of a given equation on the overall decision-making power, but as a consideration and to take concessions as you are formulating your own. This is more of a thought experiment to help you think more critically.

The first point I want to bring is for all of this time, we have been discussing an individual's learning curve. The last part of this term we have been ignoring quite heavily. We have been discussing each of these equations and have assumed that the impact of the curve is linear. And being that nobody has heard of the "learning straight line", then we can assume something else could be adjusted. I mentioned this earlier in this section more, as this becomes a psychological trait in and of itself. It starts to dive into a guessing game of individuality, which is something we have been avoiding, as it is against the entire point of the Scalability Coefficient – we don't guess, we know. Let's say we use a case of averages and we know that the average employee learns a given task at an exponential rate. That means their learning curve will have a negative impact on the company as an inverse to their exponential learning rate. Thus if we take a logarithm of learning(w, c, p), we may be fine. However, what is the base of the logarithm? Is it 10? Is it the irrational number e? I could only assume that this would differ for each person and that an exponential learning rate would also vary per person and on what they're learning. If a developer is learning Perl when they are already a master of C, I would agree that an exponential pattern would be observed. But when a developer has to learn Civil Engineering practices when they are already a master of C, I may expect an exponential rate but with a much, much smaller exponent. Evaluating the learning curve linearly is intentional, as it can remove some of the individual variability while still taking everything else into consideration.

The second is a suggestion to take heavier consideration into the current company over any past companies. This will be a trend that resonates throughout this book. The point of this is that you can trust what you know and what you see, more than what is on a resume amongst other ancillary Human Resource factoids. Not to say those are not useful; they are. It is more to say the best information may be sitting right in front of you. I will stray from illustrating this simple point, but one that is worth mentioning nevertheless. It is hard to argue with truths that happen before everyone's eyes every day, so use them to your benefit.

Choices

We have discussed three possible alternatives for evaluating the learning curve at this point. The first and simplest method takes everything into consideration while allowing for people with long tenures in an industry, with a sudden flutter of promotions, (amongst other things) to fall through the cracks. The second approach corrects this by taking a sum of the larger equation relative to each position held. The impact of someone with 20 years experience under their belt and 10 promotions in the last six months will therefore be much less. The third does little more than again changing the first equation so its denominators can be the same, and we can evaluate with like terms to get the same result. We can now take these to evaluate the differences between each to determine which would be preferable to use. We will analyze the search team consisting of our friends Exemelle and James Cartwright, for example; the smallest team of the bunch but with enough information between them to come with enough reliable information to make an informed decision.

In all cases, we need the three variables that are required for our learning functions.

w = *time within field*

c = *number of companies worked for*

p = *number of promotions received*

Let us now abstract these into terms of our search team.

Name	W	c	P
Exemelle	5	2	0
James Cartwright	1.5	1	1

Table 3.10: Search Team Attribute Breakdown

Then we can take these and apply them to our functions.

Generalized Time

$$learning(w, c, p) = \frac{w}{c} \div p$$

Name	learning(w,p,c)
Exemelle	0*
James Cartwright	1.5

Table 3.11: Applied Learning Curve
(* infinitely small number expressed as 0)

Company Specific

$$learning(w, c, p) = \sum_{n=1}^{n} \frac{p}{c} \div w$$

Name	learning(w,p,c)
Exemelle	0
James Cartwright	.667

Table 3.12: Applied Company Specific Learning Curve

We must remember to sum the relative totals for each company.

Specific Time

$$learning(w, c, p) = \frac{c}{w} \div \frac{p}{w}$$

Name	learning(w,p,c)
Exemelle	0
James Cartwright	.599

Table 3.13: Applied Specific Time Learning Curve

These are short examples with few people, so they are hardly enough to draw immediate conclusions with. That is, until you remember exactly what we are trying to achieve: find a method using facts to generate a function that will give us appropriate measures of one's ability. It is merely a function of your preference of which method to use after that.

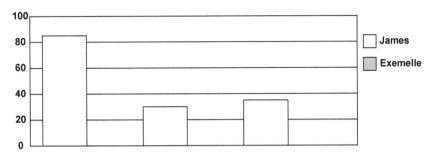

Image 3.14: Specific Time of Team

Using this approach, each function will give us the same general result at varying degrees. This folds into the dampening effects we discussed earlier in this section. As there is no boundary or rule into how you should or could express a particle, it becomes a question of what you want the equation to represent, and whether or not you understand the output so you can defend it in the future. As long as the logical concept of reality is retained, how you get there is up to you; for the most part. Taking from this example, we can judge that the latter two of the functions have the same relative impact, where the first shows nearly a two-fold difference in terms of the literal result. The issue becomes important as we continue to review the micro-portion of the practice without greater knowledge of the topics and analysis we have yet to discuss. It's all a function of the larger picture, where without it, it's just a pixel. If the pixel is red, yellow or blue makes no difference until you see the pixels together, when they build off of one another to render a comprehensible image. Let us take yet another look at our procedures through the view of the data team. Hopefully this will better demonstrate the concept in its entirety.

Name	w	C	p
John Overheimer	17	4	8
Percy Greentrain	6	2	2
Stan Keyhang	3	2	0

Table 3.15: Attribute Extraction

And with that, we can apply the values to each of the individuals.

Name	General	Company	Specific
John Overheimer	.53	.36964	.5
Percy Greentrain	1.5	.2	1
Stan Keyhang	0	0	0

Table 3.16: Individual Application Implementation

If we move the results into the same visual representation as we had before:

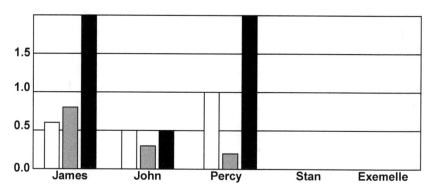

Image 3.17: Time Distributions for Team

We have taken a different perspective on the visual with the addition of three new employees. Each of the columns for each of the people represents our Specific, Company, and General methods. Looking at the data from this direction exposes a few differences between the equations. If we take the three people who have had a promotion (James, John, and Percy) and impacts greater than zero, we can see the different functions will give us different results in terms of individuals with a respectively adjusted learning curve. We can first see that the "Company" approach has completely different results if simply comparing positive values when compared to the "General" and "Specific," which are much closer to one another, which makes sense if you think about the composition of the functions themselves. The "Company" approach takes each position into consideration rather than an average of them all into a larger sum, for example. Percy scoring lower than John, who is lower than James, is therefore justified by the facts relative to what is taken into consideration. Before working at Intellicorp for the past year, Percy spent five years with another company and received two promotions. This implies that he receives a promotion every 2.5 years with little consideration to the fact that he has yet to receive a promotion at Intellicorp as the experience of his past is taken with higher regard in this sense. James, on the other hand, is the exact opposite. He has only worked with Intellicorp and receives a higher score even though he has already received a promotion in his first 1.5 years within the company. When you look at the remaining two differences in scale, you find that John receives a higher score than both James and Percy, yet to varying degrees. When you take equal consideration from each company, you will see that John's experience in the past two decades relative to the number of companies is better suited for the result. Looking further into the "Specific" algorithm, you see that the tie between Percy and James is broken and it brings James' score down below Percy, yet still above John. Explainable, as the former takes more consideration to time over promotions, where John is nearly 1:1 versus Percy's 3:1 ratio. The point here is less about which of these three options we should chose. It is about which best suits you and your company's goals. What do you want to concentrate your efforts on and where do you want to go? If you take the attributes that define your company into full consideration when designing your functions, you will find people having a tough time arguing with you. If you work toward this level of breakdown and analysis, you will quickly find that the explanations of your decisions are easier, as you have likely already considered their alternatives. You know the differences, the people, their past and their habits well enough to make decisions intelligently based off of facts. Thus, feel free to take one of these algorithms but also feel free to design your own. Once you know your organization to this level, which you should, you will be a force to be reckoned with.

When taking Intellicorp's goals into consideration, we know few things given our relationship and tenure: they want to be more efficient with what they have, simple enough. Of the three algorithms we have worked with, we will continue from here on with the "Specific" approach. This approach best demonstrates how experience dominates the lack thereof, while suggesting the course of short-term, positive gains by individuals without consideration for other companies. Intellicorp wants to care about what people are doing now, not what they have done in the past. When the management of your local sports team recruits the best coach in the league, do you care how their wins and losses stack up after the dawn of the first game under his or her regime? No. You care about how your team will do now with the new coach. Hardly will you ever hear a fan say "Well, we never won a game but that's OK - the coach used to be *really* good back in the day." This idea holds true with Intellicorp. We care about the employee's performance now, while taking some consideration into the past. Even with coaches, their past can help paint an optimistic future in the wake of a horrid season. It is more common to hear "We'll do better next season." which is a cue to this.

So there we have it: our learning curve. Individual results may vary.

$$learning(w, c, p) = \frac{c}{w} \div \frac{p}{w}$$

Last, before we move on, let's compute our learning curve as we have determined it to be for the entire organization.

Name	w	c	p	learning(w,c,p)
Strider Johnson	3	1	3	.3333
Arwen Little	7	15	0	0
Erwin Little	7	15	0	0
Chet Smith	5	2	0	0
Grace Hopset	7	3	1	5.33
Perl Wall	3	2	0	0
Exemelle	5	2	0	0
James Cartwright	1.5	1	1	1
John Overheimer	17	4	8	.5
Percy Greentrain	6	2	2	1
Stan Keyhang	3	2	0	0
Caleb Alan	10	4	5	.8
Addie Lane	8	3	1	3
Therese Jean	5	2	0	0
Bill Votex	10	5	4	4
Jason Watcifer	8	3	1	3

Table 3.18: Computed Learning Curve

With this drawn, we can continue onto the next portion of analysis. Congratulations! We now have the first particle of our organization fully analyzed. We'll break this down quite a bit further as we build to a conclusion of the full analysis of the people that make up Intellicorp to see how these numbers will better compute, and how they can help us make better decisions.

Compensation and Effectiveness

Compensation is more than how much a person makes. It is a window into their intelligence, experience and general worth to the company. One would hope that a person who makes $30,000 a year plus $5,000 in benefits will return more than $35,000 to the company over the same year. That would make sense, wouldn't it? Furthermore, this may be one of the most scrutinized, analyzed and highly managed numbers that float to each person within the company. Everyone thinks they are worth more, work to justify this stance. The only line of defense is to review performance as an individual, respective of the team and the general importance to the company (will a janitor get as much consideration as an executive when one asks for a raise?), and comparing those to market equivalents. I have rarely seen a company that doesn't employ an entire team to these non-trivial facts. One's is a number that has been given to them with everything surrounding them, with the local and national industry taken into consideration in terms of their talent. The great thing about this information is that we can use this number to our benefit in determining the relative contribution differences between individuals within the same general role. Let's take Intellicorp back into consideration for a second - the QA team specifically. We have Addie, Therese and Bill who have the titles of QAE II, QAE II and SDET IV respectively. We know a little more than that about each. We do know, however, that Bill is somewhat of a control freak that basically takes the work that he wants, while Addie and Therese are joined at the hip with sister-like similarities, both in terms of experience and throughput. We could nosedive into the different psychological characteristics of these three, but let us again take a step back and look again at their titles - what do *they* have to say?

QAE Team

We can see that all three positions have two designations: title and level, the former denoted by an acronym and the latter by a whole number. From the three people in this example, we have two titles: Quality Assurance Engineer (QAE) and Software Development Engineer in Test (SDET). We also have two levels: II and IV. What we don't see is that there are levels in between these levels. We know there must be at least a QAE I. If not in practice, in theory. Similarly for the SDET position, we can assume the level I, II and III also exist, at least on paper. A betting man could also assume HR has job descriptions for QAE positions with levels higher than II. Therese reveals that the position's promotion path rises to IV just as SDET position does in this case. We now not only know the three people's positions and levels, but we have quickly figured out the range of possibility with these positions as well. Although we may not know it directly from looking at their business card, we know from earlier conversations with these three and their HR department the salary of which each makes: $25k, $25k and $35k respectively. Somewhere near each of these suggests the salary of each position. This all may be obvious, but what does this telling us? All of this says exactly what we want to evaluate: ignoring the personality traits that effect an individual's effectiveness on a team, using their physical salaries relative to the number of levels that are available for the positions as a reliable gauge of their effectiveness. The difference of level of contribution of a Junior Developer and Senior Developer is, in part, a functional difference of their salary applied as a mathematical function, where the number of levels available for a position will dictate how big of a difference each position holder will make. Let's go into some examples that will start to prove this case before we dive into some of these equations. Let's look at Addie and Therese to start. The two were characterized to be near identical twins in nearly all cases. We know they hold the same position with the same level, have the same experience and make the same salary. Holding the same position and level both suggest they should be on the same professional level, and that is more or less emphasized with the two raking in the same amount of dough each month. As it turns out, they are the same. They contribute the same and Bill and Caleb both use them interchangeably for the same tasks. This should be the case and for nearly all companies, we should expect this case to varying degrees. We should expect that people are in the positions they deserve to be in. If they are not, they should be moved. If nobody is, then the positions should be changed. You could consider this an opinion surging its elbow into a theory which disproves the entire thing, but it's not. I won't hire a young man fresh out of college to be the Directory of my technology organization, and I would expect nobody else to make the same fatal mistake. I would expect someone with the right experience to be in the position they have worked towards and proven themselves to excel at. In terms of this book, this is something I will have to continue to assume. Of course, real life doesn't usually sit two peas in a pod like Addison and Therese, and so we should look outside of this life of perfectness for a second as well. Most people do have personal traits that will dictate how much they contribute. Just because someone is fresh out of college doesn't mean they can only code at two characters a second. They may be defaulted into a Junior position and work quickly to dig out of that spot into something that's more appropriate for their quickly learned skill set. On the other hand, there may be a tired veteran of the industry that is the utmost senior software architect you have ever met, but contributes more to the uptime of the bathrooms than that of his job. These two are polar opposites and both will demolish the point made earlier. Before I go into the destructive details of how this will all impact our decision making, let's first start with looking into the first points I brought up and work from there.

We must first believe that salary ranges have been appropriately assigned. As I was describing earlier, a well-established tool for determining differences in performance and expertise is the money they make respective of their position and ignoring their level (as in most cases the level also explains salary range changes). What this means is that two people who are each QAEs can be compared with one another, whereas you cannot take the salary of a QAE and compare it to that of a SDET because you have crossed the relativistic boundary of comparisons. The two have different jobs, different responsibilities and own a completely different portion of the development life cycle. Although they work close together, the positions encapsulate different roles and responsibilities. Like a home's fame to its foundation, they need one another to be a solid and long-lasting structure and one without the other would be useless but they're still different. I won't hire a framer to pour my concrete foundation, I'll hire a framer to frame and a concrete and foundation specialist to pour my foundation. I may even ask the two to meet, shake hands and discuss a schedule. Of course, it can be argued that people within the same position with different levels have different roles and responsibilities as well, and will also cross the relativistic threshold of comparisons. Although these statements can be true, they are not always. The same general job function and end goal is to be completed and they all own the same part of the development life cycle; they may just hold different responsibilities within their team, not within the larger organization. You could imagine that the tier of one's position indicates little more than experience and with that comes efficiency. If it doesn't, then you may question whether or not that person fits in the position they are in. This is the larger picture I am trying to paint: if you attack a project with 10 Senior, level IV staffers versus 10 Junior, level I staffers, would you expect a difference of a projects pace or quality? We will talk about the countless issues that affect this answer. The 10 Senior, level IV staffers would generally finish before their Junior counterparts with a higher level of quality and at a higher price. The reason for this is nothing more than experience. People gain efficiencies over the course of time, making mistakes, discovering tools and methods; and learning the appropriate skills along the way. They do this to the degree where it becomes an art and becomes faster than their early, junior counterparts. Yet how do we express this? First, we have to take the differences of salary which will give us a range between each position. To make things simple, we will take the average of a given level's range. If the range is from \$10,000 to \$20,000/year, for example, we will assume \$15,000. We can do this as the function is exclusive of individuals, and inclusive of the position. Let's do this for Addie and Therese's positions helping to draw a clearer picture.

Number	Position	Average Salary
1	QAE I	20
2	QAE II	25
3	QAE III	30
4	QAE IV	35

Table 3.19: QA Salaries Respective of Position

This first step was nothing more than copying down what HR has on file. It states nothing more than the four positions that are available for Addie and Therese if they stay in their career path at this point: QA I through IV and the average salary range for each of them. Taking this a bit further and to what was stated earlier:

Number	Position	Average Salary	Difference
1	QAE I	20	5
2	QAE II	25	5
3	QAE III	30	5
4	QAE IV	35	5

Table 3.20: QA Salary Differences

This example is simple enough, but the point is clear. Each position has a $5,000 per year difference in payment for experience. The first position, in this case, is assumed to be 5 as well, even though there is nothing to compare it against. In this case, it inherits its attributes from its next highest position. Now what this difference suggests is not only the monetary payment offered at varying levels, but the perceived value difference between the differing positions. It is somewhat substantial in this case, just as well as $5,000 is 20% of the QAII and 14.28% of the QA IV position respectively. Even a pop from III to IV is a raise to not shake a stick at. Regardless, this is all example but the point is drawn: the difference relative to the number of positions is nothing more than a gauge of experience, where experience is nothing more than an accumulation of knowledge which includes efficient use of time. Therefore, if we express the range difference respective of the total number of levels, we can find the difference each should be expected to contribute.

$$ContributionalDifference = contribution(r, t) = \frac{r}{(t-1)}$$

Where:

r = *Difference of salary ranges*

t = *Total number of position levels*

It's a simple enough equation that demonstrates everything we've been talking about. The difference in expected output is a function of reward over levels of opportunity. There are, as always, still discussion points that should be brought up. The first thing that can be noticed is that this equation assumes everyone at a given level of a position contributes the exact same as the next. This is never true of course. There are a few answers to this argument. We are first allowed to assume the average of people. If we believe that our HR department and hiring managers are doing their job, then the difference of skill and contribution between different people in a level should be minimal. If they're not, then adjustment should be made to the organization to make sure people are in the right position, not the equation that evaluates the right position. The other answer is much like the answer we gave to evaluating the learning curve: adjust it on an individual basis with an arbitrary weight. Be careful of this as there is a good chance you will be taking other characteristics into account in other equations we come up with. For example, if you want to adjust the difference of contribution of someone because they are extremely new to the team, you have to ask if you are adjusting the correct value. This would be a valid case of someone falling to the lower end of a position with the assumption they will move ahead over time. We are talking about the ability of a person to learn over time in this case, which is nothing more than a person's learning curve and have already been computed. If we take both into consideration, then we will be adjusting for a learning curve twice rather than the single intended time. Although it may be difficult at this point to see the larger picture of how this will fit together, we have to remember at this point we are determining the Scalability Coefficient at a particle level, the smallest level possible. We are still looking at a sapling at the edge of a rain forest. We will continue to plant these new trees. Once we have completed, we will take a step back and evaluate the forest to see what we can do to make it proper over the years. We are working on small functions and ideas that will be combined into a much more rigid and powerful decision-making machine as we continue. This is the reason why I suggest you take arbitrary adjustments with even more care, and for even more reasons than I have stated before. It's a slippery slope if nothing else and besides, we're looking for near accuracy, not perfection. Suggestions, not scientific fact. It is OK to take the average of the people who fill the level and assume we can categorize them into a single function.

You may be asking yourself a number of other questions at this point regarding this individual function. Again, I urge you to think of the bigger picture. One good argument is taking us back to the ten Senior versus ten Junior Developer at a project example where we guessed which team would finish first. I said if we could assume everything else was equal and free, the ten Senior Developers would contribute more and be victorious in the proverbial race. However ten Senior Developers will cost considerably more than ten Junior Developers and maybe the cost savings is worth the loss of time. It is a valid argument made daily for this reason, and for the fact that there is a finite amount of resources available to everyone. There is also the case within this example that could be suggested that ten Senior people would start to cause inefficiencies, as they would be stepping on one another's toes. Another valid argument made; if the task is to build a single HTML page, then assigning ten Senior Developers would likely produce ten individual HTML pages, each a little different and none fitting the requirements. Whereas the ten Junior Developers may struggle, but may come out with something closer to what was asked, as their concentration was on finishing the task while learning how to do it rather than rushing through a medial task (as compared to the Senior Developer). Each a valid case and will be brought up later.

Now that we have talked through some of the issues and how we have gotten here, let's break down Intellicorp starting with the QA team and branching out to the rest of the organization. Respective of the QA team alone, remember what we started with:

Number	Position	Average Salary	Difference
1	QAE I	20	5
2	QAE II	25	5
3	QAE III	30	5
4	QAE IV	35	5

Table 3.21: QA Salary Differences

Using the algorithm we described earlier and knowing the salary difference is 5, with a total of four levels for the position, we have:

$$contribution(r, t) = contribution(5, 4) = \frac{5}{(4-1)} = 1.667$$

Before I dip into the description of how we can apply this, we will adjust the equation a bit so we can better explain what to do with it, and so it can be applied with accuracy to the growing set of functions. Therefore, we will have:

$$contribution(t, r) = (\frac{r}{(t-1)})/100$$

The alteration does not need much explanation, but it's a simple change bringing the number to a multiplier we can apply to future coefficients. When you think about it, we are currently working on the effect that people in different levels of their position will have. The approach I recommend, and that you will continue to see, is using it as a multiplying adjustment again. Not to be confused with an arbitrary multiplier, as we were discussing with earlier equations, but a computed multiplier that will have a real and justified effect on the outcome of our Scalability Coefficient as its applied across teams.

Now with our change, we have.

$r = 5$

$t = 5$

$$contribution(r, t) = contribution(5, 4) = (\frac{5}{(4-1)})/100 = 0.0167$$

Now this number is a constant relative to the entire spread of levels in this example. The next step we take is to apply it across the field as a relative reduction and increase of output from the middle of the levels as a percentage. With that description we have:

Number	Position	Average Salary	Difference	Adjusted Contribution
1	QAE I	20	5	.2166
2	QAE II	25	5	.2333
3	QAE III	30	5	.2767
4	QAE IV	35	5	.2934

Table 3.22: Adjusted QA Salary Differences

The sum of each of the adjusted contributions should total 1 (with some intentional ignorance applied to the rounding). We can now apply in different situations to take different positions into account. This is just once piece of a larger puzzle. There are a few issues with our approach up until now, but let's apply this function to the rest of the organization and see what evolves.

Web Team

Much like the QA team, we have information about the web team from our interviews and Intellicorp's Human Resources files. Five people comprise the team with two positions and a total of eight levels; Software Development Engineers (SDE) and Web Development Engineers (WDE) each with five and four levels respectively. We also know each's salary ranges and the ranges of the positions and levels that have nobody associated with them. Let us expose our contribution function to our SDE position with a little depth as they hold one of the largest possible position sets.

Number	Position	Salary Range	Difference
1	SDE I	30	5
2	SDE II	35	5
3	SDE III	40	5
4	SSDE I	60	20
5	SSDE II	70	10

Table 3.23: SDE Salary Differences Respective of Position

Most of the teams fit to the cookie cutter design of the QA team; five positions, each with an even distribution. This is an unusual case, but the point of this exercise is to demonstrate how to take differences like this into account. There are only three things I want to demonstrate before we move on. The first is the combination of SDE and SSDE (Senior versus not-Senior). It's with the same argument as before in that the classifications of roles in terms of seniority is less important than the partitioning of responsibilities in terms of actual job. In this case, a Senior Software Development Engineer is still a Software Development Engineer. And a SSDE II is still a Senior Software Development Engineer which is still a Software Development Engineer. This deviates from earlier points, but the different prefixes are nothing more than level changes, ego-boosters, and possibly bonus structure changes. I, for one, would prefer a "Senior" prefix than a "IV" suffix. Maybe you're different. More importantly, accompanying this prefix change is a jump in salary. You can see from the table above that this change gives us a different twist on the difference of salary ranges when respecting the contribution function we have been working with. With this small slice of reality to now take into consideration, we have at least two ways to evaluate the fluctuation in differences between positions. The first and simplest way is to simply take the average of the differences, giving us 9 in this case where $(5 * 3 + 20 + 10 / 5 = 9)$. This will spread the differences evenly across all positions, which seems like something we don't want to do. If we follow the same line of thought as before, we have assigned a $5k difference between an SDE I and SDE II, and a $20k difference between SDE III and SSDE I, not $9k. Yet this generalization is still acceptable as it will adjust each position by the relative adjusted contribution, smoothing the ripples of its effect. Another method of reconciliation is to be much more specific and adjust each contribution by a function of the difference, respective of other differences taken into consideration. This method is more precise and is why I will go through it. So let's break down this method.

We first know the differences of salary per position:

Position	Difference
SDE I	5
SDE II	5
SDE III	5
SSDE I	20
SSDE II	10

Table 3.24: Raw SDE Salary Differences

With an simpler algorithm, we can then determine the relative contribution as a function of the size of the difference, with respect to the size of all differences. Taking the full range all the levels in the position, we can then determine what percentage one level takes within the full range of the position, giving us the formulated result we hope for. This draws the same conclusion as what we drew earlier, yet we can now have varying degrees of contribution based on the level, rather than linear contribution as we would other wise experience by taking the average of each of the positions as a single difference. If we take this new paradigm into thought, we would come up with:

$$contribution(r) = \frac{(\sum_{n}^{n=1} r_n - 1) + r}{\sum_{n}^{n=1} r}$$

r = range (or difference)

n = the number of subordinate positions

We can now see that the difference of contribution as we have outlined it. It can be expressed as the difference of salary over the sum of all differences. This will give us the following table:

Position	Difference	Difference as Percentage
SDE I	5	.111
SDE II	5	.222
SDE III	5	.333
SSDE I	20	.777
SSDE II	10	1.00

Table 3.25: SDE Salary Differences as Percentage

You can see the difference in the result. Now the highest level for the position will achieve maximum contribution if we can assume that is the best one can be within their respective position. We also continue to get the benefit of varying levels of contribution, respecting many of the points we raised earlier. You can see if we were to take the above formula and compare it to the averaging of differences, you would see:

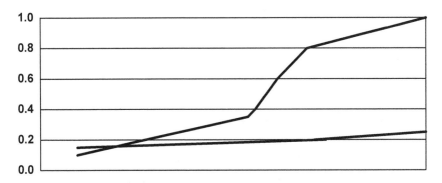

Image 3.26: SDE Salary Differences as Percentage

What you can see here is the immediate difference between the two functions. Which method better suits your organization? This point was made for the sake of demonstration of course, though it would still be a question on myself as Intellicorp's consultant to determine if an SSDE II really is expected to contribute nearly 89% more than an SDE I. In a normal situation, with a non-fictional company, this range is possible. The question becomes: is it correct and how does it apply in terms of future analysis? These questions we will get to shortly as we work with our results to find out exactly what our continued evaluation delivers.

Choices

We have some choices based off the information we have at this point. The choice is a matter of goals, objectives, logic and appropriateness, and remembering it's not a matter of dramatics. It is a matter of accuracy which can even be feathered a bit. With this in mind, let's refresh ourselves with what we have:

General Method

$$contribution(t, r) = (\frac{r}{(t-1)})/100$$

For a lack of a better term, we have the "General" method. It is a fair demonstration through the averaging of the full range of differences between each position and their type. This method is less an image of reality and more a display of fairness while continuing to give higher consideration (in terms of real, positive numbers) to those who have a higher position and level than their peers a bit lower on the same ladder. We have already computed the Software Engineering classification (and is again below), but let's compute a few more to get a better gauge of what we are comparing against. In terms of taking an average of all the differences as we spoke to earlier, the real function is more along the lines of:

$$contribution(t, r) = \frac{(\sum_{n}^{n=1} r)/n}{t - 1}/100$$

Position	r	t	contribution(t, r)	Contribution %
SDE I	9	5	.02250	.15500
SDE II	9	5	.02250	.17750
SDE III	9	5	.02250	.20
SSDE I	9	5	.02250	.22250
SSDE II	9	5	.02250	.24500

Table 3.27: Computed SDE Compensation Percentage

Let us take the other team that we've partially analyzed to see what we come up with again. We can continue to use the slightly modified equation to take averaging of the differences into account, even though it won't matter as much with this case, as the differences are each the same anyways.

Position	r	t	contribution(t, r)	Contribution %
QAE I	5	4	.01666	.21668
QAE II	5	4	.01666	.23334
QAE III	5	4	.01666	.26666
QAE IV	5	4	.01666	.28332

Table 3.28: Computed QAE Compensation Percentage

We can now have two positions with a total of nine levels between them. We see the difference between a well spread expectation and a less-so distribution. Let's carry on.

Specific Method

$$contribution(r) = \frac{\left(\sum_{n}^{n=1} r_n - 1\right) + r}{\sum_{n}^{n=1} r}$$

Our second method is to take the percentage of the difference as it relates to the entire salary range for the position. The result is far less of a linear progression that what we saw with our "General" method, and a little closer to reality. Let's take the time to compute the SDEs (again) and the QA team with this method before getting too deep too fast.

Position	r	contribution(r)
SDE I	5	.11111
SDE II	5	.22222
SDE III	5	.33333
SSDE I	20	.77777
SSDE II	10	1.0000
QAE I	5	.25
QAE II	5	.50
QAE III	5	.75
QAE IV	5	1.0

Table 3.29: Computed Product Development General Contribution

We now have each of the algorithms in place; let's now compare them so we can determine the reasons behind their output and make the best decision between the two. We must first remember that each team must be evaluated separately, as they are only relative to themselves. We can then see the difference between the two method's interpretations of Software Developers:

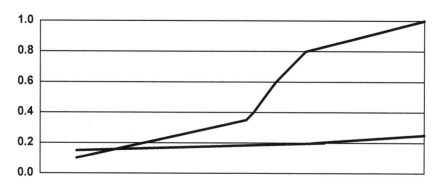

Image 3.30: Computed Product Development General Contribution

And their peers in the Quality Assurance organization:

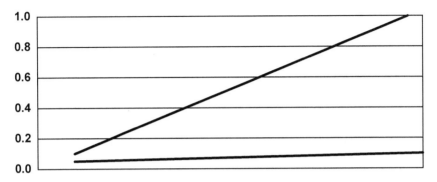

Image 3.31: Product Development Contributon

We have our visualization of what we have been conceptualizing. The question continues: Which is most appropriate for what is best for the organization? We must first understand what we have to choose from. Second, we have to explain it. Third, we have to decide. We will take each step while taking the organization's best interests into consideration. Let's start with the first two steps. Reviewing our data again, we have a difference between taking the organizational difference as an average, or specifically for each level of each position. We can see that the first image does a good job of staggering the responsibility as it relates to the pay scale for the level. The second algorithm does too - at least for the two teams we are working with. Naturally, the biggest difference is the consideration that is taken for the positions that fall within the middle of the curve. By taking the range as an average of the differences, it brings the relative Coefficient up to ensure the linear pattern, whereas the specific approach ensures the varying degree based of the perceived responsibility. For any given example, this would ultimately be the case. The highs and lows will remain relative to one another. In terms of scale, it's more about the middle that will change. Thus it becomes a question of complexity as a function of the dynamic of the organization. In terms of Intellicorp, we *do* care about the middle. The middle has the widest difference between the two, where the jump between a SDE III and SSDE I is a bump of $20k per year, which is about 44%

of the range of the entire position. This is a considerable amount. Averaging this bump across the rest of the levels would present unfair prejudice against them, setting Intellicorp up for failure. A fair question then is whether or not the jump is appropriate for the position. Does a difference between an SSDE I and SDE III justify a near 50% pay increase? From conversations held with the team, it's nearly impossible to say and dissolves into rather a moot point. At the point of our interviews, there were no Senior Developers in the organization at all. This means that off of paper, there is no bar at all. Writing down an impossible job description is one thing, but hiring for and promoting into it is completely another. In the case of Intellicorp, it will be hard to answer the definitive question of whether or not the first Senior developer of the team is worth the extra money. If they carry out the responsibilities that are written to them such as training, coaching, etc. - bringing each of the non-Senior members up to their level over time, then maybe. But maybe not, too. There is always the evolving question of having too many high-authority people on a single team or within an organization. In fact, there are countless terms and phrases that have been adorned over the years that explain this very phenomena. Whether or not the position is justified for the increase, we do not have to take it into consideration. For the positions we do consider, it's a linear scale regardless. We will continue to have a large difference between ranges in some positions, and the job descriptions are written to justify this difference. Without filling the position, we will never know if we should raise or lower the range but still need to assume it will remain until we can. With taking nothing much more into consideration and knowing only this, it would make the most sense to stick with the "specific" method for our further analysis.

$$contribution(r) = \frac{(\sum_{n}^{n=1} r_n - 1) + r}{\sum_{n}^{n=1} r}$$

With the decision of which to use, let us next apply our function to the organization. We have already accomplished this for two of our positions and we have three left: Data Analyst, Web Development and Managers.

Software Development

Position	r	contribution(r)
SDE I	5	.1111
SDE II	5	.2222
SDE III	5	.3333
SSDE I	20	.7777
SSDE II	10	1.000

Table 3.32: Computed SDE Contribution

Quality Assurance

Position	r	contribution(r)
QAE I	5	.25
QAE II	5	.50
QAE III	5	.75
QAE IV	5	1.00

Table 3.33: Computed QAE Contribution

Web Development

Position	r	contribution(r)
WebDev I	5	.2777
WebDev II	5	.5555
WebDev III	5	.8333
WebDev IV	3	1.000

Table 3.34: Computed WD Contribution

Data Analyst

Position	r	contribution(r)
Data Analyst I	2	.1428
Data Analyst II	5	.5000
Data Analyst III	7	1.000

Table 3.35: Computed Data Analyst Contribution

Managerial

Position	r	contribution(r)
Manager	10	.5
Sr. Manager	20	1.00

Table 3.36: Computed Managerial Contribution

Let us finish this conversation with a few more points before we move on. These have been intentionally broken up into their respective positions for the cases we've outlined earlier: each are different and should be analyzed as such. Second, now that we have brought this approach to the larger scope of the organization, we have to review a few more points that we had not before. There are a number of positions that are not filled and some that are split between two teams. Stan Keyhang, for example, is a Data Analyst who is also a Software Developer. Even deeper is that he is also under the managerial wing of John Overheimer of the data team, yet makes a Software Engineer's salary. The obvious question becomes: where do we put him? In the case of our analysis of Intellicorp, he will be applied to the Data Team under his respective title of Data Analyst I - even with his difference in salary. Another approach would be to classify him alone respective of his own amalgamated position. These are eventually your decisions to make, each requiring the same level of hindsight review; not everyone will fit into the same cookie cutter. Another finding after the expanded analysis is the bi-level managerial position. With the description of our analysis given, the question from earlier arises: is there really a 50% difference in contribution between a Senior and non-Senior Manager? In the case of Intellicorp: it doesn't matter as there are no Senior Mangers (phew). In another company who may have the two levels filled, it would be a safe bet to say: no. To what extent could a single promotion suggest that that person would suddenly be 50% more effective than the day before? Nothing. That analysis is still looking at the tree instead of the forest. It depends on so many more attributes and the context of the generalized or specific analysis we will take for the given situation. In other words, if you are satisfied with the function you have chosen, then trust the output of the data; it's that simple. Last, we should take some time to understand the data we have built a bit deeper. In the examples we have drawn, we see that the most senior person receives a score of 1, while each level underneath has a proportionately lesser score than the former. When taking the concept of lowering the overall Coefficient, we have to consider that by taking the contribution of something into account, we would expect the most senior people to be able to contribute the most. With an increasing number, however, that becomes hard to accomplish. Since we have defined this as the contribution of an individual at the level of a given position, we can also take this as multiplier of particular segments of a larger equation. This would continue to have the issue of an increasing coefficient with growing experience contradicting the assumptions we have taken about the efficiency of Senior employees up to this point. A simple adjustment would be to subtract the result of contribution(r) by 1 and inverting the values. By doing so, each of the senior members would be given a multiplier of zero and likely giving them an unfair advantage over most relative to methods that were applied to this. If you believe this to be the case, then consider an application to reverse it by multiplying it by -1. Any multiplier will then be given a larger negative number than it's less senior counterparts and, when summed, will reduce the coefficient appropriately. These are adjustments that can be done once the particle equations that we are creating now are applied to a larger context and analyzed. Thinking of it now is important to keep consistency as we continue. In any case, whether or not this approach is feasible at "run-time" (the time when we take these equations and actually apply them to decision making), we may come up with something like:

$$contribution(r) = \frac{(\sum_n^{n=1} r_n - 1) + r}{\sum_n^{n=1} r} * -1$$

Versus our earlier function from earlier:

$$contribution(r) = \frac{(\sum_n^{n=1} r_n - 1) + r}{\sum_n^{n=1} r}$$

You can see the point from each angle and have hopefully thought through the situations as I have. We now have our equation for the effect of contributions of individuals and we can move on from here.

A Time to Reflect

We have thoughtfully decomposed the different pieces of the team into each of their evaluable particles, analyzed them, and found appropriate methods of assigning metrics to each. It is easy to point out that we have not yet covered each of the physical attributes we have outlined. At any point of the analysis, it is impossible to believe everything has been taken into consideration. Above that, it is bordering on irresponsible to believe you should. Let your thoughts and approaches grow with your learning. When you realize you have missed something, figure it out then and take it into consideration as we have with the limited things we have thought about thus far. All this aside, we have taken the majority of our thoughts into consideration, enabling us to create two functions that can tell us a number of things based off of nothing but facts. Before we move on to the next set of analysis, however, we should take the time to read less into what the composition of the functions are, and more into what they can actually tell us. This is a useful strategy as we continue to grow our knowledge of the organization. The more we know of what we covered, the more intelligent decisions we can make in the future.

Take the equation we built to evaluate individual learning curves.

$$learning(w, c, p) = \frac{c}{w} \div \frac{p}{w}$$

We know the details about this equation we have already talked about, but what can we actually get out of it? It helps to remember that the goal of this equation is to bring the result as close as possible to zero where we assume the sum of all equations will result in the most efficient decision. Find the most appropriate method, be consistent and stick with it.

Looking at the learning equation we have designed, we can take a look at the first half to start with. We have a simple design of the number of companies one has worked for, divided by the tenure in years they have been within their respective field. The first thing this tells us is that there is a widely negative impact for people who have worked at a lot of companies in a short amount of time. When the number of companies outgrows the number of years a person has been working, we start rubbing shoulders with positive numbers, which will do nothing but grow any other multiplier or summed value with quick speed. The opposite tells us that the fewer companies a person works for over the course of a period of time is a great positive benefit. Where if a person has been employed in a field for thirty years, all of with the same company, we would find that person to be wildly valuable. As the higher the ratio of years worked to number of companies grows, the leftward portion of the equation shrinks. This is not the undeniable truth, as the result of this is the numerator for a larger equation which we must consider. The rightward side of the equation tells us we have a similar ratio to consider between the numbers of promotions received over the time worked within an industry. Looking at the denominator alone will give us skewed results and are not worth talking much about. We need to look at these together. We will see together that the best result will come from an equation where the numerator is small and the denominator is large. This tells us that we can expect the most efficient person to be someone who has worked at few companies over their tenure, yet has received a large number of promotions over the same time frame. This says that same person who has worked at a single company for thirty years must have also received a string of promotions over the same number of years before we would consider them to be of large value to the organization. Someone who has been job-hopping over the years embodies an immediate, negative impact, unless the same person has welcomed an unprecedented number of promotions while doing so. As the first equation we have completed, this is, unfortunately, as far as we can look into it. There is nothing to compare it against to determine relative increases of efficiency. Keeping the tired analogy, all we can do is look at the tree and remember its composition for later. We can take three simple memories onto our growing suite of equations, however: A balanced learning result is the equality of companies and promotions over the same amount of time, the best or most efficient is someone who has received a very disproportionate number of promotions over time, and the worst or least efficient is someone who has been stagnant at a company over a period of time. To have it worth much of anything, we can finally begin the trek of walking backwards to gain a better perspective of the forest we are beginning to construct.

Review of our contribution function is a little less obvious when staring directly into its light, but we still need to understand what it defines before we should move on. Much like how we interpreted the learning function to better gauge what we can or should look for in a highly efficient person, we need to be able to do the same with a person's contributions.

$$contribution(r) = \frac{(\sum_{n}^{n=1} r_n - 1) + r}{\sum_{n}^{n=1} r} * -1$$

We break this function into its numerator and denominator to evaluate them separately before we combine them. We must also remember that the goal is to reduce this number to zero when possible (where a value of zero implies the person does not exist which is the most efficient person). The numerator is the sum of all levels of the position and all underneath. I will remind you, however, that we are hunting for the result of *contribution* to be as close to zero as possible which suggests we need the numerator to be as small as possible relative to the denominator. But the inverse of the product is taken by multiplying it by -1, which tells us we actually want the absolute value of the result to be as far away from zero as possible. Therefore, we need the numerator to be as large as possible relative to the denominator, which is the sum of all the differences. Ignoring the sign reversal, if the numerator is the sum of all levels at and beneath the one being evaluated and the denominator is the sum of all, then we know the largest number we can obtain is *1* (*r* / *r* = *1*) which will translate to *-1* as we reverse the sign. We know we want the smallest number; the number whose absolute value is the furthest away from zero as possible (-1). This function tells us we only want the most Senior people for the position across all positions. This cannot be true, of course. Not many companies can hire the most expensive people for every project they work on, and in most cases they would not want to anyways. This consideration will be taken later in our writing. Yet from the perspective of this single particle, the one thing we know is the most Senior people will give us the largest gain for the organization.

We have evaluated and understand two functions independently for the first time, which suggests we should step back a bit to see if or how they interact with one another. This will become an important and significant portion of the book as we move on, and is still something that is necessary to do even if there seems to be no obvious interaction between anything. The exercise of evaluation after understanding is something we need to do, starting at a small scale like this and eventually growing to an analysis of a much larger scale as we continue. We need to see what impact the learning curve has on an individual's contribution and vice versa. For this example, there is little - but not none. A learning curve is the value over time that a person's performance will negatively affect a task as it applies to multiple tasks for any project. A person's contribution factor is a percentage of a task they can complete for the entirety of a project. If someone with a score of (absolute value taken) 1, we assume they are the "high bar" in terms of total contribution a person can give, where anyone in a level under him or her will be a percentage of that bar. We can already see a similarity in that either will impact what we can expect from a person. When working together, combined, we know more. Both functions will impact the levels and waves of contribution to expect from a person; they will likely not interact with one another directly. They are similar enough where they will be used as associative functions to increase or reduce different and larger results. We will cover larger project evaluation using these and other equations we have yet to cover, for example. It is foreseeable that both of the functions we have discussed can be used to help determine what the overall effect people will have on a project in different and more reliable ways, rather than having the two affect one another. If we determine what a project will look like using similar methods that we have so far while taking the people, products, components (and everything else) into consideration, the adjustments these functions can give us will be to the coefficient of the people as they impact the project. If a member is working on a new piece of software, and they are junior compared to the rest of the team, they will have two things riding against them: a steep curve to begin with and a lesser factor of contribution. These two will then increase the project cost, as the price of both of these factors will have to be taken into consideration. At the same time, they are independent factors which also tells us the two cannot change one or the other - but other things that will be impacted by them as independent entities like a project or team at large.

These thought exercise will evolve into a much more advanced decision-making tool as we work to get our. We will be able to take into consideration, when looking at interactions, what we have already learned and know, where the example we theorized above will be able to evolve into a larger function, allowing us to make effective decisions with it; not just by looking into what they mean when they have been put together as we have here, but churning out a larger equation for different situations. There are still a few things we have intentionally avoided, such as finding the coefficient as we know it for the team at this point. It is something that could be entertaining and thoughtful, but something we will do as we continue further down the road. At this point, we have so little information that there is less than a formulated coefficient for the team - which would presumably be the sum of their collective learning and effectiveness. It would arguably be a worthless number in any event. We are exercising a paradigm through examples and very few for that matter. The cases and proofs are nothing more than examples of a thought experiment I am taking you on. When it comes to the application of this design, you must continue the progression we have made up into this point. As with most everything, there is no necessity to this but the recommendation is made. You will find we can make sound decisions with what we will outline in this writing. The fact is that this book will stop and remain static until its continuing revisions are published. Your business does not (or should not as the case may be) ever become static and neither should your implementation of your Scalability Coefficient.

Internal Components

Remembering back to earlier portions of this book, we went through an exercise of diagraming the full network of interactions your team works with. We included the people, their positions, what tools they use, their social and integrated computer networks, the products they work on - the pieces of your organization that are easily forgotten about but impact everything we do and every decision we make every day. We have made the critical leap into dissecting some of the parts of this organizational map in terms of the people who make it happen, but this will slowly erode into only being the surface of our Coefficient. It is revealing as you look into the components people work with, both in terms of tools they use and the products they build. This is in part because the analysis we have given individuals leaves itself to be adjustments to larger equations. The larger reason behind this fact, however, is that there is no behavioral correction that can be made if something is to go wrong. If you have a product that has had no control, is impossible to work with and everyone who tries quits almost immediately - you have more issues than if you have a disgruntled or inefficient employee. You cannot fire your product. You cannot train your product to be a better product. You cannot kill the entire product and start fresh with a new idea, either. You have to fix your product. This is the reality of business. Whether you are offering manufactured good(s), services or something - you have a product. Your product may be your approach to analyzing a company with efficiency deficiencies within a consulting company, or it may be a 1-ton, quad-cab, over-sized monster truck with a 6,000 pound payload and 24,000 pounds of towing capacity. You manufacture *something* and at least one person has bought it, or will. You can certainly change your product. You can give it a complete overhaul if you want. If you sell cars, you can overhaul its design or the method of which you manufacture it. If you are a contractor or consultant, you can work on changing your skill sets or work to achieve a differentiating advantage over your competitors by writing a book. If you are working with a software team, you can redesign and re-implement your software. All things are possible. What goes up can come down and can go back up again. The questions become: why and how? Let us first assume there is no such thing as a dynamic market and no matter what you sell, you will sell a lot of and make a good enough profit to insure your life-long goals. First you should ask: how do you know where your efficiency is going? How do you know it is really your product doing it and not something different like a morale issue? If you know it is the product (development process is taking an obviously extended period of time for example), then you need to ask what part of the product is it? In terms of development cycles, where in your methodology are you losing the most and why? The last and, perhaps, the most important, what can be done to reverse this? Is it changing your methodology? How do you do it to make sure you don't get trapped in the same circle again if so? Is it redesigning a core piece of software? What other impacts will that have and will it really fix enough to relive its costs by the gains of efficiencies if so? Each of these things are independently related to the components that are used in your organization. There is the chance that a third party piece of confusing software is taking hours of productivity away from an entire team each day, although this is likely not the case. Are the benefits of this software worth all the time that is spent using it? These are all questions that should be asked every day for every decision that is made. As we have concluded, your organization is an interconnected network which suggests a single change will effect multiple, connected and independent parts. The question of "how" still looms. These are the questions we will answer with the methods we have already started to unfold. The network is a defined piece of work that will change slowly over time, regardless of how agile you are. You will not be losing and gaining 50% of your code-base every day, nor will you be experiencing employee turnover rates of the same percentage. Therefore, I can begin to show you where your energy is being spent, what can be done to resolve it and what you can do to sustain it. The last two things I want to mention is that at this point, we will not consider the markets. They do matter of course, and should play one of the most critical roles of your decision-making. The second point is that although we have mentioned both internal and external (third party) components, we will be using this section to only work with our internal components.

Physical

The method for analyzing any particle of your organization is the same in general, where things are removed from each as we continue. This is true for physical properties of your organization as well. This is not different from the internal components of an organization, where internal components are defined as components or a sum of components (to make a product) that is the intellectual property of an organization. As a proof of the earlier statement, the largest difference you will see between this and former evaluations is there can be no psychological attributes as those are only defined as biological hazards of the workplace (humans). They are great to work with, but hard to understand. The most notable part about this is the wave of rich information each of these physical attributes hold that will give us cues into what we can expect in terms of its solid design. With the exception of day-to-day activity, there is little that changes. Your product won't be directly effected by a massive layoff during a recession, nor will it be hungover on the 5th of July. Furthermore, it is defined by humans, not by other indefinable forces. Because we have illustrated what the product is and have built it to specification, then we can use those facts to tell us what we have done right, wrong and what we should do better in the future.

To step back for a second, we should remember the facts about Intellicorp and how it relates to our working conditions while we take deeper strides into this exercise. We are going to take the facts that we know about Intellicorp and work solely with those. This means, of course, that everything that evolves from here will be in regards to Intellicorp's needs and you will have to adapt them to fit yours. You can continue to take the paradigm with you, leaving the literal context. Now that you have (I assume), as we have before, we must look for the facts. The truth will be in the immutable details rather than in the assumptions that surround them.

Network Nodes

Proprietary software can grow in complexity by many forms. Since the dawn of networked computing, an obvious factor of complexity is forged by the nodes within a network. Perhaps one of the most discussed methods laws that helps define this concept is *Metcalf's Law*, which defines the concept that the size of a network can be expressed by the number of unique connections that are made in that network (or n^2 asymptotically). This helps us conceptualize the growing complexity based off the network. Although this law defines the size of a network but not its complexity, it is still a decent place to start. Starting with this law, we can believe that the complexity of a network is not directly linked to its size. Is the Internet any more complex now than it was yesterday even though it is growing at a rapid rate? No. Yet, the size of the Internet *is* growing at an exponential rate as defined by Metcalf's Law. However, growth is still a factor as the same question with a broader date range should change your opinion. Has the Internet grown in complexity over the past ten years? Yes, it has - a lot. Stepping back again, it is hard to associate the growth in complexity of the Internet to the number of nodes who connect to it, as it mostly depends on how you define the complex parts. For example, a web developer may suggest that the growth of complexity can be most seen in the advancement of dynamic languages in the browser and the ability to give richer experiences than we could a decade ago. In the same light, a back-end software engineer may say the growing population of worldwide Internet users is causing complexity in simple problems. Serving a video is easy when you have one user and quite hard when you have one billion spread across the globe. Both are true, but only one has anything to do with a growing size of a network and the latter still cannot adhere to the degree of growth that is defined by a network effect. No matter the spin, complexity still grows as more nodes are connected to it. Every network will be different, every node will be defined differently, particularly when describing a proprietary product. Nodes could range from computers or servers to any other interconnected object that relates to a product, just as basing decisions respective of the Internet will draw different results than when determining the number of nodes that effect Intellicorp for our examples. No matter how it is accomplished, nodes are a direct multiplier to complexity in some flavor. If the Internet had zero computers connecting to it, it becomes a rather simple beast. When a few billion connect, it evolves into a horse of a different color.

We will become closer to the accuracy we seek the further we break apart a network into its appropriate pieces. When we try to encapsulate our mind around what a node in a network is, we quickly find different resources within it. As we have discussed before, we need to articulate the smallest entities without getting too specific, and that sometimes means evaluating particles, breaking them apart and evaluating those sub-particles. Nodes in a network hold to this concept well. Depending on what a node is defined as, this deeper exercise may not be necessary. Although since this book is an example study of the analysis of Intellicorp, a software company, we will break the nodes of the network into two smaller sub-particles: sources and dependents.

Network Sources

The first sub-component of a network node we will evaluate for this example is a network source. In terms of our analysis, this is nothing more than a client who receives content from another source within the network. If we fall back to the Internet example we started earlier, imagine we are browsing our favorite website. If doing nothing else than reading a few static pages, we are acting as a network source node to the organization's network we are visiting. We are consuming their input and have become the destination of their output. We want to separate this, as there is a definite differences in terms of complexity when judging between a source and a dependent (which we will define next). The truth of this is that a disconnect of a source will not disrupt the network as a whole. If our browsing pleasure is suddenly interrupted by a power outage, for example, someone else visiting the same page across the country will never know the difference (assuming it is a simple and localized outage). This does not negate the fact that a growing number of sources will alter in any way the growth of complexity, but more to suggest that it lessens it by some degree.

Network Dependents

The inverse of network sources are its dependents. As we will define them, network dependents are nodes that will be dependent for sources to exist and survive. Following the same example, let us assume that we were not only browsing a few static news sites but we were also maintaining them. In browsing, we accidentally knocked over our cup of coffee which drenched the server - and in a clamber to keep it from shorting - we disconnected the power supply. This act of clumsiness would result in both myself (as a user and administrator of the site) and the person across the country who was also viewing the site.

Thinking in these terms brings two points to our attention. The first is the departing of source from dependent. The fact that the disablement of a dependent will effect more than one person is a general use case into why it is more complex as there are more considerations to take when maintaining a network dependency versus a network source. Before we dive into the second portion of the analogy brought up, we should first discuss more of the theory behind the statements just made. It begins to fall onto bases of argument brought up earlier in this book, which is suggested by the perceived amount of complexity that is brought into an organization. An easy contradicting argument to this is that you may not care at all if your service remains up at all. This concept is thrown around a lot and commonly tagged with some buzzword to make it feel a little more edgy. Your uptime likely matters a whole lot more than you give it credit for. Imagine any site you regularly use. Does it or did it ever say "beta" under its logo? If the site was down and later suggested to be the result of something "beta" that happened, were you any less perturbed about the fact that you could not access that service for some amount of time? The truth is that if you give someone a product or service that they find of value, they could care less about whether or not it is in early stages of development or not. They want it to work and they want it to work correctly. Furthermore, very few companies can do a good job of defending against any bad publicity, and when the calls start ringing in about a site being down or a service being buggy, I have yet to hear a customer service response be "Oh yeah, well didn't you see the 'beta' label? Well, an awesome, new startup so just deal with it until we're not." The likely response is something a bit more professional and along the lines of "Thanks, we will look into it" as the issue is quickly escalated to the development team for a hot-fix of some nature. Being the latter situation is the one that will find its way to the resolution, the actions that took it there immediately tell you that it does matter what your customers think, which also means that anything that is dependent on your customers satisfaction will have more complexity than things that do not, plain and simple.

As we veer our eyes to our rear-view mirror, let our focus be brought back onto the example of the systems administrator of the news site losing power to the server while browsing their own site. We have gone over the case of being a dependent, and although it is not an exact definition, it brings up the case of a node being both a source and dependent. This situation happens often, but it does not redefine what a node is. As it is still either a source or dependent at one time. A decent argument could be made that it would be a third classification, although it would be more work then it is worth. Some combination of both being a source and dependent will be sufficient to produce our desired effect, and is a valid example that occurs regularly in most software and general product designs. For our examples, we will ignore this argument and leave it to you and your peers. Rather than creating a third classification, we will have the sum of the other two act as the third.

Product Installations

The number of product installations is an easy number to obtain and describes an incredible amount of the application's complexity. We can ultimately think of this attribute in two dimensions: off-line versus on-line installations. The difference of the two is extremely important. We will define the former as any piece of software that is installed on a remote, client machine. Imagine Microsoft's flagship product, Windows. Windows is currently installed on a majority of computers across the globe. This puts the number of installations in the billions. Alone, this number is not only staggering, but it paints a generic picture into exactly why the product is so large and complex: they have to satisfy billions of customers. Continuing this example - with the aid of your imagination - changing the design of the installation structure and look into a different computer operating system that is based off the Internet - a web-based operating system. Although the consumer market may very well be the same size, the number of installations can be greatly reduced. With the number of installations reduced, the variables that are interfaced with the application are far more controlled and well known. When in this example, you are able to concurrently run multiple consumer's operating systems on the same machine, where each machine powering all your clients are running under a single, unified hardware and software configuration. Suddenly your operating system itself doesn't have to consider the countless variables that go into multiple-vendor hardware selections. Compared to when one user may install your software on a Dell and another on an Acer; fundamentally the same but with subtle differences which all have to be taken into consideration.

Furthering this concept in regards to the number of installations almost immediately feels like any time you move into the client-installation market, you gain complexity. This is not always true, as there are gains and losses from both sides. For example, putting your software onto someone else's computer means you no longer have to maintain the physical environment it sits on; if you have a localized installation with remote connections, you do. If you are serving web pages, you need to make sure the server is running. If you are installing a remote RSS reader (trying to keep the news reading analogy), then you could care less of the client fails as long as they stay a customer. You lose the cost of support of the hardware, which can be staggering when you consider payrolls, fixed costs and depreciation. We will dive a bit into a number of these things, as they are all contributing factors into the complexity of any application. Yet they are all hinged to a single business concept: how do you want people to access your software?

Environments Supported

This attribute is tied to the hip of the one we just completed analyzing, as it heavily relates to the number of product installations. Jumping back to the example we started - we know that Microsoft chooses to install the majority of their software on external computers, by the billions. One of the downsides to this approach is you then have to consider the number of hardware and software environments you need to support. How many operating systems do you support? Obviously, Windows will support only one, but Office may hold support for Apple and Microsoft products. What type of processor interfaces should be supported? Luckily there two major vendors of residential computer CPU's: AMD and Intel. And it's a pretty safe bet they will continue to be the forefront of the market for some years to come. However, each have released numerous products in the years since their inception, most of which come with varying Application Programming Interfaces (APIs), which Microsoft (or any other vendor) support. Do you support 32-bit, 64-bit or both architectures? Do you support single or multi-processor processing? If you interface with external pieces of hardware either directly to the machine or through software, how many driver versions do you support? Each of these questions should be answered with a combination of market penetration analysis and long-term cost structures. Which markets are growing the fastest and have the most steam? Are there many? If so, what are the costs to maintaining a piece of software that supports current and future trends? It is a classic return on investment (ROI) analysis, but one that is usually only looked at from a consumer base and not rigidly into the cost base, which is partly within the product organization. Now on the other side of the coin, we still have the example situation that any company can potentially produce the same software behind the cloak of the Internet. The benefits include the instant reduction in the environments supported, as they are under your control. At the same time, there are more added costs to this route which can actually lead to higher costs than the former, depending on the situation. A smaller online market with higher costs would all but incinerate the benefits reaped from having a controlled environment, and is one of many thought paths that must be taken and I can help you with.

Versions Supported

Much like the number of environments that are supported by software, there is a similar space: the number of versions that are supported. Much like most things in this space, we can argue cases for and against controlled environments. With client-based installed products and software, you will have adoption stragglers; customers that love your product but will constantly shy away from any upgrades. To what extent do you support the ancients as time progresses and your product advances? What happens if you run into your fourth overhaul of the underlying software over a decade and you still have 50% of your users on the first version? Will you keep training your customer service, managers, programmers, quality assurance engineers, product and project managers (and anyone else who interacts with the product) about each of the current and legacy versions? How will the market react to the sun setting of a version? Will those costs outweigh the costs of its continued support? This is again an ROI question, but one that needs to be taken with care and heavy consideration into each of the pieces while understanding their effects on the other portions of your organization's interactive and living network. Once you disconnect the direct interaction between your organization and the client, as you do with client-installed software, you can never really force upgrades as they happen without violating your customer's rights to privacy. While having your product installed locally will let you control the versions, it will come at a cost as well; the support of doing so. Which cost is bigger and which one will effect your market penetration the most, and therefore your bottom line? Once you decide, how can you evolve your thinking to continue to be the most efficient organization while maximizing your profit? This is where we can begin.

Customers

Customers are the necessary evil for any company that is trying to sell something. As without customers, nobody would be buying what is being sold. The fact that we are considering customers does stray a bit from the analytical path we have taken through the evaluation of the technical organization of a larger company. There are a few ways to pick this thought apart, folding it into justification. The first and most obvious is that the customers are too important to ignore. We may be venturing into more of a marketing analysis than technical analysis but we must also consider how related these analysis are. There is nothing to say that we cannot take an engineering centric approach to determining what our most optimal market is, furthermore. Not to say that market exists, it may not. We can say what we would prefer in terms of input translating to output. The second is just because we are considering something now does not mean we have to take it into consideration at all. This process is a mental exercise to think through each of the variables. If the decision is made to ignore a particular attribute - this one for the reasons we have already mentioned - then so be it; there is nothing stopping you. Regardless, ignoring your customer base for any decision is likely a bad idea. Up until now, we have been talking about the end consumers of a company's product. The thing is, we are not talking about an entire company, and we are talking about an organizational unit of Intellicorp: the technology wielding organization to be specific. Technically there is no paying customer for the tech group but they do have customers. Any organization without customers is likely an organization that need not exist at all. HR's customers are the employees of a company just as the technology team's customers are either other employee's or other integral technologies within the company. Homage must be paid to the paying customers; without them, there is no product and without a product, there are no jobs. There are exceptions, certainly, but they are few and far between. In a technology group for example, we may have an entire team dedicated to administrative tools whose only consumers are employees of the larger company. Let's take a piece of software that is the core communication layer of a search engine - much like what Intellicorp has. This engine is not the web layer as well, therefore has the web layer as its customer, so to speak. Within this engine, different features have been built and maintained, coming to a point where there are thousands of interconnected features. If we look at the single customer, the web tier, there is no real gauge into what could be scrapped to reduce the level of complexity that has built up over the years. One would have to look at the customers' customers to get a better idea: the people who use the web tier. Looking at their trends and what translates into active features is a good indicator into what can be removed to help simplify the search tier and in an attempt to reduce the time of development for new features. This example can carry on as we determine effective methods of measuring ROI for the reduction of features over time, as the gains may be low enough where new features' complexity will overtake any gains made. We will get into these complexities later, but the point is still valid: everyone has a customer. In most cases, if your customer is not the end consumer buying and using the eventual product, the customer will eventually be found up the product delivery supply chain, and you must take them into consideration. To continue the example from earlier, if the web team requests for new feature from the search engine that will likely double the number of searches conducted and will also double the load on the search servers, the search team has two customer bases to satisfy: the web team and the web team's customers - everyone and everything in their product delivery supply chain, each lessening the impacts the more distant they are.

We have taken a long trail in thinking about what is perhaps the most influential attributes any company has: their customers. However, it is important to think of the largest influence the most as there is an urgency to attribute their factors into your decision-making. The point in summary is this: your customers matter and they are always right. Your customers rely on their customers so you must take the entire chain into consideration, else one group is likely to be dissatisfied and will affect you and your organization. The question then becomes: how can we do this simply?

Bugs

One aspect most attributes do not carry is cascading effects on behavior. Some do, telling us we need to be careful with each one we take into consideration, as the effects of incorrect choices can become cataclysmic. The inclusion of bugs could have some great negative impacts on the general morale and daily team rituals throughout the organization if attributed incorrectly. On one hand, it should be obvious that the number of bugs an application has directly relates to the overall complexity of the product. This is not exclusive to software, but any product that can have anything go wrong with it. A steep accumulation of bugs over time will add to a growing headache of maintenance. Bugs provide a layer of cost, complexity and inefficiency, as any effort spent on keeping something running is less time you have to build a better product, generating more revenue. We can never truly expect constant perfection as humans. The issue builds a counterbalance between setting expectations and creating an environment where people make less mistakes. By attributing metrics solely to the number of bugs can be a counterintuitive task. If there is any communication about the fact that an increase of number of bugs will have a negative and personal impact on employees, you will run the risk of having people hide bugs, not filing them, or simply trying to fix them without anyone noticing. This sort of reaction to the evaluations is bad and we need to shy away from it as far as possible. Where if we are hiding or ignoring issues, only the customer will be affected. Although we may have freed up some time to work on new products and features, we are letting the current product degrade to what could become an unsatisfactory level respective of the customer's expectations. To the latter example, if there are people flying under the radar, hot-fixing issues, pushing solutions to the customer before their proper review becomes a recipe for disaster. It's like pouring rubbing salt in a fresh paper cut. The point with this is that we need to take bugs into account when making decisions, but we must stray from putting any negative connotations behind the rise in number of them, or the degree of their severity. The number of quality bugs is more of an indication into a good Quality Assurance team, not a bad programmer Everyone will make mistakes, it is the great that will find them. You *must* know about the issues you have or risk losing customers and money.

This is a good resting place to reiterate the thought that must go into the evaluation of each particle, whether you use it or not in your global or local decision-making. Your analysis and methods therein will likely make it to everyone in the organization over time. Although there may not be a negative effect to any individual, knowing an action can have a negative impact will likely change behavior to reduce the negativity. Everyone wants to keep their job and therefore reduce negative consequences as best as possible, this is human nature. This is the first example of a situation where we want to know as much as possible of the faults we have with a product, yet we don't want to discourage people from finding or making them. As we know a rising number of bugs in any product will add to the time it takes to maintain, particularly since a rising number implies that the maintenance is under-shadowed by the development in some regards. This does not mean we need to stop finding new issues, but find ways to prevent issues from happening in the first place and making sure bugs are being filed and managed correctly. There are many other reactions that can be taken for a product that has fires igniting faster than they can be extinguished, and one should not be putting walls up to prevent yourself from seeing the fire. Now the trick has become: how do we evaluate bugs while minimizing the negative effect on the analysis.

Size

The size of your product will affect its complexity. Although, you must be careful in how you define size, as it is (usually) not the physical area in which it consumes but other measurable aspects. Take the difference between the 1908 Ford Model "T" and the 2009 Ford Fiesta. Both are roughly the same physical size but which do you imagine is more complex to maintain? There is the old adage "I can't work on a car newer than 1980" (or your personally appropriate model-year). There are countless reasons for this, most of which are not from the physical size of the car. The first production model "T" didn't have a radio or air conditioning, where the Fiesta does. The model "T" didn't even have windows that rolled down; a feature that has become standard with today's Fiesta. Although small, each of these features add a level of complexity to the product. The model "T" did, however, have an exhaust system. The Fiesta does too, but it is much larger and much more complex as it tries to battle its own forces with the release of carbon emissions and road noise. Size matters. Moving into something more relevant for our conversation: software. What would you imagine is easier to maintain and work in: a piece of software that is one file and 100 lines long or a piece of software that is 297 files and 73,205 lines of code? I would be willing to bet, without any more information, the first noted piece of software would be the easiest to maintain. Although the physical space taken is the same, the latter example is more complex and will reduce efficiency than the former.

You should urge yourself to consider the impact of any decision you make. Much like bugs, unforeseen negative consequences can come if you assign rigid evaluations that reduce other complexities of the formula. If, for example, Ford maintained an ongoing evaluation that noted the size of any component within a vehicle could not rise at a specific rate, we would likely be stuck somewhere in the 40's in terms of technology we have come to expect as standard in today's vehicles. There are many natural driving forces beyond the market that need to be taken into consideration as well, but the concept is true beyond the auto industry. In software, for example, it is impossible to say that web framework that is comprised of 50,000 lines of code compared to one that is comprised of 75,000 lines of code is better just because of the reduction of lines of code. There are plenty of languages out there that will let you minimize the lines of code yet increase the complexity, where other languages force you to have line breaks in particular places. Even if we know both frameworks are built in the same language, it is the physical code that will give us the level of complexity rather than the size, although the size still plays a part. We cannot suggest to any developer that the number of lines of code needs to be reduced to gain efficiency. If this were the case, I imagine the first thing to go is comments which is a shame. The second could be unit tests. The third may be line breaks and other obfuscations that make it increasingly difficult to maintain the code-base all while satisfying the directive of size reduction. All of which would satisfy the individual dictation, while suffering a loss of maintainability and overall sanity. At some point, though, the size of the application must be taken into consideration regardless of the impact it has. However, there are different approaches that can be taken to counter this effect. We analyze the changes that can be made to reduce our coefficients while not allowing the negative connotations to encapsulate the thinking of our product developers. We can change how we operate to gain efficiency rather than forcing negative traits to hide the reality of inefficiency.

Age

The age of a component also matters to some degree. In reality, the age of an application matters less unless it is used in conjunction with other attributes that are involved with the application. Specifically, age as a percentage based off the tenure of the team working with the component is what matters. This has, in part, been justified throughout our earlier learning curve analysis. Products come with a number of things as you start working with it, including each of the elements we have and will continue to talk about, but also less quantifiable metrics like: history, evolutionary patterns, documentation, etc. Imagine one of the

Internet's dawning (and now extinct) companies: CompuServe. Through the couple decades of its dominance, they had surely learned quite a bit about the market they led. As time told, their long-term strategy killed their strong run with a purchase by the company, driving its final nail into the coffin of its once illustrious life. The point is not about CompuServe, but more about their competitors that were the beginning to its end. To avoid catastrophe themselves, they had to learn from not only their mistakes but also the mistakes that were made by people in the past. Imagine a world where a collapse and other dismal failures were forgotten and their memories were left behind faster than their successes. Where would we be? To advance, we must learn from our own, our peers and our fore-fathers' successes and failures to ensure the road we take in the future is the wisest road to travel. As is the case with CompuServe's competitors that learned from what the decade-old on line mammoth did wrong in order to dismantle them, the same case can be made in smaller scale with products within these and your companies. We must learn from what has been done in the past to make sure we don't make the same mistake over and over. Unlike the gestures made by major corporations, however, the traditional wealth of historical knowledge tends to be embodied deep in the long-term memory of the people who have worked with the product for the longest period of time. The longer and individual has worked with something, the more knowledge they gain and retain where a good portion of it will never be written down. That which is documented can become lost, making some people invaluable to a team and to an organization. It is this value that we will discuss. As a product grows in age, its history continues as well. Without people next to it for the entirety of its life, struggle nuggets will be lost along the way. It is these lost nuggets that will effect your product and efficiency, at some point and to some degree. When you try to recreate a failure without knowing the failure occurred, you will fail, losing time and money along the way. Simpler yet is to imagine a product that is 100 years old but the eldest member of the team has only been working with the product and company for a month. Could you imagine there may be something lost in transition? Yes, without hesitation, the answer is "Yes".

Other Particles

There are countless other particles that we haven't started to think about or discuss. This is not to suggest they should be ignored, just that we haven't considered them. On the other hand, there are many concepts we can start merging across into one another as we continue to build a bigger and more robust decision platform. A great example of this is how, through this section, we haven't broke any physical ground on concepts of constraints like money. I would be willing to bet that together we could make a die hard, highly efficient, brilliant, beautiful, tall, famous team; each with four hands that are equipped with twenty fingers a piece (great for software development) ... for a price. To the same chime, we could also make a great application that had every bell, whistle, appliance, thirty wheels, six engines (impressive for a web site, no?) and every current top-ten artist to promote it ... for a price. Yes, we all want a team full of super stars and to be able to hire new undying superstars every time we start a new project. It is a sad reality that we have silly constraints like available resources and money - it's a free market we challenge ourselves with in terms of the available people we have at our disposal and not all of them have centuries worth of experience under their belt. Yes, constraints will get to us throughout this process and to the point where we will cover a number of these as we continue through the book. Following the same crescendo, we are talking about one of the more sensitive and variable organisms of your organization that cannot be described through ten physical attributes. The tone is much the same here as it is with every other encounter with this situation: that's fine, continue thinking. The intriguing part of this analytical tool is that there is no definitive and invariable method for drawing your conclusions. It is a designed thought process that you can grow outside of your readings. Therefore, these aren't the ten particles that you can only use, these are nine examples that can help us make decisions when respect is taken for Intellicorp.

Psychological

Inhuman entities will not have psychological attributes, this I hope you already know. It takes a psyche to have psychological attributes and corporate products do not have one. This truth is not the case with all companies. Imagine a company that specializes in animal related procedures (training, boarding, sales, etc.). Albeit a market for smaller shops, the likes of which would likely not benefit much from this level of analysis, the case is still relevant. My assumption (which are things I suggest we not make many of as they are likely skewed with bias and usually wrong) is that you work for an organization that sells a good or service that does not live or breathe. The exercise is still valid as the entire foundation of this analytical strategy is to think. Think through each of the scenarios, breaking them apart as you go along. Just because something appears to not exist on the surface, it doesn't mean it is not inches below. In this case, there are no psychological attributes of the technological organization at Intellicorp But we not only know that, we are confident about that. No argument or decision can be unbeaten unless you have all the information, which includes the lack of information. The greatest defense to a counter to your decision-making is a thorough analysis. If you have a solid, thoughtful answer to any question, you will find people start trusting your decisions, which is what you want.

The Collective

It is now where the true analysis will start to evolve. Not only is the analysis of the core components of an organization perhaps the most complex and telling of actions to take, but this is the first time where we will be able to apply equations we have previously formulated into those that we will create. In other words, the true cross-pollinating effects of our analysis will start to peek its head out into a rich utility, fueling a fury of simply made decisions using countless factual and unarguable attributes. We will be able to apply them to our previous leanings, growing our decision making power each time we do so. For example, if we believe efficiency can be adjusted by varying degrees by a function of the age of a component over the average age of the people who work on it, we will have merged concepts covered throughout different sections of this writing. We will be able to cross-apply metrics from our analysis of individuals from earlier, all while using some of our learning curve algorithms to determine the impact and length of a function of age over tenure. Without our previous analysis, this may not have been possible. It now becomes a growing suite of methods that will interact with one another, and that is where the fun and power breeds.

The design of this portion of our analysis will be structured a little differently than before to illustrate two points: there is no predefined method of drawing a conclusion, more that we have a paradigm of thinking and we need to apply it in a rational manner. The second is that every sub-group of analytical particles (individuals versus internal components expresses two sub-groups in these terms) can deserve a different level of analysis. We will use a method similar to what we used with evaluating individuals, as it deserves a higher level of thinking and discussion before we draw our equations. Although not completely necessary, it is a change that is due and one we will use.

Implementation

With any conception comes its implementation, followed then by its practical application. We will now proceed with our concept's implementation, where we will break down our conceptual design into an implementation we can later apply to our organization.

Network Complexity

We talked about the different levels of network complexity earlier in this section when we discussed the differences between source and dependent nodes. Before we dive much further, we should briefly reiterate our thoughts on this matter. First, a source and dependent node is to a network architecture as a master and slave is to a database architecture. The source receives information from a dependent, where a source is not critical on the survival of any other node in a network; a dependent is a commonplace location of information and is critical to the operation of a network. Even more granular is how we define a network. A network is nothing more than a larger application that has interconnected pieces but does not indicate bi-directional communication (in general terms). For a simple example, imagine a web site that uses a database. That has a two-node network with one dependent and one source: the database and web applications respectively. With our definitions, we know what we could lose our web application while still having the database application operate smoothly, where if we lose the database application we will also lose the web application. This, alone, defines our dependent and source relationship.

The previous example is well suited as our next classification is what can be considered an internal application at all. In Intellicorp, we remember our unappreciated data analyst, Stan Keyhang, had the freedom to work with just about any technology including MySQL and Postgres. In this example, we cannot include either application as an internal application node, as there is no development effort into the product itself, even though they may be necessary for the revenue generating product(s) to successfully sustain the overall product. Because Intellicorp does not contribute to the database engines that Stan is using, they are not internal applications, they are external. Just as Microsoft Windows, the operating system of choice at Intellicorp, could never be considered as an internal application, neither can software packages that are not considered core products of the company. Think of it this way: a product or component (or node for our examples) should only be taken into consideration once, globally - much like household dependents on your annual tax forms. Sun Microsystems (the right holder to MySQL) is the only organization that can claim MySQL and PostgreSQL Global Development Group (the right holders to PostgreSQL) are the only ones who can claim PostgreSQL - exactly how only one person can claim their children as tax withholding dependents when reporting your income to the government. Of course, Intellicorp also maintains "C", the shared cache environment; their web application amongst other proprietary works. These are dependent applications that can be considered internal applications, as Intellicorp is the only company that can claim them. Therefore, we must dissect each of these and classify their nodes within each of the applications. As with anything and everything else, there is always a gray area and Intellicorp is no exception. An example of this is the evolution of the search team, headed by Exemelle. If you remember, she had taken the open source data indexing framework, Lucine, and modified its underlying architecture to fit their ever-changing requirements. This is an interesting situation to be in for a few reasons. The addition of custom, proprietary code into a 3rd party application first becomes a management nightmare. You either have to upgrade to future versions, reverse engineering patches along the way, or stick with the old version as long as necessary. Accepting the risk of having to re implement core changes to the product that may have been better thought out, implemented and tested by a larger community through the open source network at the Apache Foundation (the current project host of Lucine at the time of this writing). With this taken into consideration, does this modified version of Lucine become an internal or external component of Intellicorp? The answer is going to be variable depending on your own analysis. Since we know Exemelle has modified the current production version of the Lucine distribution to the point where the raw source of the product has been muddled with by introduction of proprietary (to Intellicorp) changes, we will consider it an internal application. Although a technical product solely, Lucine is a product of the search team that has come to fruition over the years Exemelle has worked with it. It started as a product of a larger and open community, it is now, however, a hybrid of its origin, out of date to the point where any merge with the most recent Lucine release would reach near impossibility. Being that this is a managed product by the technical product development team, we will consider it an internal application even though it is a hybrid of the two. Its classification can be met fewer than one of its originating categories.

Although there will likely be contingencies to nearly every rule you define for any group of attributes like this, there is one more I would like to call out specifically for this exercise. By definition, the end consumers of your product, the ones who will give you money, are dependent nodes of your network. You can figure your customers into the larger equation we are about to work through, rather than calling them out as a separate, larger and more impacting entity. In terms of Intellicorp, however, we will be separating them entirely for two major reasons. First, they are the true bread and butter of the company. Without them, there would be no investors, revenue or cash in the bank to pay anyone to build and sell a product, deeming the company non-existent. They are a very important group of individuals and should be taken into consideration separate from every other affecting node. This may not be the case with your organization and if not, simplify your strategy and define them as a dependent node. The second reason is this will divide the complexity. We are concerning ourselves with the generalized complexity of an internal product and its effect on productivity, efficiency, cost and time. Regardless of these traits, there will be customers. Customers don't care if a new feature takes two versus four weeks to deliver what they hadn't been expecting in the first place; they will use it when it becomes available to them. This is the case, anyways, with Intellicorp and most small-to-medium sized software-based companies. There are exceptions to this as there is with anything else. If you are a huge software company as the likes of Microsoft or Google, the press can be all over your proclaimed release dates and these dates suddenly matter. Another company, alternatively, could beat you to the market. In either case, the time it takes to develop your product begins to be a bigger and concerning issue. Very few customers know when a site redesign, code re-architecture, new data sources or any other new yet substantial product enhancement comes down the line. As the general rule of thumb (for now apparent reason other than safety) is to announce features *after* they are released, no matter when they were scheduled to originally be released. Do you remember the last time you anxiously awaited a new feature in Google search result pages, only to be let down of yet another time-line slip? Probably not. Though if any of those features slipped, do you think people inside the walls of the Mountain View compound would notice? Yes, and that is not an assumption. This does not mean, of course, customers do not matter in terms of the complexity of the problem, even if they do not notice a slipped release. If you have 145,000,000 (approximately) people coming to your front door every month as Google does, you can bet there are scalability challenges. We will work with these challenges in the future as we bring everything we have learned throughout this section together as we take customers (which we will have then covered) into a larger consideration. This again may be different for your situation, but not for Intellicorp They provide an on-line service and generally don't say anything about a new feature or product enhancement until after they release said change. In terms of our analysis for Intellicorp, and between the two points regarding the importance of customers and the quest for distinct separation, we will cover customers and apply them appropriately in a later section.

With each of these principles covered, the meat is in an actual analysis of the network we have been diligent in describing. With a solid definition and through thought process behind us, we can easily come to conclusions about how to evaluate the complexity of a particular network.

Let's start with what we know, taking source and dependent nodes into consideration. This can be simply defined as the following:

d = Dependent Nodes

s = Source Nodes

We know there is added complexity to any interaction to a dependent node. If we remove a dependent node from the network, the source nodes will fail. This level of dependency will always cause more confusion in the development of the product, particularly in software. Although we have not touched on the concept yet, most organizations of medium size who make a good portion or greater of their revenue through networked software coupled with dependencies will attest to the fact that they need to reduce the amount of downtime. Every minute customers cannot come to a site is a minute of lost revenue. This translates into a redundant layer of dependent nodes where each node is an identical replica of another, yet not dependent on the other replicas. Therefore if one is to fail in some way, the others can pick up the remaining load. This is not the best time to get into the greater complexities of scalable software in these terms, but you can see the problems crop up with dependent nodes that you won't see with source nodes. The question is how do we measure this? What is it about that complexity that we can illustrate mathematically? One method is to visualize a simplified network, similar this following diagram:

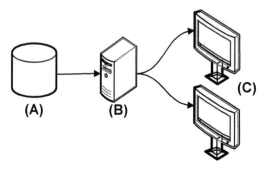

Image 3.37: Source and Dependent Model

This is a simple representation of countless architectures across the world, including that found within Intellicorp. To better illustrate, we have a database (A) serving content to a central server (B) - the Lucine search index - then feeding requests to any client who needs it (C). A straightforward 3-tier architecture. Taking this example with respect to what we are discussing, we can see that the database is a dependent node for the server, where the server is both a source node to the dependent for each of the clients (C) who are themselves a source node of the server. This still does not tell us the arithmetical difference between a dependent and a source node, but does start to illustrate the delta better. One method of consideration could simply be taken by putting each operation on equal playing ground. Assume that a source and dependent node can equally have a "value" of some integer, where any node that is a combination of the two will simply have the sum of the two integers. This would work out to be something as the following:

$$NetworkComplexity = \sum_{n}^{n=1}(s + d)$$

Network complexity is then defined as the sum of all nodes, represented by the sum of the integer value respective of a source and dependent node. This is the simplest method and will draw a general idea of the complexity your network has. The drawbacks to the simplicity are two-fold: first, it is a linear equation. A growing network will never be represented with anything but growing complexity in a linear pattern. One node will equate to the same increase of complexity as the one before. In many cases, this is not true. There are three thoughts on this, depending on your particular situation. The first consideration to make is that a linear progression of complexity is correct given the circumstances in which case this equation will work in this context. The second and third thoughts are that complexity will either grow exponentially or logarithmically respectively as new nodes are added. The former is an argument that suggests the *wider* a network grows, its complexity will grow exponentially to some degree. Adding more server tiers (not replicating the same server), more database tiers and more client needs will add to the complexity and a growing rate, as the number of interconnected pieces becomes more to think about, and more paths for failure to occur. On the logarithmic side, the suggestion is that adding a node to replicate the behavior of an existing one is no more trouble than adding the first, where each successor to the original node will grow the overall complexity lesser than the first. Imagine our web tier as it is one of the major source nodes to the Lucine search index. When the company first launched, there was the necessity for a single web server. Although there may have only been one, there was a large effort put into making sure that one got there. The original cost of development, installation, configuration and troubleshooting all need to be taken into consideration when evaluating the cost of the very first web server. As the company grew, the same costs could then be ignored for its replicants as lessons, as it is nothing more than a clone of the first. No new code, configurations or troubleshooting were necessary - simply the setup and install of a new server, just as had been done before. As each server is added, lessons can be learned from history in order to smooth the process and streamline it, making the growing complexity lessen as time progresses. All of this is true, although it subsequently depends on how much of it you want to consider. There are varying levels of complexity that you will have to take into consideration depending on the width (non-replicated nodes) and height (replicated nodes - like our web servers) of your network. Our first equation takes the former of these issues into consideration. For the sake of simplicity, this equation may be all right, but it comes with the loss of accuracy. Stepping back to our original conversation - the two-fold issue with our equation - we have already covered the first: it's linear. The second is that we have considered both a dependent and a source to have the same complexity value, but this, again, may not be true in all circumstances (and likely not many at all). A simple adjustment to this is to change the integer values of what a source and dependents are attributed as. This will change the value depending on their network role and continue with the simplistic path this method takes us.

There are numerous ways to dice this, but up into this point we have not covered what we should consider for Intellicorp, which is the same thing you should do for your company. What Intellicorp is concerned with is a combination of simplicity and accuracy without being overwhelming. We must take the two sides of the complexity argument into consideration to suit accuracy: a taller network will generally gain in complexity exponentially, while a wider network will gain in a logarithmic pattern. To level this theory with simplicity, we will apply two concessions. The first is to have a simple equation to adjust for the varying levels of complexity between a source and a dependent. We will state that a dependent is twice as complex as a source. The justification of this is simple: a source is only that, a source to an information flow where a dependent is not only relied upon by others but is also a source of information or computation. Given this, we are to simply state a dependent is twice that of a source and can be expressed as the following:

Source = S

Dependent = D = 2S

The second concession we will make is to adjust the concept between the logarithmic and exponential properties of the network's multiple dimensions we have been describing. We will adjust the justification behind the theories a bit. After doing so, we will express growing complexity as a function of the total number of sources and dependents as they apply to a network, each growing the complexity of the network exponentially. In other words, we will ignore the theory of a wider network growing complexity in a logarithmic pattern and conversely state that both a network growing in width and height will grow exponentially, but by varying levels based off the number of dependents and sources it is growing by. We can do this by applying the sum of the value of each of the dependents and sources as an exponent of the total number of nodes in the network. Therefore, a growing number of sources will continue to grow the complexity exponentially, but at a slower rate than that of a dependent. Perhaps a better explanation is to express the theory in math terms. As we will have the complexity grow as expressed as an exponent of the total number of all nodes, we must first state the total nodes.

t = Total Nodes

We can then express the function as we have discussed as the following:

$$complexity(t, S, D) = t^{(S+D*2)}$$

This is still unpolished, as the most immediate impression of the result set will indicate an extremely heavy advantage applied to companies with larger networks, no matter how many Dependents or Sources they have. For example, is an organizational unit that maintains 1,000 simple web servers serving nothing but static content (*S = 1000, D = 0*) any more complex than one that maintains a single web server for the same purpose (*S = 1, D = 0*). Yes, of course it is. But is the former *1e3000* times more complex than the latter? Absolutely not. Is it even 1000 times more complex? Likely not. However, the latter argument is one we have already taken: a wider network has a growth pattern that is logarithmic. To take both reality and the simplistic human mind into consideration, we can simply use the current exponent of the complexity function as a numerator to the total number of nodes. The result of this is that a growth of Sources is linear and one of Dependents is exponential. This somewhat flies in the face of a few things but still takes our general goal into heavy consideration. We want a simple way to express truths using truths while being relatively accurate. Yes, the ignorance of some of the discussions we have had will reduce accuracy but it will vastly improve simplicity, and if we remember this is only a small portion of a larger equation set, then we will remember the smaller details matter less in a larger scale. With all of this in mind, we can take our last update to our complexity algorithm and express it as follows:

$$complexity(t, S, D) = t^{((S+D*2)/t)}$$

We have, at this point, sufficiently satisfied each of our goals to determining the general complexity of a network. We know the growth of a network will grow the complexity of a network, where Source nodes will have less of an impact than Dependents. Furthermore, we know now what we have ignored to generate this function to keep the level of simplicity to a controlled chaos. As I have said before, knowing what you have given up to gain something else is as important as getting something in the first place. We may have a simple and generally accurate method of determining complexity of a network, but we also know how to adjust it and its applications to these same properties. We could gain accuracy and lose simplicity by breaking down Sources and Dependents, determining if they are nodes growing in width and height, and applying different functions to them depending on their action to the network. Our stance is, however, that this will become too complex of a direction to take something as simple as network complexity into account. We know why though, which is half the battle.

Choices

It was mentioned earlier that a different approach was to be taken at this point and this is where the majority of the difference is. After previously evaluating different equations, we broke each down to gain a further understanding in order to come to a better conclusion. I'm using this example to demonstrate the fact that it is really only necessary if there is a lack of confidence with where you were going with any of them. It is fine to have a lack of confidence and proving any one of them to yourself is a very necessary step in making sure you are choosing the correct algorithms to make better decisions. A different approach is to accomplish this earlier in our process as we have in this section. If you can take the time to make the critical analysis it takes to come to a conclusion, it is more likely that you have already indirectly evaluated countless different expressions on the road to the one you eventually will chose. This is the case here: we ended with one which negates our need to choose. Although getting to the one equation took longer in terms of thought and speed for a single equation, the total time to come to it was shorter than finding two or three alternatives we would then have to evaluate again. Over and over, this is will save time and allows you to skip an unnecessary step. Once you realize we won't be publishing our findings in a nationwide scientific dissertation, or lead people to believe we have discovered an infallible approach to determining and measuring the scalability and efficiency of your organization, you will see the value in concise applications.

Choices or not, we still need to take the time to determine this particle's coefficient - for Intellicorp in our case. To do this, we have to refer back to the original interviews. As with the style of the general Scalability Coefficient, we want to break apart everything into its smallest parts first, while being mindful of how small we get. In our analysis, we are lucky enough to be working with a medium-sized team each with distributed and isolated functions... for the most part

Web Team

The web team has two primary internally maintained and developed products: the web application and the cross-team cache tier termed endearingly as "C". We also have our original diagrams we pieced together to add to this after we covered the interviews with the entire technology team. The next best step is to refer back to the original diagrams we made of our organization and apply a similar pattern we added in the "Proprietary" (and "Open Source Proprietary"), respective of the applications the web team develops and maintains to generate a visual diagram of what we have. For the sake of our analysis, we will combine the development and production environments into a single entity. This is a logical step to reduce complexity in our evaluation. Furthermore, since the only difference between a development and production environment is the scale - both in the overall size but also the number of consuming agents - there is little argument to say one environment is less complex than the other. If anything, the more environments you add, the more you add to the overall complexity of the network (though we will assume this does not happen for our examples).

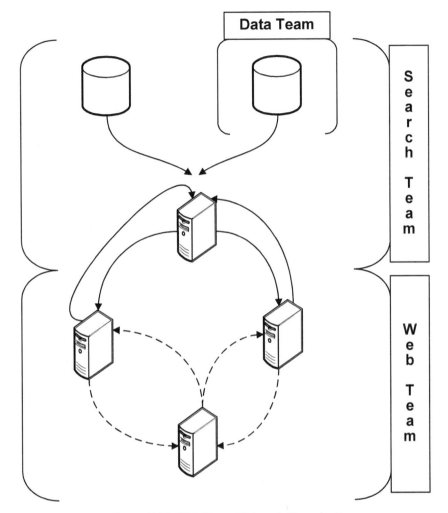

Image 3.38: Web Team Network Complexity

The lesser reincarnate of the original diagrams we created earlier reminds us of the most immediate internal software network of Intellicorp. This includes the ten web servers and two cache servers. To best understand which tier is a dependent and which is a source, we need to traverse past the most immediate team into teams that consume data or that are consumed. Extracted from the diagram above, this will include the data team's search engine and data store, along with the loosely coupled data team's single MySQL instance, a queried source for the search tier. This should bring into question: how far back does this analysis have to take us? The depth of the immediate analysis should only take you as far as the immediate, internal components reach in a single network hop. Continuing this example from above, this would mean we must include "C" and the web tier. Included in our analysis would be the search tier's search engine as the cache tier is within a single hop from the web tier, which is maintained by the web team whom we are analyzing. As for the search teams' internal data source and the data team's 3rd party data set, we need not include them now as they will be included in the analysis as we get to that particular team.

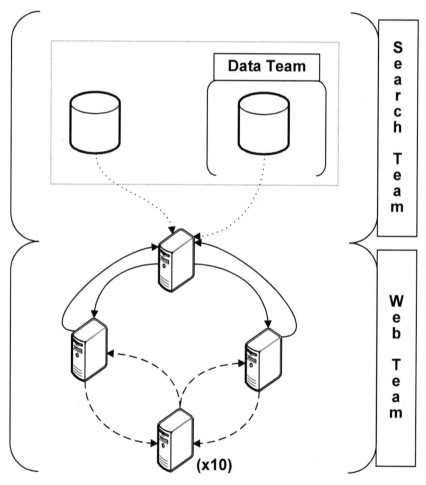

Image 3.39: Search and Web Team Intercomplexity

The same teams, but only including a cross-team distance of one will simplify what we are working at in the immediate time frame. Another pulsing issue should be the fact that with ten web servers, there should be some consumers - the customers. We will first treat the customers a little differently, as their importance weighs a bit more than standard internal components. Second, customers are not internal components of a product, and we should not take them into consideration while we are investigating internal components. We will take them into consideration in the future, just not at this time. Although the customers are worth considering again since they are the primary consumers of the web servers and they are the direct consumers of the web servers.

With a diagram such as the last one we have looked at, the dependent and source relationships are clear. We can first look at the cache tier in this example. As was described to us in short detail by the web team during our interviews, the cache tier is read and written to by both the search and web teams respectively. The read and write functions alone tell us that, by our definition, the cache tier is a Dependent node. For those of us who know a little bit about web architectures, it is generally of sound mind and practice to not have any site or service depend on a cache tier. If it goes away, don't use it - if it's there, do use it. They are generally intended to be a central processing cache that should not be relied upon. At this point, we simply don't know enough about Intellicorp to know whether or not the cache tier is in the critical path of its dependents, and therefore a true dependent based off of our earlier definitions. There are two ultimate paths we could take with this. The first and most obvious is to find out the answer to this. If it is a true cache tier, then we know it is not a reliable dependent to the network and therefore *could* be taken into a lower consideration threshold than those who are in the critical path. The second (and the one we will take) is to ignore this question altogether. The justification of doing so is that we are measuring complexity and efficiency, not the true scalability of a piece of software. In terms of determining the

Scalability Coefficient of a component, we do not care if the right decisions were made (in terms of the design), we really only care of *what* decisions were made and later we can use these to determine what there is to fix (if there is anything to fix).

The second tier of the web team is the simple web application components. We have already discussed the relationship with their dependents, the customers, and can ignore them for this portion of the analysis. Because of this, we have nobody depending on this tier which tells us, by our definition, the web tier is a Source tier. An interesting attribute of the web tier we have yet to discuss is the fact that they are sourced by two independent components: the cache tier and the search tier. We will ignore static content or local disk as we will wrap them into a single component. This would not be the case if we had a detached network device or similar as the source of static files, for example. This brings us to another decision that needs to be made: how do we take multiple sources into consideration? We can measure each source as an independent entity or group them as a single entity. To better explain, when considering the web tier alone and the ten servers that comprise it, we have the option of considering twenty-three sources (the search engine as one and the cache tier as two more) or ten (considering the web tier a source). You could even combine the two for a total of 33 (although that is stretching our definition a bit much) for us to take into consideration. It's really a question of what makes the most sense for your application. For Intellicorp, we are going to take a different road and consider any input as a source; any output as a dependent. This not only suffices our definition of what a source and dependent node is, but it will also demonstrate a growth in complexity as we add more things for an application - the web application in this case - to reply upon. We now have two input methods (per individual server at a time) with our current method in place for ten web servers, giving us a total of twenty sources for the web tier. In terms of the cache tier, we have two servers each with two input devices for a total of four sources, summed to give us 24 total. We already know, with dependents, the web tier has no output dependents while the cache tier has two *output* dependents for two servers, giving us a total of four further dependent nodes; a total of 28 total sources and dependents.

We still have the rest of our teams to evaluate: Search, Data, QA and SA; these with less verbosity as we have covered about all the bases.

Search Team

Remembering that we only back-trace our network by a single-hop outside of the group immediately being analyzed, we have:

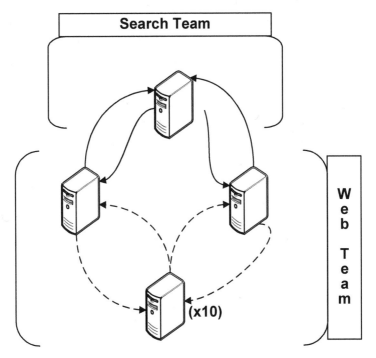

Image 3.40: Web and Search Server Connectivity

With the search team, we have a few more points of difference from what we have experienced up until this point that we can now address. This is, the second group we will be evaluating, and by the nature of a networked technology organization (through their respective products), they will be using services provided from another team. These services will have already been attributed through the evaluation of the team that owns them in many cases, that is the case here as well. Some of the components on the new team we are evaluating - the search team - will have already been considered on other teams. That's OK, we will include them again. *How* you include and address these re-evaluated components will mostly depend on how you count a source and a dependent node. For Intellicorp; we chose to attribute each input method as an incrementing factor for a dependent and source, depending on the respective responsibility This combined with the fact that we are evaluating the complexity of a single group as a function of all the dependents and sources therein, we must include each component as many times as it plays a part with another group. The cache tier, for example, will be accounted for against the search and the web team, as its existence increases the complexity of both teams. It could be suggested that the web team's complexity is higher then the search team's since they not only use it but also maintain it. In our case, we will justify ignoring this claim as the added complexity of using a third-party API - when compared to the maintenance and usage of an API cancel - one another out and therefore need not be considered. This may not be the case for you and your team, however. The application your team works on may be an API itself rather than a stand-alone, hardly-thought-about off-shoot of a necessity that blossomed into something much larger than anyone anticipated still remained a "hack". The latter example is the case with Intellicorp, and is why we can take our stance. The second experience we have touched on without a direct stance is the use of multiple components as we have with our Lucine search engine. We have two sources of content that stream into the index for searching; one internal source to the search team and one external source from the data team. We can first take a look at the internal source of information. The source itself is not proprietary. It is sourced from third party vendors via the Internet. It begs the question of how we include and evaluate it. The most logical answer to this depends on how proprietary the source is and the method in which it gets into the searched index and data files. In this case, even though the source is not proprietary, the sourcing mechanisms are quite proprietary. With this, there is a new level of abstraction that will add to the overall complexity of the model. Where we should update our image to represent this difference.

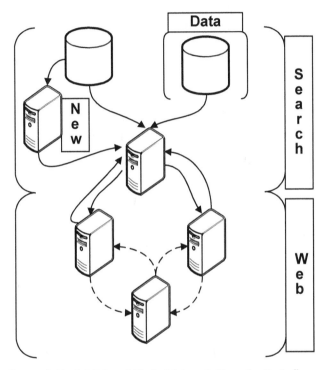

Image 3.41: Additional Node Network Complexity Influence

Adding this new node, even though it is more of a connection between two physical nodes, is a good representation of the separation of responsibilities. We must take the processing into account. The source for the processing does not and should not be considered, as it is an external component rather than an internal one. To finish this line of thought, we still have the data source from the data team to take into consideration - the MySQL database silently provided to Exemelle from Stan. To know whether or not we take this into consideration at all, we can use the same approach we have for the external source we recently finished discussing: how proprietary is it? This is a much easier node to analyze, as there is absolutely no proprietary works to consider whatsoever. It is an externally maintained piece of free software that provides everything you need to connect, store, index, query and modify the data within it. Furthermore, Lucine (Java) provides the JDBC interface which together implies there is no maintenance or administration from the product teams perspective, and the entire application can be shoveled as an external application.

With our internal network further defined, and how it applies to the search team, we have yet another new diagram that will describe all the pieces we will need to take into consideration for the internal application Scalability Coefficient for the data team.

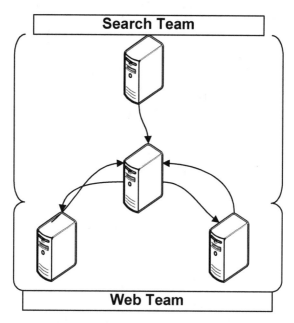

Image 3.42: Search and Web Intercommunications

Having this, along with what we have defined a dependent and source node to be, we now know that we have two source nodes for the search tier - both from the cache tier – and three dependent nodes, one from the sourced processing device and two from the cache tier (using the same qualifications about this as we did with the web team). This gives us a total of five nodes to take into consideration for the search team.

Data Team

With the data team, the next team we will review brings a lot of the same problems we have faced in earlier groups, which should help bring the analysis to a quick resolution. As with the previous groups, we should first take a look at the groups network as it stands, including all components a single hop away and less from the group.

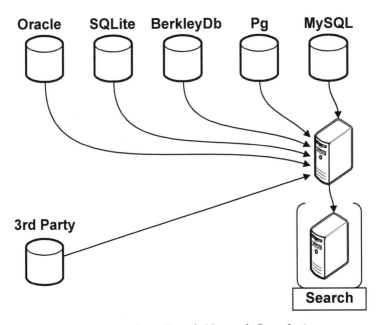

Image 3.43: Data Team's Network Complexity

Due to the nature of the team, the better part of the network is not proprietary to the data group. Between a large cluster of varying database engines and few third party sources they are continuously monitoring, all the team manages from a product perspective is intellectual (which is not analyzed at this point). And the processes that move and manipulate the data. Once we remove all the third party sources and dependents, we end up with a rather simple network as is detailed below.

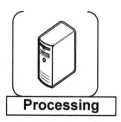

Processing

Image 3.44: Data Team's Server Complexity

With the same justification as we used to ignore the MySQL database for the data team, we can do the same for the Oracle, BDB, SQLite and Postgres databases as well; along with any external sources of data. As the table is now turned away from the search team, we can also ignore them for this portion of the analysis. While we are ignoring the MySQL link between the two groups, we can ignore the connection to the search group. Ignorance is bliss. All that is left is to determine how many sources and dependents are encapsulated into the single box. With a single node, we have a total of one node. However, this box not only manages the processes that import and add data to the databases, but the multiple methods with which it evaluates them. It manages the source of the data while being a dependent of itself. In other words, just because multiple tasks are on a single node does not mean it cannot hold the properties of multiple nodes; just that you have reduced the total number of nodes. Therefore, we have two total nodes: one of the source management (as the dependent) and one for the data evaluation (as the source, who depends on the source management to correctly work before it can work itself). With this perspective, the illustration we derived our earlier conversations from is a little unclear and could likely be redrawn as the following diagram. It demonstrates to show the relationship between a single node with the attributes of multiple nodes as we have found within the data team.

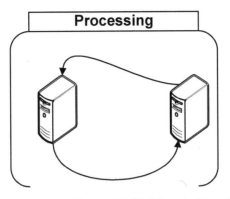

Image 3.45: Data Network's Multi-node Complexity

Quality Assurance Team

With the two teams remaining to evaluate, QA and Systems Administration, we have little network yet to understand. We also have a new level of definition we must consume before moving on. To do this, we will start with a glance at the QA team. As with many organizations, they usually have a software network that emulates their production network, with the only difference being scale. And through our conversations with Caleb, the QA manager, we know that this is also the case with Intellicorp, regardless of whether or not they can keep up with the demand that pressures them. To accommodate this scaled down representation of the entire application cluster, they have three total servers: one for the web tier, one for the cache tier and the last for the search tier. Scaled down databases piggy backing on the search tiers' servers.

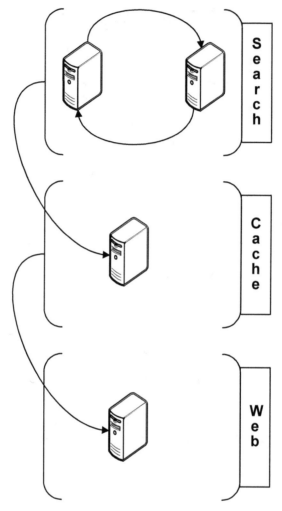

Image 3.46: QA Network Complexity

This diagram is nothing that breaks new ground since we have already taken a look at the teams themselves. This is simply an amalgamation of each of the three environments. The point of this conversation is not how to form the defined structure of the QA team, it is more a function of determining where the complexity is. In other words, what team should the complexity of this network be assigned? Intellicorp's QA team does not have a role in developing the software, nor do they have a role in configuring or managing the network. They are, however, using each of the components as much as possible to riffle through any issues before they eventually meet the customers. Because the QA team is using advanced methods of consuming the applications output, from one perspective, they are much like the customers we have not evaluated. They are going through the same actions and viewing the same output as the eventual customers will and it begs the question: is there any real difference between the two groups? The answer to this is cemented in the foundation of your organization. Where if the QA team is decided to be a subset of the larger customer analysis portion we have yet to start, then we still need to apply the complexity that is inherited from the network of the combined teams, and there are a number of methods that can be used to tackle this problem if the need is there. The first of these is to change the function we have already designed and determined to be fit for our continuing evaluation by allowing node complexity to be shared amongst different groups. The case would be justified as the code maintenance and knowledge still resides in the respective development teams corral while the deployment and server maintenance is managed by the Systems Administrators. This is a dirty hill to slide down, as it is commonplace to neglect the complexity and efficiencies that are within a Quality Assurance team. They may not manage the servers or write the product code, but they *do* manage the entire IP as a scaled subset of what every other team manages a small portion of. More specifically, the QA team must keep track of 100% of the connections in the network, rather than 33.33% as is the case into this point (1/3 for each of the 3 teams is a generalization, but the point should be clear). With this, we have the other option, which is simply keeping the Scalability Coefficient within the boundaries of the QA group, and this is what we will do to further the analysis at Intellicorp. Although the system is scaled down from our former examples, we still have similar connections. The tally we will therefore consider at this point is: two dependent and one source node for the web tier, two dependent and source nodes respectively for the cache tier, and two source and dependent nodes for the search tier; giving us a total of 6 source nodes and 5 dependent nodes for a total of 11 managed nodes.

Systems Administration

The last group we are to take a look at for Intellicorp is the single-staffed Systems Administration group. We saved this group for last intentionally as they have the most to take care of. From the version controls, to each of the nodes in each of the environments, it is this team that has the responsibility of understanding and maintaining these systems, ensuring they run as continuously and as well as possible. To add more fuel to their fire, the active engagement that envelopes their internal component network includes all environments, including anything that they have created to help them with their jobs such as monitoring plugins and maintenance to release scripts. There is a lot to manage and maintain. There is a major difference with this group than from the rest of the product development landscape and this difference comes with the lack of advanced development respective of their responsibilities. In other words, once a server is installed, monitor plugins are working and release scripts are finalized, there should be little work to be done if the environment is working well. But to the same chime as the rest of the group, any major additions will cause a flurry of complexity as everything is managed in threes. Within the software group, there is one piece of software that can be replicated throughout the environments without much change. With QA, there is only one environment they really have to concern themselves with. Yet for the SAs, there are physical installations to be made in every environment. And although most installations should be the same with each passing environment, there is hardly ever a case where everything will be perfectly the same. Networks are different, scale is different, sometimes servers are from different vendors and hardware types - and the list goes on. With this all in mind, there are tradeoffs to the discovery of the relative complexity, where each of these differences in the group must be taken into careful consideration when deciding how to approach the team - every individual team in Intellicorp is linked in one way or another, and yet all different at the same time. The few things to remember when making these decisions are to consider the balance of complexity, particularly in terms of a project or task basis. This is what we will use the Scalability Coefficient for in most cases once we have completed each of the individual evaluations. For example, we will only take the SA group into consideration of a project when they are needed. If a project consumes the web, search, and QA team for a massive software update, yet there is no added need for new hardware, network configurations, or similar, we likely will take little or no consideration into account for the SAs. This should hardly be the case, but the point should be clear. Now in terms of SC, Inc., we will take the entire network as we know it into consideration. The foundation is first: we will only take into consideration what we need to when we need. Second, there is no point in avoiding the fact that a SA's job is never an easy one. Even toasters have their issues so you should be able to understand that servers with miles of integrated circuits running over silicon wafers will have periodic issues. Although the amount of work is dependent on the sanity of the people installing and maintaining the servers, the same case could be made with every group. In other words, because the work is different does not mean it is any less complex and we will treat it as such. The one difference we will take relates back to the first point of our justification: we will only take into consideration what we need to when we need to. We will begin by breaking apart the generalized network of the SA into four equal pieces: the Production, Development, QA and Internal Networks. We have been taking the entire network into consideration for the individual teams in the past; the SA network will be a combination of four independent networks. The case for this is simple: there are a lot of times where work is impacted differently to this team in the different environments. To scale the web tier, for example, is sometimes a necessity in Production, but can be ignored in the Development and QA tiers. A little sluggishness is better absorbed when you are not the customer, paying the bills.

In this example, we would only need to take the added complexity into account for the Production environment while ignoring the other environments. It can simplify change if we abstract each a little differently. It will simplify our measurements since we have already found the metrics for each of the respective teams. Although we will take them into consideration again, as the application of the same nodes is different between multiple teams, they will have the same attribution as the other teams as our definitions of dependent and source nodes have not changed. The one caveat to this is any added nodes the SA team must claim. Particularly for Jason's work, this includes the custom monitoring and release procedures he maintains (without more reasoning, we will exclude the version control systems as they are external components). This is seeded by the fact that the general attribute of any SA's node is that they are a source. And is the case for Intellicorp as well. Of course a running server is a necessity and could, technically, be considered a dependent - we will consider only the interactions between servers as we have before; primarily for simplicity and consistency. However, in terms of the monitoring and release systems, we have a few more nodes to take into consideration. Before we do so, let's take a look again at the network as it sits, each of the quadrants fused for this example:

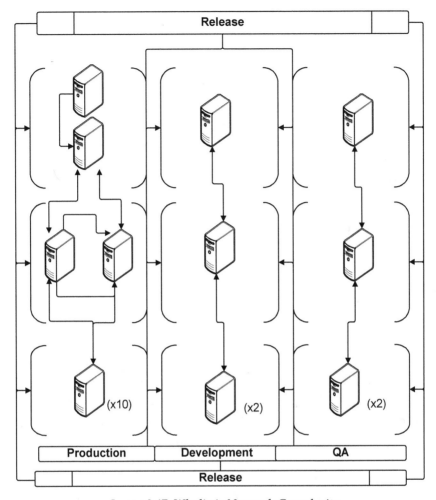

Image 3.47: Wholistic Network Complexity

The monitoring, as an example, is only plugged into the production environment and therefore only needs to consider the production environment. We can understand that monitoring software is not needed to keep anything running. Each connection can be considered a sourced node, and will translate into 14 source nodes; 10 for the web tier, 2 for the cache, 1 for the search engine and 1 for the source feed processing. On the other hand, we have to take the release processes into consideration as well. To contrast our previous example, this process touches every node in every environment that has anything intellectual on it. Although to the same note as the monitoring services, each connected node can be considered a source, as there is nothing that relies on the release process to run. We know we already have 14 nodes in the Production environment. Either by referring back to earlier analysis or by simply counting again, we can see we have four new nodes in the Development and QA environments, giving us a total of 22 total nodes between each of the three to take into consideration for the release process; summed to 36 for the entire internal sector. Before thinking too hard about this number and what it means - we will take it into further consideration later through further analysis while retaining the memories of analysis we have had up into this point.

More Time of Reflection

We have, at this point, covered each of the groups we are concerning ourselves with. We have discovered the number of nodes that are within the scope of responsibility for each team, and the only thing we are going to do is summarize our findings as they relate to the network complexity function we have outlined. First we must remember this relation, as there has been a relatively substantial amount of thought between the time we completed it and now.

$$complexity(t, S, D) = t^{((S+D*2)/t)}$$

Internal network complexity, as we have defined it, is a function of the relationship of source and dependent nodes respective of the total number of nodes available. Now that we have defined this and have outlined each of the internal source and dependent nodes of the organization, we can complete our summarization and move to the next topic:

Team	Sources	Dependent	Total	Scalability Coefficient
Development	24	4	28	85
Search	2	3	5	13.13
Quality Assurance	6	5	11	32.72
Data	1	1	2	2.82
Sys. Admin.	36	0	36	36

Table 3.48: Internal Network Scalability Coefficient

We will look into what these numbers mean and how they relate best to the rest of the organization after we have completed the component analysis. We can, however, extrapolate these findings into something to visually carry us along.

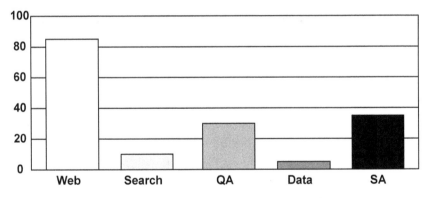

Image 3.49: Network Complexity Respective of Division

With our algorithm applied to each of the teams, we can start to make more sense from the haze of math and analysis. The data and search teams appear to be the least complex of the other five teams; followed by the QA and SA teams, which are roughly at the same playing ground; all led by the web team. This distribution of complexity makes a lot of sense both logically and through the analytical functions we have designed. The larger the network and number of components, the more complex you can expect to be. This is a simple concept that can now be proven across teams with each point rigidly defined and analyzed for accurate deliberation and discussion.

Physical Product Complexity

The network of any product is only a single, lesser defined attribute of a much higher level of definition behind a product. It takes a considerable amount of information into consideration while leaving more out. In our examples, there are eleven attributes available to consider, yet we have only taken three into account at this point. There has been little differentiation up to this point between the product and the network, even though the reality of this is quite the opposite. It is the product that neither defines nor illustrates the network it resides on. The only true, physical relationship between the two is: one cannot live without the other. This is a strong relationship, but only to the extent as the relationship between hydrogen and oxygen; without one, there is no water. Significant as it is pointless when considering our analysis. We need to know about both, but independently. The product is the physical piece of value to a customer or consumer, while the network is the protocol in which it provides a service. Imagine sitting at your favorite restaurant, waves of flavor rolling from the kitchen as they describe the day's special. The waitress walks up and you rise an inch off your chair, your voice rising to an awkward pitch as throwing your order to her at an auctioneer's rate. Your order arrives, the aroma rushing past your face faster than you can enjoy. The main course falling victim to perfection that can only be described by the memory of the taste and flavor that could cure the deaf.

Let's still a look back at this somewhat dramatic restauranteering scenario. There are a few objects in motion here: you, the waitress and the main course (presumably a chair, the restaurant its self, a urinal in the men's room, etc. but we can disregard those items). You are the restaurant's customer (we have yet to cover your impact into the restaurant). The network is to the product what the waitress is to the meal. The waitress is the network into which the product, your dinner, is served. Their job is complex in its own right as it includes a number of things we have talked about in all our earlier sections; length of the tenure, size of the menu, preparation options, number of tables sat, number of people at each table. Her job is a combination of things, but the primary focus of her job is a distribution and communication channel for the product. The delicious food that is presented to you is the product. It is what people come to visit the restaurant for. Certainly a well mannered, patient, informative and attentive wait staff will keep customers coming - just as a well established network at Intellicorp is crucial to the delivery of the product. A great product will keep people coming, regardless of the network. The dinner you are about to indulge in carries with it entirely different attributes that should be considered independent of the method of its delivery for this and other reasons. We could change the restaurant into a self-serve establishment, all but removing the network and loading it back onto the customer. With the same menu, kitchen and cook staff; the end product will remain the same. It can still be prepared with the same care and complexity yet delivered via a different distribution system. It is with this that we must consider the two separately while ensuring that we do not lose focus of either. Regardless of the design of the tables, the wait staff or the presented menu, we must take both into consideration in order to come to our best decisions. This brings us full circle to here: evaluating our product.

Bugs

To begin, we can take a quick look into each of the easily obtainable metrics we can consider. Of those we discussed at the beginning of the section, we can gain easy statistics on bugs, size of the applications, and the age of each of the applications. Let us take evaluate the bugs known in the system in terms of Intellicorp. This is a simple task as only the search team has enlisted the help of Bugzilla, an open source application dedicated to the categorization and tracking of issues found with a piece of software. Before we gather the information that will be of use to us, I will reiterate a point that was made earlier due the relative and important impact this and the next few attributes can make on your organization. What will come of the further evaluations is that the more of anything we have - the number of bugs, the size of the application or the age – the more negatively the Scalability Coefficient will be affected. Your decisions into what defines your equation will drive your business. If we know, for example, that the larger the stack of known bugs equates to a larger Scalability Coefficient (i.e. a less efficient organization), it suggests the reduction of the bugs is a goal to undertake. There are few statements that hold a purer truth. *How* you reduce the number of bugs, however, is a topic you must consider. Bug reduction through deception can be a common reaction, leading to a masquerade of hidden and lost bugs that are skirted due to the negative connotations that come from them. If there is reprimand to a growing bug-base, you will find the rate of growth to taper off and possibly shrink as individuals will care more about their job than the quality of the software they are maintaining. This is a horrible and slippery slope to take. The number of bugs, the size or age of an application, or anything that could create an environment of this nature does not have a direct correlation to the performance of an employee or team. There is a root cause to some of these issues where they may all be related; in all cases individual punishment is never the answer. The filing of bugs is a necessity for all products that take quality into consideration. This is not a bad thing, even if your Scalability Coefficient suggests that it is. There is always a root cause outside the work of the people developing the product. High bug rates could be an indication to an elderly product that needs major work from the inside out, an overloaded team struggling to find enough time to work on new products while fixing legacy issues, or a great and efficient quality assurance team. An unbalanced atmosphere, perhaps, was making people rush through the development process leaving behind an incomplete, vulnerable product. Each of these examples are well outside of the hands of the product team. Each of these issues can be resolved with change that will cause the Coefficient of the particular particle to be reduced (the effect we want) without the direct punishment of the people doing their job to their titled description. When anyone receives negative feedback for an action, you can expect the action to be reduced by methods that only have immediate benefits. To use the Scalability Coefficient effectively, it must be applied to the long-term effects rather than the short-term gains that can come of them. The latter will result in a long-term loss and is never a situation any organization wishes to find themselves in. We can eliminate some of this impact to a certain degree. We can demonstrate this first with our evaluation of the bugs at Intellicorp. No matter the amount of eliminated consequence we take, the careful steps I have outlined must still be taken in order to sustain an environment that will continue to operate efficiently and productively for the long-term. That was my soapbox, I hope you enjoyed it.

Stepping back to our list of metrics that can be gathered quickly and with precision. We can start first with the bugs out of the search team. The best first step is to categorize the bugs by the date they were created. We could use a different date, such as the date in which the bug was last modified, but the create date is an attribute that will tell us more about the importance of the bug.

Month	Number of Bugs
June	2
July	4
August	2
September	17
October	20
November	17
December	5
January	34
February	40
March	32
April	43
May	44
June	49
July	43
August	50

Table 3.50: Monthly Breakdown of Bugs Filed

By categorizing the issued bug counts by month, we can immediately see a few things. First, the number of bugs are growing as time progresses. This suggests that people either are adopting issue tracking as time continues, the concept of bug tracking has become synonymous with something else as time progresses, more bugs are presenting themselves in the search engine, or they are being resolved at a reasonable pace. Second, issues have only been being tracked for the 14 months prior when we know Exemelle, the developer with the longest tenure on the team, has been there for 18. This may or may not have any implications into these numbers, and as these are the only reputable, factual hard facts we have to work with, we must assume the first four months of her tenure will not impact our decision-making. We only want to consider undisputable facts for our Coefficient and continues to be the case here. We must next decide what these numbers equate to in terms of effect on the efficiency of a team. For Exemelle and James, this is a simple function of work to be done; nothing more, nothing less. All the work they will accomplish is detailed to varying degrees within Bugzilla. The impact of this is somewhat implicit yet very real. Most teams that will track bugs encapsulate two functions: maintenance (managing and resolving bugs) and new product development. The two do not have to be tracked using the same method, as they are at Intellicorp; although this does make our evaluation a few degrees easier. This difference will still be taken into consideration to demonstrate the impact they independently make. We can then think about what this collection of bug statistics means. We can easily see that each month has a number of outstanding bugs. The number, when compared to the average of the months in its future, the further back, but will continue to be positive. We must take make some concessions for priority of the issue. We can see in this example some active issues being tracked that have aged to greater than a year. In terms of our analysis for Intellicorp, we can say that the longer a bug or feature adjustment stays active in the system will affect the level of priority it receives. Any operating team cannot procrastinate important issues and products that are making everyone jump. Our interviews would have also exposed this behavior if it existed. In fact the opposite was outlined: the search team works in order of priority assigned to the issue relative to descending date; the oldest, highest priority bugs first. We know, within this paradigm, that the elder the bug, the lower the priority. The first object of our infatuation is the raw number of bugs. This is nothing more than the sum of all active and known bugs.

We can use the following expression to refer to this attribute from here on:

b = Sum of Total Active Bugs

We next need to find a way to express the priority of the bugs. We will follow two indicators to prioritize to do this: the priority assigned to the bug and the physical age of the bug (the difference between the current date and the date the bug was created). The former of the two attributes works, as Bugzilla has a default bug attribute which indicates the assigned priority (though not all tracking systems will necessarily have this). We assume, by using this, that it is either used with religious tradition or one that is not used at all. Behavior that is somewhere in the middle can skew the overall Coefficient, as adjustments will rely on constant behavior. Though this scenario is intended to be less of a case to exclude this metric and more of a suggestion to change standard operating procedures. This metric also comes with the same stipulations we have already discussed with bugs in general: be careful of what impact the Coefficients of bugs and their priorities have on your organization (I can not say this enough). While I'm back on that soapbox, as we were reviewing usages of bug priority, we had lightly touched a very important concept. The concept of adjusting your operations to accommodate assumptions is not a light one to take, and is in part why I am bringing these contrasting topics together. Using the Scalability Coefficient in your organization should help to bring the best and most efficient business to light. In one case, this means ensuring good standards and operations not by punishing employees for an increased bug count, but to find why there is an increased bug count. On the other hand, it can mean changing the standards and operations of a team to tighten the consistency of how things are used in order to build sharper decisions. You need real information to build real decisions which begins by fostering an environment that will give you natural and real information. It is up to you in how to accomplish that.

Back to the topic at hand, let us now redraw our bugs, grouped by age (in months) and priority. For those who may be more familiar with Bugzilla, taking this further (as with priority and any custom fields) is an option that could be enlisted if need be.

Month	P5	P4	P3	P2	P1	Total
June	2	0	0	0	0	2
July	2	2	0	0	0	4
August	1	1	0	0	0	2
September	6	9	2	0	0	17
October	5	7	6	2	0	20
November	17	0	0	0	0	17
December	5	0	0	0	0	5
January	10	5	15	3	1	34
February	13	17	5	5	0	40
March	23	7	2	0	0	32
April	22	12	5	4	0	43
May	17	13	10	3	1	44
June	20	10	17	2	0	49
July	7	5	30	1	0	43
August	8	10	26	4	2	50

Table 3.51: Summation of Active Bugs

For those of you wading in the dark of Bugzilla notation, the "P" with a numerical tail is an indication of the assigned priority of the issue. Priority 1 (P1) is the highest and 5 is the lowest, assuming you follow the recommendations they have outlined. Aside from the fact that you are now the guru of Bugzilla intelligence, we still must find a way to use the statistics we have in a constructive manner. If we look at the effect we want, this is an easy metric to come by. Essentially we can believe two things with the numbers. The first is that the age of the bug suggests the priority as we have suggested; the older the bug, the lesser the priority. Second, we know that the assigned priority is the physical priority that has been assigned by a person through some level of internal triage. The higher the number, the lesser the priority.

Starting with the assigned priority and knowing that the higher number indicates a lower priority, we can also consider that the difference between each incremented priority is the same, where the difference between P1 and P2 is the same difference between P3 and P4. This is nothing more than a point to suggest we do not need to take sliding scales of reason into account. When by means of triaging bugs, there is always discussion of "It's not *really* a P2 but it's not *really* a P3". Reasoning always adjusts perception to a degree, but we cannot take that into consideration, as it is counter-productive. Knowing the maximum priority is the lowest, we can use that as a function against the priority of the given bug to assign it an appropriate weight. With a function that declares the maximum priority as the numerator of a fraction containing the assigned bug number as the denominator, we would have a method that produces a linearly increasing adjustment as the priority increases.

$$priority(p) = max(p)/p$$

We still must apply a method that suggests the same behavior while also taking the bug's growing age into consideration. This is as simple as the last equation because it holds the same properties. If we use the age as a function of the number of bugs assigned for the given period, we may have what we are looking for. In terms of finding this, we need to decide what a good categorization of bugs will be in terms of age. We have already gone ahead and categorized them by the month they were created in the table we created earlier and will be satisfactory as we can consider each month to be an additional 30.5 days or so, summed to that of the ones prior to it. Perhaps a less confusing explanation is that the number of total months a set of bugs is in the past multiplied by 30.5 (the average number of days in most months). If we use this as the denominator of a fraction, with the number of bugs in the same allocated amount of time, the result will be a declining quotient as the past grows more distant, assuming the same number of bugs. This is precisely what we are looking for as it fits the rule we have outlined that the more time an active bug exists, the lesser the priority it has.

$$priority(m, b) = b/(m * 30.5)$$

Where:

m = Number of Months Active

b = Number of Bugs Categorized for the Month

We will have to account for the bugs that are assigned in the current month ($m = 0$) and we can adjust the function to consider the current month as the first (1) month. Explicitly drawn, we can use the following expression as a replacement to the first we have drawn.

$$priority = (m, b) = b/((m + 1) * 30.5)$$

We have already confirmed that this function will react the way we expect, although it should be noted that it will also react in the opposite fashion as we would like it to when the number of bugs outgrows the number of days within the working month offset. This makes little logical sense at first. Though it does suggest that too many bugs outstanding over long periods of time has negative consequences, and for the analysis we are applying for Intellicorp, this is precisely what we want to suggest. There is little argument into why a single bug would relate to a single day in this manner, the point is still clear: keep bugs to a minimum and manage your ongoing bug list effectively. If you have a lot of old bugs that are being ignored, decide whether or not you want to keep them at all. If you do, fix them; if you don't, deactivate them. Regardless of either, keep filing them as well. The negative effect of a large bug list is present, but not nearly as much as the negative effect of not knowing about them in the first place. Take the stance of finding your bugs before your customers do.

At this point, We have two effective measurements for priority that are independent of one another yet still related and should be paired to make an even more accurate priority scale. What we want to demonstrate is that the lower priority (higher number) and higher age bugs have a lower impact than those who are brand new and with a higher priority (lower number). The entire point of this is to help deflate the criticality of long-running bugs, first off. Secondly, since we are studying the evaluation of the generalized complexity and efficiency of a system, we need to study where time will be allocated for a team. One of these points is in the scope of the bugs that are entertained. Yet not all should be considered equally. The amount of time and effort put into a bug is a function of its freshness (in terms of when it was created) and the priority it was assigned. Although this is not a rigid fact etched into the walls by early human ancestors, this is a fact of logic. Do not spend hours a day on a 2-year old P5 bug when there are three P1's recently triaged into the same queue.

To successfully reach our goal of lower priority bugs receiving a lower Coefficient can be accomplished using any functional method depending on the scale by which you want the two to be related. In our case, we will do nothing more than simply multiply the two together where the product will be the Scalability Coefficient for the categorization (month and priority) we are working with.

This will allow us to have a decent relationship between the two functions so that either one is not outweighed by the other, while both resulting in the product of the Scalability Coefficient.

$$priority(p, b, m) = \frac{max(p)}{p} * \frac{b}{(m + 1) * 30.5}$$

We now have a simple method of translating some of the attributes that are accessible for a bug to help determine its independent impact on the team. We should apply our learning now, as we have with every other high-level of analysis up into this point. This is an easy process as there is only a single, centralized issue tracking system at Intellicorp. Although it is used by near every team, it is only for work assigned to a single team: the search team.

	P5	P4	P3	P2	P1	Result
Jun	3.9	0	0	0	0	3.9
Jul	4.3	5.3	0	0	0	9.6
Aug	2.1	2.6	0	0	0	4.7
Sep	15.3	28.5	8.1	0	0	51.9
Oct	13.7	24.0	27.3	13.7	0	78.7
Nov	51.9	0	0	0	0	51.9
Dec	16.8	0	0	0	0	16.8
Jan	38.1	23.6	94.6	28.2	19.3	203.8
Feb	56.4	92.2	35.5	54.1	0	238.2
Mar	116.8	107.8	16.6	0	0	241.2
Apr	134.2	91.5	50.6	76.2	0	352.5
May	129.7	123.9	126.5	25.3	38.1	443.5
Jun	203.1	126.9	286.5	50.3	0	666.8
Jul	106.8	95.3	759.4	38.1	0	999.6
Aug	244	381.2	1215.1	305	305	2450.3

Table 3.52: Active Bug Queue Influence

We have gathered the Coefficients for the different categories, grouped by both date and severity; we can work to verify that the functions we have chosen meet our specifications. Our goal is as simple as the design of the measurement, we can see a high rate of growth as both time and the number of high priority bugs grow. A good example of this is by comparing April and May. They both have nearly the same number of bugs and an even match-up of moderately prioritized bugs. Yet as May is closer to the present, we see a jump of nearly 80%. This large of a jump is arguably higher than we may need to suggest the facts as we have outlined, but the jump as we see it was our primary goal. We can see this pronounced when we outline the points visually.

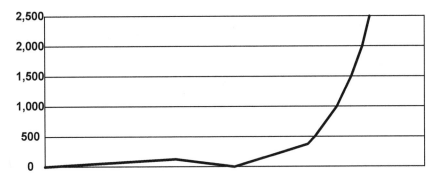

Image 3.53: Visual Representation of Bug Impact

In terms of the goal we keep reaching for, the exponential growth may be a bit of an exaggeration, it screams to the point we are trying to draw. Thinking too much into the numbers at this point in our analysis is premature. There is much we have yet to uncover. We do know some of what we have tackled up into this point. With those numbers we know that the Coefficient for the bugs has an eclipsing effect. Although this means little now, you can remember these arguments when we sum the Coefficient of the respective particles together and begin to make decisions. This would give bugs quite a big of significance any time the search team is included in a decision. We have covered this thought process many times already, but never with as much history and knowledge of the organization as we have at this point. Having the knowledge we have, we could absorb some of the effect of the rate of increase by shadowing the results as a logarithm (in base 10) as a function of the original design.

$$priority(b, p, m) = log_{10}(\frac{max(p)}{p} * \frac{b}{(m+1) * 30.5})$$

This will absorb the exponential effect while keeping true to the logic and goals we have outlined. This is an apparent fact when we look at this visually again.

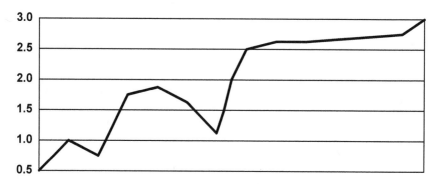

Image 3.54: Visual of Bug Impact, Adjusted

We know we can adjust the function to lessen the unbalanced effect with respect to its neighboring Coefficients, but this is not the time to do so. We will be applying these to scenarios that will be presented to you in our further analysis of Intellicorp. Rather than playing with our crystal ball that has yet to be invented, let's wait until the time we apply the algorithms before we adjust them too much. Therefore, we can keep what we originally tallied against.

$$priority(b, p, m) = \frac{max(p)}{p} * \frac{b}{(m + 1) * 30.5})$$

Distribution

Although the known issues of a product add to the complexity of a product, it is far from the only thing we can take into account. One of the largest and most overlooked contributors to a product, particularly in software, is how it is distributed and used. The interesting part of this analysis is that it exposes many places to not only improve your organization, but sheds a level of transparency into your product that is commonly missed. This section will cover a lot of details, each of which is critical to the understanding of the product you are always making decisions about. Each must be understood to continue to make *good* decisions.

The first particle of distribution is, simply, the customers. Although this is our first adventure with this influential group of people, it will not be our last. We consider the customers at this point because they fuel the decisions that are made about a product, existing or new. Although there are a few things to consider in how they apply, the first attribute we will look into is the raw number of customers. Consider the difference of a product that has two components to it. The first attracts millions of users a day and the second a few thousand. Although both are significant numbers, it is reasonable to believe that an issue, new feature, or enhancement to the former component will be given a higher urgency and developed with a higher level of care than the latter as it will effect two orders of magnitude more people; assuming for now that revenue-per-customer is equal. The more people a change or update will effect, the more consideration will be taken into the modification or enhancement; everything else being equal. Consider our friends in Mountain View, California: Google. In 2006, they bought a cannibalistic competitor to one of their products: YouTube. Nearly 2 1/2 years later, they stopped allowing for users to upload their videos to their legacy product. Why? The company claims it is so they can concentrate on their revolutionary search technology that drives Google Video. Do you think the same would have happened if they either didn't buy YouTube (the 4th largest Internet property at the time of this writing) or if the Google Video product gained market penetration over YouTube? Although we will never know for sure, the answer is likely to be "No". All of these stipulations, and the Google example expose the grim reality that the number of users alone is not the only color to use in our portrait. The value of these customers to the product is also a factor. In the first example, we had a two-component product with an unbalanced distribution of customers. If the smaller group was the only population that spent money, what does that mean? What concessions will be made to one million customers who pay nothing versus ten thousand that spend one hundred dollars every month? Does our original evaluation of inherited complexity change? Of course it does, for-profit companies can hardly exist without money. The tough part of this is how to evaluate the value of a customer. Although some may not physically give money to a company, they may provide value. This is a highly volatile question that cries for a lot of research. What is your power of referrals, good or bad? How many non-paying and paying customers return to conduct more business? What is the level of conversion between paying and non-paying customers? In a period, there are churn rates, discount rates, retention costs, and revenue evaluations amongst so many other things. The core of these results, however, is a static number, the Coefficient of the customer's value. We can harness some of these results to build the first part of our customer analysis in determining their value as a function of the complexity they will bring to the product.

There are two approaches we can take. The first is for the customers who buy something. There is a lot of research into this very topic and is generally termed as the "lifetime customer value" (LTV). In most cases, the abbreviated estimate to this is a simple formula based off the average purchase multiplied by the number of times a customer returns for purchase.

$$LTV = a * p$$

Where:

a = *Average Purchase*

p = *Number of purchases made per customer*

This is a much studied topic in most marketing concentrations as applying a value to a customer under a given scenario is a great way to measure their value. A more specific approach to the equation we have uncovered includes decisive measurements that include the revenue generated from a purchase less the cost of getting the customer to pay (customer service, product maintenance and marketing per user). Then divided by the organization's discount rate all with the customer's acquisition costs subtracted. The sum of this function as a product of each customer is the total lifetime value for the organization.

One of the more complex mechanisms of this method is the discount rate. The concept is to take delayed payments for a product over time in exchange for a fee or interest rate. Because the LTV is calculated at a particular time, the discount is applied to demonstrate the delayed income from the product. Think of it this way: when you buy a pack of gum, you pay it all up front; a discount of 1. When you buy a car, you will likely put it on a delayed monthly payment plan spread over some number of months in exchange for an added interest payment that will be applied to the original price. For the latter case, if we assume the delayed payment structure is for 48 months at a 7.5% interest rate. The rate in this case is a function of the future value (what the loan will mature at), the present value, and the time it takes for the loan to mature. So what we have to work with is:

$$i = (FV/PV)^{\frac{1}{n}} - 1$$

This equation demonstrates that the future value as the dividend to the present value to the power of a slice of time as defined by the length of the term. In other words, the discount rate is how much you got today, divided by how much you will eventually get, to the power of how many payments you will receive. In terms of the new car that was just loaned, the future value is the price of the car, the present value is the down payment and it is brought to the power of 0.02083 (one 48th of one). Commonly, this is simplified to the interest rate gathered per payment installment. Although this is a simpler method of finding the discount rate, it is not actually the discount rate; it is the interest rate.

Now that we have passed Finance 201, we can get back to the LTV calculation.

$$LTV = \sum_{t=0}^{r} \frac{(p_t - c_t)r_t}{(1+i)^t} - AC$$

Where:

p_t = Price paid by a customer at time t

c_t = Direct cost of servicing the customer at time t

i = Discount rate or cost of capital of the organization

r_t = Probability of customer repeating

AC = Acquisition cost per customer

T = Time horizon for calculating LTV

Either of the equations we have unearthed to assign value to each customers will work, depending on your situation; the second is much more specific and accurate than the first. However, they both rely on a single premise: the customer pays money directly for a product. For the majority of profitable online entities, including Intellicorp, this is irrelevant, as the majority of revenue generated online is through advertising networks. Online entities that take advantage of this business model can usually be found with ads littered throughout the pages and interstitial between each click as you find the free service they are providing. In these cases, there is no monetary exchange between the customer and your business, it is their interaction with your service that will direct the money into your bank account. Although the shift in advertising-based revenue models has been strong in recent decades, the concept of the valuation of a customer still remains the same. The biggest difference is the scale and the source of the income. I did not just drag you through a horrid flashback of a monotone professor standing in front of you and 150 peers spilling ongoing dribble about cash flow and net present values. The two differences in this asynchronous model is that other companies pay your organization rather than the customers themselves, though it is still the customers that give you the value. If you have no customers, you have no clicks. If you have no clicks, you have no revenue. The second and somewhat more subtle difference relates to the size of the payments. Depending on a number of attributes of your business and advertising model and techniques, each click produces a relatively small amount of revenue to your company - somewhere between a few cents and a few dollars. Due to this small amount, there is no need to factor in discounts over time, as your revenue is paid immediately. These two differences together mean a simpler calculation of your customers LTV and a change of terms; using the CPC generated rather than the price paid by a customer.

$$LTV = \sum_{t=0}^{r}(p_t - CPC_t)r_t - AC$$

Where:

p_t = *Price paid by a customer at time t*

CPC_t = *The cost per click payed by the advertiser at time t*

r_t = *Probability of customer repeating*

AC = *Acquisition cost per customer*

T = *Time horizon for calculating LTV*

There will continue to be calculations of direct and acquisition costs and probability of repeat customers. The former two are simple enough to obtain, as they are fixed costs in your organization. For a web-based advertising agency such as Intellicorp, determining the probability of repeating customers is a simple metric that can be gathered by tracking the users that visit the site. If you have any level of advertising on your site, it is more than reasonable to assume that you are also tracking your visitors. By knowing your traffic trends, you will know repeating customer trends. Depending on how closely you track your visitors, you will be able to come to a specific number of repeat customers and how many of those click an advertisement more than once. This is nothing more than taking the delta between the total users to an ad, and the unique users to the same ad, for every ad

$$r = \frac{uc_a}{tc_a}$$

Where:

tc_a = *Average clicks on an ad*

uc_a = *Average unique clicks on an ad*

We can now add this to our LTV calculation.

$$LTV = \sum_{t=0}^{r}(p_t - CPC_t)(\frac{uc_a}{tc_a}) - AC$$

There we have it: the value each customer brings to Intellicorp's organization. The sum of each is the total value all customers bring to the company. As with all the particles we have been evaluating up into this point, the value of your customer is as important as the customers themselves. You want them to keep coming, and you want them to generate the most bang for your buck. You need to know what they bring and if they are worth spending your precious time and money on. At this point, if we were to follow the tradition we've outlined thus far, we would travel through the equations we have discovered and work through them to determine the most appropriate one to choose. However, this section is a little different, as the true evaluation of a product's complexity spans well beyond the customers. Without each independent particle designed with consideration for one another, we would have a set of powerless functions. To get a true pulse on the complexity of your product, we need to take everything into consideration.

Installations

We discussed the importance of the number of installations as a function of complexity earlier. Although the term "installation" is a term loosely used in software, we will use to the scope of how you distribute your product to your customers. There is, in some cases, only one way to allow your customers to use your application. This is the case with the sale and distribution of physical goods for example. The principles we will consider can be applied across industries, however. Lets compare two fictitious companies: one that sells computers and one that sells software. To survive, the computer company (let's call them ComputerCo), must ship their products to sales vendors and outlets to get them in front of their customers. No matter the packaging, the included components or the type of material, ComputerCo must assemble, package, ship and sell each individual item at a particular price and at a particular volume to meet their profitability margins and goals. Each time a copy of ComputerCo's product starts this process of being sold, from the time it is assembled and accounted for, we can consider it an installation. It is a redefinition of a commonly used term, but the concept is still the same. It's a copy of a specific version of the product intended for the view of a customer. A custom built entity that can be delivered and "installed" to the specifications the customer sees fit.

To compare with a case we are comfortable with, let us now take a look into the software company: SoCo. For a company that distributes hard-copies of software for installation onto a computer, the term defines itself. The only reason to bring it up in the first place is to draw the differences between it and ComputerCo's sales model. The question really becomes how a computer can be considered an installation in the same terms that a piece of software's installation on a computer. The truth is that there is little difference between these two companies in terms of their definition of installations. They are both measured by the number of copies of a version of the product they sell to their customers, regardless of how many they sell or get turned on. The complexity of the distribution has a direct correlation to how many copies they make. If SoCo makes one million copies of their product and sells only one, it is still just as hard to sell that one copy as if they sold one million. And if ComputerCo made one million copies of a particular computer configuration, sold all one million yet none were ever installed; the complexity of the product manufacturing is the same. Therefore, an installation is how much is made to install and this is the figure we will use.

Versioning

The next particle we will take into consideration relates well to the number of installs: the number of supported versions you carry. The number of installations in terms of its evaluation is nothing but a count of total available versions your product team actively supports. The relationship between versions and installs is that total installs are the sum of all installs per version. Where, for example, if your product has 10 supported versions, each with 100 installs; the number of installations (as far as we would consider) is 1000. Regardless of how they are calculated, the number of supported versions effects the complexity of your product. Maintaining frozen copies of a product with continued maintenance adds to the workload of your organization. The question really becomes *how* does it effect it. There are a few things we can take into consideration including the relationship between the design of the product and the customers who use it.

One of the largest contributors to the effect of multiple versions can be drawn to the design of the product itself. There are a few disclaimers that have to be flagged before we continue. You must only take consideration to the measurable facts that can be attributed to the design. That means we can look at the size of the application, as we can accurately measure it, but not the design philosophy that was used. Speaking in terms of a software product, an argument can be made that a choice of a highly abstracted object-oriented design will draw countless efficiency benefits, over one that avoids objects and embraces repetitive code and business rules. This is a completely valid argument, and one that may even stand depending on the product that is being designed at the time in the context of the business at hand. However, this is not the sort of analysis we can draw, as there is no inarguable metric that can be used to compare the two. There are, however, some (very few) direct measurements we can take that can come to the same conclusion that the design argument would have. With this continued analysis, we will be able to find the most desirable design. This is one of the benefits of this approach to your businesses research. In other words, we can use the facts and methods we gather along the path of our analysis to tell us which design would be best suited for a product. We should not try to take an existing design and explain why it is bad, we can only gather the available facts and interpret their meaning.

The design of a product into consideration can be sliced in more ways than the number of oxygen atoms in the Earth's atmosphere. We will consider only the software products that effect Intellicorp. With these, we will have to find the most prevalent measurable attributes of the given product applications. We can do this by quickly generating a list of each of the attributes of software that we can include.

Size of Product

- Number of languages used
- Number of individual classes
- TCP/IP Network
- Time-based network
- Networks

This list is complete enough to get started, with a number of points needing to be stressed when evaluating this type of organizational particle. Starting from the bottom of the list up, we see the first two measurable portions that came to mind are network related. I want to stress the point that was made many times earlier: the analysis we will and have already accomplished will affect our decision as we finalize our analysis. Of course, both attributes will play a part in the overall complexity and efficiency of a product.

Code base (languages and classes)

Further thought can be applied to the code base, as it's components are not only figures we can obtain and use without argument, but they are both directly related to the complexity of a piece of software. The number of languages used will bring a function of time and money in terms of training and hiring. The fact is, to maintain a language, you need someone who knows it; preferably someone who knows it well. To maintain multiple languages, you either need a more skilled person (more money) or more people (more money) to maintain the code in different languages. This does not include the effect of context-switching people experiencing when swapping between programming languages. Languages can require elementary syntax and logic similarities, which will ease the transition. Yet each language can be different and are critical to the operation and compilation of the language itself. There are costs to running a business that supports more than one language. However, there can be benefits as well. This brings us to the next point. This analysis should dictate the design of a product (ring a bell?). This includes language acquisition and usage. A choice of a language should be a thoughtful one, taking careful consideration into the alternatives, with respect to the problems it needs to solve while taking in the context of what it will be integrated into. The second point is that negative connotations made to choosing more than one language is a bad idea. An elegant way to foster a bad idea. Every language comes with pros and cons; where each should be evaluated when given an opportunity to choose a new one. An obvious con is the price of hiring new developers and/or cross-training the ones you have. But the pros may eclipse this just as negative attributes could as well. When making the same concessions for bugs earlier, we noted this while continuing the evaluation as their impact on the organization suggested we should. In this case, the same argument could be made but we are going to chose a different path: we will exclude this attribute from our analysis. We will do this for the two reasons we outlined: we don't want to cast a negative shadow on decisions that have not yet been made for products that have not been envisioned. A third and more subtle reason is that Intellicorp in particular has stayed with a relatively small number of languages. This fact weighted with the previous two tell us we can leave out the language analysis for now while remembering that we can take it into consideration again if the product landscape changes to suggest we should. We are doing this in writing to demonstrate the flexibility of our craft.

The number of individual classes walks the same line as the number of languages used, though we will not go into as much detail into why we will exclude them as well. The other consideration we will make to this reduction of analysis brings into question of how much of an impact a large number of classes will make in an application. For example, it is completely possible to create an entire application within a single class. This file would likely be a muddle of confusion and obfuscation for a number of reasons, namely maintainability and readability. If we consider a reduced number of classes, this would prove to produce a paradox. On the other hand, an application could be built with thousands of classes, each meticulously documented and logically located on the file-system with a well thought out namespace and naming convention that perfectly maps to the operations, data, or business rules it manages. For all intents and purposes, this is a good design that will arguably reduce the time to develop throughout the product. To contrast the earlier example, this would prove contradictory in that a good design would receive negative merits based off the raw number of files that lay on the disk. We can take both examples into consideration. Our point remains clear: there is no need to impede on design unless we can use immutable facts to prove beyond a reasonable doubt that it adds to the overall complexity of the product. There is a good argument that a poorly designed namespace and naming convention of files at a large scale could be harmful and breed inefficiencies, but this is based off of one person's interpretation of what confusing is. There is no reliable way to measure *confusing*. It is because of this that we will not take them into consideration for our analysis of Intellicorp. This is our prerogative for our analysis yet this may not be, nor has to be yours.

Although our analysis of Intellicorp will ignore some code-driven traits, this is a design that suggests thought experiments to come to any rigid conclusions. Although we have traversed down this path, we can still take some time to evaluate what a logical method would be to include these attributes if we did see the need. We will not for our practices, but in the light of education, it is still worth the time. To start, we can take a look at the number of languages and how they can be applied to the Scalability Coefficient. There is more to the raw number of languages we will need to take into consideration, as we have mentioned before; even more we *can* take into consideration. Things to consider are very similar to what we evaluated a companies components. Tenure, for example, is a big piece. The amount of time an individual has spent with a language, paired with their performance over the same amount of time, is a direct representation of how fast a product can be developed by that person, in the particular language; along with how well it will scale over time. The age of the language will also play a big part, just as the age of the component will suggest the relative complexity - though the relationships are somewhat inverse. The longer a language has been in existence, the more public questions have been asked, the more open communities have been formed, and the more help there is. This is a function to the popularity of the language, as a language that has been around for 100 years with a single user may not be as resourceful as a language that has been around for 20 years, boasting 100,000 known active developers. This concept falls close into the next: the ratio of community and professional documentation. The more documentation that exists, the smaller the learning curve there is to pick it up. However, there is a difference between documentation that comes out of desperate community members versus those that come from technical writers. There is also a function of coverage that has to be taken into consideration respective of these traits. Where some languages are known world-wide to have well documented and fully covered classes packaged with the distributions, others are better known to have only major functional pieces of community code lightly peppered with poor documentation. Let us consider each of these particles and how they could apply to our overall coefficient. Along the way, covering the basis of why our ignorance will override the implementation.

Most of the attributes we have discussed up to this point we can be considered to have a linear relationship to the end coefficient. We can entertain other relationships, although the necessity of this is low since we have already built the conclusion. Tenure, for a good example, is the suggested relationship between the number of years working within a particular language respective of the time within an industry. The logic is sound, as the time of your exposure to a language grows, your experience and expertise grows as well. We have talked about these types of relationships , as much as we have talked about the business world never being predictable. What evolves from this spiral of thought is as complex as it is valuable to reiterate. Regardless, the points of tension that change our dreams of linear, predictability remain the same. Remembering the first introduction to the similar topic, we discussed the different attributes that are effected by one's tenure with a company.

As was then, it becomes portions of a larger function that helps define the learning curve of an employee.

$$learning(w, c, p) = \frac{w}{c} \div p$$

Where:

w = Time Within Field

c = Number of Companies Worked For

p = Number of Promotions Received

There is little variation from this earlier equation from the approach one would take to determine the impact of seniority with a particular language. The only difference being in how we define each of the variables. There is some level of logic that would suggest most of the variables could even remain exactly the same. The same truths that defined our earlier learning curve would apply to this definition. The ultimate method of realizing the impact that the knowledge of a language provides is mostly one's learning curve with the language. The difference between the learning relative to a language specifically, and that of a more generalized approach, given a person's expertise, is that the latter is a sub-component of the former. In terms of the learning curve, one approach is simply redefining w to the time working with the language, rather than the time within their respective field. The others can remain the same as the net relationship with time spent in their industry cancels it out. For example, a developer can be working with a language for a decade at one company, hidden in a corner, known by few other than the payroll department. Compare this person to a more "junior" person, recently graduated from college and working with a language for the first time in their career over the previous six months, working in a world of brightly lit desks, parading senior developers dedicated to the well-being and growing knowledge of said junior developer. The student grows over the six months that follow, growing with two promotions and beginning an illustrious career in product development throughout the nine years that follow. Do you think there is a difference between these two otherwise equal developers? Yes. Yes, there is. Learning and growth is still a good indication of being able to tackle tasks with an elevated level of potential energy, while leaving a trail of bread-crumbs for the future to follow or avoid. As for the guy with the red stapler hiding in the corner, is there any proof that, if there was a new application that had the requirement of being written in another language, he would have any luck picking it up with any level of authority? That question is embedded deeply in the psyche of either person. The truth is either one could excel, however, a betting man would likely put his money on the younger chap with a richer background.

We mentioned earlier this is a small part of the larger picture of how each language will impact your organization. With plenty of other attributes to consider, we have to determine how they effect one another. There are two we have discussed that are defined by each language independently: the age of the language and the level of available documentation. The first, is a pretty easy number to obtain. Visit the respective site and search the page for "history". For one reason or another, every language likes to brag about itself to some extent, always at least to the degree of mentioning the v1 release. Of course, we need not lie to ourselves at this juncture; age most certainly does matter. Just as I would trust my three year old son to design and implement a multi-tiered, randomly distributed hash-indexing system; I would trust a v1 language to build the same platform. It matters. The second attribute, the documentation, is partly related to age, and we will represent it as such when we get to that point. However, there are divergent paths of what level of documentation is available. Let's compare Java and Perl for a moment, both languages I have far too much experience with. Java has taken it upon themselves to build a brilliantly simple documentation syntax with integration into the compilation/build phases of the language. Java's documentation is, of course, ushered to excellence in part from the highly typed and available reflection APIs that enable the output to be a well formed, albeit ugly, HTML document framework that consolidates every bit of information in a clear, concise, informative and consistent manner. Furthermore, the overwhelming core API that is packaged with J2SE is extensively well documented above the automatically generated blisters of useful information. Even if the developer doesn't take the time to add any JavaDoc, the JavaDoc compiler will still be able to generate a well formed stream of good documentation that is enough for even a novice developer to pick up (that may be putting it on too high of a pedestal, but you get the point). Perl, on the other hand, has taken a completely different approach to the entire matter. As a community-driven, loosely typed and interpreted language, it would be hard for many people to believe they could compare. In all fairness, there is a defined method to Perl documentation syntax which is itself well documented and readily available. However, it's the looseness of the language that strays from the road when compared to its counterpart. If you type nothing, you get nothing. The problem is, a lot of people type nothing. Although the underlying documentation frameworks differ, the wealth of information in the documentation has turned out to be the same. There are a number of reasons into why this is. The Comprehensive Perl Archive Network (CPAN), for example, is a place where 20 years of Perl's existence can come together to freely distribute open extensions of the language through a widely distributed network. Although the documentation therein will suffer from the lack of introspection, giving way to lazy developers; you still can find a wealth of great modules with spectacular documentation, both in the form of developer-written and technically written (depending on the size of the project). Certainly, I am not here to fight between which language is better than the other; here more to argue that the age of the language will bring with it good documentation. Good enough for even the biggest n00b on the block. Whether two decades bring you a rich online network like CPAN or lesser years give you something that's immediately rich such as JavaDocs, the longer the language is used, the more people will write about it; the more people will develop and comment in; the more problems will be solved with it and the more Google will index it. It cascades like a waterfall. The relationship should be nearly as brilliant to you now as the sun is bright. What do you think the level of documentation on CPAN looked like on the first day of its first incarnation? What do you think it was relative to todays? Do you think progress has been made since October 1995? I would imagine so.

Although there is the obvious link between the age of an application and the level of its documentation, the limiting factor to this conclusion is the number of adopters the language has. Not long ago, we covered the Perl Archive in its brilliance. The fact is, the power of this archive is in the community. Without it, not only would there be a lack of horribly documented modules and sub-version-one applications, there would be a lack of the great ones, too. There would be no documentation without a community to write it, nor the code. The language would exist, but it would lack the power. This is an extreme case, but extreme cases are the best to prove a point. The fact of the matter is hidden in that stretch, where there are many languages that exist that are fine to use to solve just about any problem. However, the learning curve that will be experienced while introducing this language into your organization is impacted by the amount and accessibility of good documentation, as well as the size and activeness of the community behind it.

A natural end to the ongoing saga of documentation's importance into the effect a language will have on your business is its coverage. This should be a concept that is pretty easy to wrap your mind around, therefore we will not spend too much time on it. We must be effective in realizing there is an effect to the percentage of the language's available API, relative to what you want to use. This would include packages, classes, scripts, etc. that are bundled with the language itself, along with any 3rd party extensions. This will likely be a function of the community (in part) behind the language, but it still must be an independent attribute of the language itself. There is no law stating that a language with a community of one million active users has to write documentation. We must consider the language that has only 10% of the available instance methods documented, versus one that has something closer to 100%. There is a difference. The more you know about the language, the more of an expert you can become. The more of an expert you are, the more productive you can be. It is yet another building block to the larger learning curve we are working to implement.

This process can continue unto the edge of the universe if we need it to, finding and evaluating each of the subtle differences between each language to formulate the most precise method determining whether or not one should be taken under the wing. But why? I cannot repeat enough that too much is too much. We need to be able to take a few big steps and avoid the never-ending, long-tail of the analysis so we can get on with our day-to-day. In terms of languages, we have done this. Perhaps you will have the preference to trudge on a bit further than we have here, or you may prefer to ignore all the concepts we have covered in the last few paragraphs. As long as you can make a well informed decision with the information you have, you will be successful. Now in terms of a language, we have started down that very path. To recap, we have our original learning curve function that exposes the relationship between tenure and performance, along with the general community and different dimensions of documentation to take into consideration. Where does this all get us? A more specific learning curve method that we can use to evaluate the impact one language has work. The truth is, the biggest road block with most modern fourth-generation languages is much less a question of whether or not they can take the job on, but more of a question into how long it will take to develop a product in the language of choice. If it takes a month to develop a concept in one language - generating a highly extensible and issue ridden application versus taking the same amount of time and continuing to incur rising costs through maintenance as the developers knew the logic, but without the intricate details of the language - which do you prefer? Even more than that, how do you know which to choose before the project has started?

We still have our original learning curve function to start and as follows:

$$learning(w, c, p) = \frac{w}{c} \div p$$

We have adjusted the definitions of the variables within as:

w = Time Using the Language

c = Number of Companies Worked For

p = Number of Promotions Received

To follow up on this, we can take what we have earlier considered with respect to the community. The relationship to the learning can be as simple or complex (and therefore precise) as you want. To keep with the tone of our overall analysis, we are going to be as simple as possible. Since we have only taken the scope of the size of the community into consideration, this is all we will take into consideration respective of the existing learning equation. We are going to take a few more concessions into consideration as well; primarily the number of major and supported community groups with their respective size, both in terms of active human population and the availability of resources as a function of the entire known community. Although more complex than taking the community as a whole into consideration, it is a small step towards precision that will take only a little more research to make a much bigger step to the most optimal decision we can.

The first step to this is to take the community into consideration. Assuming a larger community will impact the learning of an individual positively, the simple adjustment can be as follows:

$$learning(w, c, p) = \frac{w}{c} \div p * \left(\frac{1}{C}\right)$$

What this gains us when compared to the original learning function is that the impact of the rise and fall of the relative community will respectively pull and push us towards the optimal place. In other words, a very large community can lend a huge helping hand to those with little experience or a lack of proven ability to pick things up quickly. On the other hand, someone whose superpower it is to learn with as little effort as flicking a dead fly from your windowsill may have equal success working on a new language that has a very small following. Of course, this all assumes we know how C is defined, which we have yet to describe. Guess what? This is up to you. It could be any number of things for any example. It could be the raw average over past decade, with a divisor of 1000 to reduce the impact it can make on the learning curve; it could be a scale between one and ten where each appropriate language can be tagged with a particular integer somewhere in the middle as determined by your co-workers. In all cases, the entire concept is really up to you, it's the principle of what you are trying to accomplish that will take you there. For our example, we will chose an arbitrary figure for the moment: a rounded average of the size of the community over the previous twelve months. Depending on the magnitude this decision will impact the rest of our equations, we can factor large numbers out with constants throughout. Again, no matter the definition of C, it is the positioning of the value that will paint our picture.

Before we throw some numbers towards this, we should take the latter part of this conversation into consideration; the documentation. As with everything we have dug into thus far, there is more than one way to do it, so we will choose the one that best fits our needs. First, we know that the documentation is not necessarily tied to the size of the community. There are some arguments that they are mutually exclusive. Think about the .Net languages and framework that is provided from Microsoft; a corporate-driven language with a large community and a plethora of well covered APIs. In this case, does the documentation have any relation to the community? Perhaps, in that the community would not have arrived if there was no indication of how to use the framework. However, the counter argument is that Microsoft drives the larger portion of all software being used in the world, and if anyone ever wanted to make a dime using their OS, they would be forced to write at least a little bit of code. The analogy may be slightly pulled by fiction's gravity, but the point is hopefully clear. The size of the community is driven by the same factors that make the newest mobile phone popular. If it's shiny, powerful, smells good and all the right people say it's cool: it's cool. If it is actually useful, they will stay and it will continue to grow over time. Regardless, the community is driven to a language just the same as one is drawn to any product: their market factors. Furthermore, in the case of Microsoft's .Net framework, if the entire community that uses .Net in any scope were to suddenly disappear off the face of the earth, I would be willing to bet the next release would have more documentation to detail the changes.

On the other hand, we have purely community-driven languages. We know these culprits. Usually without a large corporation behind them (that owns the intellectual property), it is the community that writes the documentation. They may be organized to a point, and releases will largely come after the documentation is written, but the reverse case is true: without a community, there is no documentation. The point here is that although the community can be the driver behind the truck that hauls the documentation, they are not mutually exclusive. This is the biggest takeaway of the discussion. It is your decision of whether or not you agree with this conclusion. You can consider it with respect to your situation in your own right. However, one thing should be universally agreed upon: the better the documentation, the flatter the learning curve will become. In other words, if people can read documentation and understand the language to the point they can learn well and implement their solution intelligently, it will take less time for further development through the same developer and language. People learn, as it turns out. The trouble comes when we try to define this interaction. What makes some documentation good and others bad? To one person, a simple list of inheriting interfaces, overloaded, and class-specific methods; static, and instance methods is all that's needed. Others may want nothing more than working examples they can download and play with. Some may like a combination and in most cases, preferences change over time as the developer becomes more comfortable and knowledgeable about the platform or language they are working in. So with all of these things, how can we effectively evaluate them? Well, we don't. It's to the same philosophy we have taken throughout this reading that the necessity for being atomically precise is useless when we are evaluating a particle. Furthermore, the better part of these particular attributes take the psychology of individual people into consideration, which is something we should try to avoid. It blossoms into a realm of complexity that will do nothing but blind us from the evaluation and decisions that need to be made. In terms of what we can consider can be as simple as how we evaluated the effect of learning on the size of the community. To do so, we must find the unarguable metrics of the level of documentation we can measure universally, reducing the complexity with generics. Take some of the softer attributes that make up documentation. A few that come to mind are coverage, the amount of the language or product the documentation covers, length, the raw size of the documentation, contributors, and the total number of individual contributors to name a few. Comparing different products from one another, some of these are harder to find than the other. We don't know how many individual contributors there were when we compare a community-driven language to a corporate-driven one. Although, for situations such as these, we can infer information with logic. For example, it is reasonable to believe that a corporate-owned entity will have a set of standards in terms of templating, formatting, layout, design and content that will span throughout all of the technical writers in the organization. Whereas in community-driven documents, it is far more traditional to have a much looser method of controlling their documentation. Writing styles, philosophies on totality, and general coverage all differ to some degree between authors, no matter how advanced the document formatting system involved. A valid suggestion could be that consistency in these attributes will reduce the chaos and confusion of the documentation and directly reduce the time to learn. In this case, it is logical to consider the multiple contributors within a corporate entity as a single contributor; contributors as individuals can be measured as such within the more relaxed processes of a community-driven product. Naturally, this will not always be the case for every language, but the same logic can be taken in with each evaluation. I don't imagine your organization is working with hundreds of desperate languages, suggesting this level of thought will scale appropriately.

Let us take these few attributes to determine the impact of documentation, and how it applies to the larger learning curve function we started with. We have already discussed a couple attributes, including: coverage, size and contributors. The evaluation for each of these can be as easy or as difficult as you make them. For example, do you know whether or not php.net's documentation covers each of the sixteen billion functions PHP has to offer in any detail? You may die a little inside when you realize you know the answer to this. If you do, I am sorry for your lots. Regardless of your depth of knowledge on this topic, it doesn't matter. I certainly don't know and there is no way in my lifetime I am going to dig through the endless sea of documentation to find the answer. If you tried, for the sakes of this analysis and you were an employee of mine, you would likely be my next ex-employee. What I do know is they are very deep and rich with technical details and user-contributed factoids and snippets. There has yet to be a time where I couldn't find the function, extension, module, etc. in their documentation stack. To argue, we can assume they have 100% coverage. Yay PHP! You get a cookie. On the other hand, we have the red-headed step-child that gets no attention as it cries in the corner while doing everything for the rest of the family: Perl. Our example can be carried throughout a number of languages, but Perl brings to us a particular interest as one of its arguable super-powers is its community. CPAN, the central repository of publicly distributed Perl modules, hosts the true power of the language. Sure, you can do a lot without it, but if you are interested in building something that reaches a wide breadth of function, you will certainly be installing something from CPAN at one time or another. With this in mind, it seems logical to consider CPAN part of the global code contribution of the language as a whole, and therefore its documentation should be included as well. Now the same calm, logical, sane programmer in me has looked at quite a bit of CPAN documentation. I have come nowhere near to looking at it all. I will make it a life goal of mine to never read every shred of documentation, either. Much like I can presume the total coverage of PHP is 100% (although I do not believe this to be accurate, it is likely close), Perl is would be closer to 75%. I can't tell you how many modules have been released as "beta", which means nothing more than they likely don't work when you really want them to, and you will have to read the source to figure out how to use its API as the documentation is as long as the Deschutes River in Oregon. Is this a fair comparison? Is it fair to give Perl a coverage ratio of 75% (in this area) and PHP ratio of 100%? It will all depend on what you know and discover. Truth be told, Perl has a very thorough, well covered and extremely informative document base; core Perl, specifically. It is preference above anything else of whether or not to include CPAN into the scope of Perl itself. In the case of our analysis, we must. There is no avoiding the third party modules that are provided, and with one comes the entire set. Good problem analysis will take a comparison between alternatives, regardless of the level of documentation. When you need a problem solved, an upgrade or even an API reference to core or non-core module will take an examination of the network. With this, it is logical to include it as part of the language.

Let us next consider the breadth of the documentation. We cannot consider the size with 100% precision as it becomes an aspect of personal preference. I personally would prefer to see a list of methods combined with a one-sentence description and a few quick examples of its usage. Short, informative, brief, and not very long. I know first hand that others have a different preference. People who are new to a language tend to prefer a richer description of the methods than what a single sentence can provide. Those new to programming may prefer something a bit richer. A technical author must be able to consider and satisfy as many palates as possible, which will invalidate the necessity to gauge the size overall. There is something to be said about over doing it or under doing it. Where too much information is nearly as bad as not enough information. Where is that line, though? At what point has information overload happened and at which point are you left with the remnants of your hair underneath your fingernails as your begging for only a little more information? Although we can all agree we have found ourselves in both of these situations (and sometimes simultaneously), I doubt we will be able to agree where these points are; nor if we could even define them for ourselves and even if we could, whether or not they would be the same between us. The point of this discussion is to demonstrate the impact the size of a documentation can bring, while understanding there is no concrete method of evaluation. Much to the degree we have handled similar situations, it is not impossible to do so. More that you would be infringing on personal characteristics of individual developers and will likely end up getting you nowhere fast. That said, this is another topic we have covered and another topic we can still take into consideration.

We have our original, modified function we should apply our new learning to:

$$(learning(w, c, p) = \frac{w}{c} \div p * (\frac{1}{C}))$$

We now have our two new attributes to consider: coverage and size. In terms of the coverage, we can take our example from earlier to help us apply our base logic thread. If we remember, the total coverage can do nothing more than increase our level of understanding of the language. If only 50% of the language, modules and extensions are documented, it is reasonable to believe we will only be able to understand roughly 50% of the language at an expert level. Certainly, there are arguments to this logic, but in the sea of trees within our forest, this is a reasonable assumption to make. Now, in the case of PHP from above, if we believe we have 100% coverage, we can also believe we have reached the ultimate Zen of documentation, and that it should not effect our overall learning curve. However, Perl at 75% documentation coverage will affect our overall learning due to the time it takes to understand the remaining 25% of uncovered interfaces (or whatever the case may be). This tells us that the relationship between coverage and learning is as the coverage grows, the time to learn increases. Simple enough. If we then take a simplified version of our learning curve:

$$L = learning(w, c, p)$$

Applying the theory of diminishing coverage as it applies to learning, we come up with:

$$learning = L * 1/D_c$$

Where:

D = Documentation as a Generalized Reference.

D_c *= The Coverage of the Documentation as a Percentage of the Entire Language*

The learning curve will increase linearly with the reduction of total documentation coverage. Then, to expand back to the original function, we come up with:

$$learning(w, c, p) = \frac{w}{c} \div p * \frac{1}{C} * \frac{1}{D_c}$$

The size of the overall documentation, as we have noted earlier, is something we will ultimately leave out of the equation altogether. This is because the evaluation is far too subjective to be accurate. Remember my preference, that I consider Perl documentation to be sufficient as I would rather look at the code than read the developer's rough interpretation. The opposite may be true with someone of similar attributes to my experience and history in the industry. Furthermore, the size of the documentation can also be respective of the medium in which it is shared. A paperback publication is one medium, although extremely hard to search. Sure, you can put a thorough index in the back with references to nearly every word ever referenced and the exact page within. Alternatively, you could put the contents online and have a good presence of SEO driving the search. The latter example could make it easier for some, less so for others. Yet to the same example from earlier, the coverage of documentation is universal. If it's not there, it will take longer to learn. You will catch yourself reinventing the wheel over and over again. You will find yourself thrown into unforeseen traps built of the perception of knowledge, trudging yourself aimlessly through ignorance. Not a good position to be in.

Before we wrap up what an impact a language can have, there is one more topic we can cover that brings us back more to the context of the language, rather than the external attributes that shape it: raw similarities. There are countless evaluations we can take into consideration when drawing a comparative analysis between languages. We are going to take a high-level glimpse at this level of analysis to get the gears rolling on this concept. Ultimately, what we will find is that languages have a dramatic impact on a development organization, and choosing the right one(s) is not only a complex matter but one that will make a dramatic impact on the success of your business.

As mentioned, there is a vast sea of attributes we could evaluate when it comes into the context of comparing different languages. We will only take a few into consideration for our analysis. The point is to get us thinking in this direction, but also to demonstrate a different evaluative method in determining how it applies to our overall learning curve of introducing the new language. Let us first take a look at the strictness of a language. This is the ultimate differentiator between communities and battles that rage every day within any programming circle. Which is best: a tight, secure interface that has compile-time, reflective checks into the types that are being used and where; or a loose language that has a highly abstracted interface, only exposing a few types that can all be relatively interchanged with one another as they don't apply to any signatures within the language? To do this, we can take a look into two polar opposite languages that are used at Intellicorp: Java (in the search team) and Perl (in the data team).

Taking a high-level look into the Java language first, we start with a highly typed and strict base. Every object has a literal type that is defined, directly or indirectly, by the application developer. Even with the somewhat recent additions of autoboxing and primitive auto-typing, every object still has a type that must conform to its interface or class definition. Furthermore, every method signature will contain the particular type of the arguments, return values, and exceptions thrown. Subsequently, methods and classes can be defined with different levels of protection and uses, each of which are strictly enforced by the Java compiler to ensure the definitions are followed precisely. High level, yes, but all very important aspects of the language. These specific attributes of the language generally pre-define design patterns that become very common across most Java applications. Although they are not specific to any one language, what is commonly found is a very highly abstracted, extremely object-oriented design from the beginning of any Java application, as the language itself forces you to act this way. Not to say this is good or bad, just stating.

Perl, on the other hand, is a far cry from any of the previously mentioned attributes. Perl 5 allows for the same design patterns and strictly adheres to a highly abstracted, object-oriented design through the use of highly powerful external modules. However, the key difference is that it does not force you to make good decisions. In other words, you can make anything with Perl. From a simple, hack of a script to help manage systems administration; to an enterprise-scale application, just as you would with Java or most any other language. Out of the box, however, Perl only supplies a very small handful of types. Secondly, any of the types used, when used as a scalar reference, have no compile-time checks (yes, Perl is a compiled language, folks) for the types, as the language also supports the redefinition of any variable into any other type. As the design of Java paves the way for particular designs and patterns, Perl tends to do just the opposite. Opening the code of any application, module or script, you are bound to find dramatic differences between each one. To a lesser extent, Perl does support self-defined objects and therefore an abstracted object-oriented design, but this is to the preference of the application designer rather than a dictation of the language.

There are dramatic differences between these two languages, and every language in between. The question that should be asked is what impact will each of the (and the many unsaid) differences will have on the decision making that will take place when determining which language to use, add or implement a given solution. We can normally find ourselves in a heated argument when the question is asked about which language is the best for any given application. An argument can be made that a level of rapid application development can be better achieved with a language that employs less strict typing, as it can result in less code written. To the opposing side, it can be said that the time lost in initial development will be saved in the long-term as more and more features are added. It can be further assured that it won't break as many interfaces since the compile-time checks will protect you against these simple oversights. There are countless arguments to defend either side of the fence. Yet when the rubber hits the road, nobody can defend any language to the point if convincing everybody in the industry that one language is better than another for all given situations, in part proven by the fact that so many languages remain extremely popular. There is no "one" language and that is not about to stop anytime soon. What do the differences actually make in your decision-making with this in mind? On one side, it can be heavily argued that after a rich understanding of one language, whether it is Java, Perl or any other incarnation of a fourth generation language, learning another is nothing more than referencing knowledge from one and finding the best approach to the same situation in the other. This argument is covered in the analysis we have already accomplished with respect to the community and documentation that builds the power of the language. As we hinted at earlier, the primary differences between a strong and weak typed language is the suggestions they make to their implementer's design style. From a developer's standpoint, the biggest hurdle in learning any new language is what "category" they fall into. Perl and Java are polar opposites in many ways, which is the ultimate challenge that is presented. The meat of the challenge is knowing your way around a strongly typed language such as Java, and adapting your skills into a weakly typed language such as Perl; adapting the philosophy that has drilled into to you by Java, when it is no longer a barrier in a language such as Perl. Similarly, when adapting a knowledge that has been founded with a language such as Perl, the challenge presents itself in not only learning the new syntax and available interfaces to take advantage of, but also how to change the mental approach to a problem when you have been conditioned to work in such a loose environment. Parallels can be drawn in a lesser technical world when comparing two different industries in two different regions of the United States. Imagine a stockbroker from New York City being swapped with a corn farmer from deep with in the US corn belt. Learning how to grow corn is something that can be taught and learned over time; similarly with trading stocks on the New York Stock Exchange. The bigger challenge for the two that have swapped roles is much more about how to live and survive in their new environment. There is no textbook of how to live off the land on a multi-hundred acre farm when you have been conditioned to live off the stratosphere in one of the largest metropolitan areas in the world and vice-versa. On the other hand, when all you know is how to live the rural life in the US' mid-west planes, moving into the high-rise hustle and bustle of big city living can present its own challenges as well. The differences between these two extremes are the same: it's not the knowledge or education of the new environment, it's the new environment.

How do we apply this to the language learning curve. We can first refresh ourselves with what we have thus far.

$$learning(w, c, p) = \frac{w}{c} \div p * \frac{1}{C} * \frac{1}{D_c}$$

If we adhere to the general philosophy that adopting a new languages is the alteration of fundamental paradigm between them, the first thing to determine is the number of different categories that will be taken into consideration. A language category can be based on any number of attributes as you see fit, for the sake of simplicity, we can consider only the two we have been talking about: strict and strongly typed, versus weak and loosely typed. The function will remain the same. Therefore, when we consider that a movement from one into another, with no exposure to the other, will impact on the learning curve, we can easily assume the following function:

$$L_k$$

Where:

L_c = *Number of Language Categories Considered*

Lk = *Number of Language Paradigms Experienced*

The application of this suggests that when the number of paradigms are taken into consideration, it adds nothing to the overall learning curve. This isn't the complete and natural truth. To take all the attributes of this analysis into consideration would be like trying to successfully raise four pairs of twins, each with birthdays three days apart from one another. It's possible, but will become an epic struggle. This can still take the consideration needed from the perspective of the overall paradigm differences, which is where we will likely see the biggest challenge. Buggy code will still happen, and by no means will someone who is experienced with writing Ruby seamlessly transition into writing PHP or Perl, but it will likely be dramatically less than the same person transitioning into Java or C# for the first time. Taking that all at face value, we can apply this to the larger learning curve to generate the following:

$$learning(w, c, p) = \frac{w}{c} \div p * \frac{1}{C} * \frac{1}{D_c} * \frac{L_c}{L_k}$$

We can tell that as we increase the number of categories, we increase the overall learning curve proportionately to the other factors. That is unless the individual developer happens to have experience with each of them, which is likely an expensive resolution to the problem.

Psychological Product Complexity

Products have a difficult time maintaining a psyche, which aids us in our continued analysis. Much as the internal components could not, the product cannot hold psychological traits due to its lack of humanity. We could have just as easily skipped this section altogether (and we will spend more time on this than you should), but it's another chance to reiterate a point that can't be stressed enough. It's easier, as we continue through the analysis, learning the intricate and complex details of the organization; to skip and glance through some of the details. Such would have been the case had we not addressed the psychological traits of a product. They don't exist, of course, but we must still take the time to recognize this and let it solidify. This isn't to be a nuisance but to ensure we don't miss things through our Coefficient discovery period. If walking on desert plains of old tide pools, how can you be sure there isn't life under a rock without looking under it? You can't, nor can you with this. It's important to understand every aspect of your business, even the areas that are missing. Remember this and we can now carry on.

In Summary

Defining the complexity of a product's distribution can drag to wild extents. Through all the needles we have hunted in the haystack, and all the thought we have thrown onto the table, we have dug a ditch in what is destined to be the Grand Canyon. We can, nevertheless, take the information and logic we have gathered and apply it to our business. Even though we may not have been able to cover every intricate aspect of the complexity of a product, we can get a better understanding of what it is composed of and how it can effect the decisions we will make.

We can quickly review each of the aspects we have covered. We first discussed the determination of the value of a customer when we came up with two generally equal equations, one more specific than the other. The two had the same take away, in that the value of a customer is directly proportionate to how much money they give to the company, minus the cost of doing business with them. The more complex version:

$$LTV = \sum_{t=0}^{r}(p_t - CPC_t)(\frac{uc_a}{tc_a}) - AC$$

This takes into consideration the amount paid by customer, with consideration into how much it cost per customer, for every customer. The alternative was a much simpler derivative, taking only the amount paid and respecting the number of times each customer does it. Not taking consideration into the cost per customer.

$$LTV = a * p$$

Between the two, there is a middle ground where you may find yourself. For our evaluation here forth, we will take into consideration as much as possible, therefore adopting the more complex LTV equation:

$$LTV = \sum_{t=0}^{r}(p_t - CPC_t)(\frac{uc_a}{tc_a}) - AC$$

Next was the evaluation respective of the number of installations as it applies to the complexity in terms of manufacturing and distribution. There were a few avenues we traversed for this one, yet the simplest way to explain the generalized situation was to demonstrate the growth of complexity as it relates to cloned installations as the number of total installations. Although we didn't define it then, we will represent installations from here on as:

$$I$$

Could not be simpler.

Lastly, we took a heavy look into the composition of the application itself. With a thorough review of at least one of the building blocks of the application; the languages used to create the application; it is arguable that we didn't cover enough, and that only reviewing the languages of an application is selling ourselves short. I cannot disagree. What we have is enough to use as a good gauge in our tool-belt of decision-making, and a thought experiment you can take to the next level as you apply this level of thinking to your decision-making. We came up with the following learning curve that can loosely describe the impact different languages can make on a project, application, or overall software ecosystem in your organization.

$$learning(w, c, p) = \frac{w}{c} \div p * \frac{1}{C} * \frac{1}{D_c} * \frac{L_c}{L_k}$$

The next step is to take these equations and assemble them logically together in order to determine a function that will tell us what factors into the complexity of a product will affect our decision-making. We can then apply them individually to Intellicorp. We can start making decisions from there. So, let's do this; get your party hats on. We will first take a critical review of how each of the factors applies to one another, and how we can apply them to our larger Scalability Coefficient. Everything boils down to dollars and cents, though that is not the ultimate goal of the Scalability Coefficient; no matter how related they may be. That said, the first equation we generated is nothing more than an evaluation of dollars and cents. Income minus cost. There is nothing wrong with this as it stands, as long as the proportions are adequate in their current state. At this point, we will assume they are, and will start with this equation.

We next have the raw number of installations, which is an indirect reference to the overall complexity that a single installation will take. With this alone, we know that any number of installations greater than zero will increase the complexity of the product, and by the definition we decided on earlier in this section, each installation will have the same net effect on the overall complexity (for simplicity, there are no hard-and-fast rules here). How can that apply to our LTV now knowing this? This depends on whether or not each customer gets an installation or not; i.e. is the product manufactured and distributed with a one-to-one relationship to the customer, or is it installed once per 1,000 users (e.g. a web-application that can scale to 1,000 total users)? The difference there lies within the precise approach. If a single installation is packaged as a single item for sale, it will then apply to the LTV per each customer. On the opposite front, if one installation can be multiplexed to 1,000 customers, then it would make far less sense to apply the function to each customer within the sum of all customers within the LTV. Therefore, it is nothing more than an increase of a fraction of the installation's value, where the denominator is defined by the number customers a single installation can handle. Therefore, what we end up with is:

$$ProductComplexity(PC) = \sum_{t=0}^{r}((p_t - CPC_t)(\frac{uc_a}{tc_a}) - AC) + \frac{1}{I}$$

This is nothing more than the sum of a customer's LTV, adjusted for the proportionate cost of installations as it applies to the distribution and manufacturing. I can be defined as something far more broad and complex than what we have. However, we continue with our overall thought process while demonstrating that there is a cost-benefit in distributing a single product to multiple customers, rather than distributing a product as individual pieces of sale. What if, for example, rather than having a car pull up to a gas station to fill their tank, gasoline distribution companies installed a gas pump at every house that needed one? Convenient, yes, but the complexity that is brought to the organization would be many orders of magnitude greater than they are with the most commonly known business model. The network of confusion it would have created would be overwhelmingly intense from the maintenance, delivery, upgrades, etc. There is a benefit to having only a gas station pump millions of gallons of gasoline every year, rather than the alternative, which this function represents.

Our next task is to remove ourselves from the customers and come into the light of the product team. This is a different perspective than the lower-level review of each customer from a singular plane; though, all the product team adds is a level of expense. Ignoring everything else we have talked about up into this point, if we only consider the attributes of a product and how they affect the product overall. To join these two concepts, let's start by considering two approaches: applying the learning curve directly into the current customer summation method and creating a new one that concentrates on the key member. The first we can take into consideration really makes little sense, so we will not spend much time with it. The only semi-logical approach would be to reduce the price by the cost of the learning curve. The question is immediately raised of how to actually relate an individual contributor in a proper ratio to a customer. There is not a good way. It can be done, but only if it can be determined that there is a precise linear relationship between every customer and every individual product contributor. That is a difficult and rather needless exercise to begin, as there is a more logical approach in calculating two separate equations and determining how they relate to one another in order to determine the overall complexity. We can convert the learning curve into something a little more reasonable that doesn't apply to only a single contributor:

$$learning = \sum_{ic=0}^{ic} \frac{w}{c} \div p * \frac{1}{C} * \frac{1}{D_c} * \frac{L_c}{L_k}$$

The awkward, one-sidedness of this evaluation should be pointed out as it concentrates only on the impact of the physical software. When you begin taking this approach into consideration, it should be broadened to take more groups and teams within the product team into consideration. Still for our example, we must remember a few things: we're eventually working with the Intellicorp's engineering team; we are still only looking at the minute structure of the organization, and have yet to take the big step to put everything we've learned back together. That said, we now have a basic function that will tell us the total impact that product learning will have on the complexity of a product.

Whether or not the relationship is between the working product complexity component and its application to the customers, and how it applies to our new internally-focused approach, is still a question that has been left unanswered. As we have discussed earlier, the ultimate draw from the complexity of the product is that as the learning curve grows and takes longer, the product's complexity will grow as well, therefore adjusting the Scalability Coefficient away from our ultimate goal of zero. There is narrowing enough for us to determine part of the equation, but there is still the question of the relationship: how does the product learning affect the customer relationship and vice versa. The truth is, there isn't one - at least for our analysis. It could be argued that an extreme learning curve with inexperienced developers, either in tenure or with the product itself, can move the product to a point where it is released it has already been rendered obsolete by its completion. We have all seen this happen before, particularly in technology or any other emerging, developing and volatile industry. Therefore, the total for the complexity of the product can be simply explained by a sum of the two equations, where the overall complexity is defined by the learning effect of a product and the customer effect.

$$PC = (\sum_{t=0}^{r}((p_t - CPC_t)(\frac{uc_a}{tc_a}) - AC) + \frac{1}{I}) + (\sum_{ic=0}^{ic}\frac{w}{c} \div p * \frac{1}{C} * \frac{1}{D_c} * \frac{L_c}{L_k})$$

This is understandably a little hard to remember. Of course, with the magic of algebra, we can mask the hard parts into an even simpler combination of references.

$$PC = LTV + learning$$

Simplified further into.

$$PC$$

This is what we will remember and refer to from here on

We have now formulated a method of defining the complexity of a product. Next we can apply it to our business to ensure it fits the critical points we are trying to achieve with the Scalability Coefficient. The result, when adjusted appropriately, will move closer and further away from absolute efficiency: zero. Although we have combined each of the aspects of our function into one large function, it may make more sense to take a step back again and evaluate the functions independently before we combine them back to define the total product complexity. Particularly being as there are the two categories of affecters: internal and external. We can start with the complexity of the users and customers to do this.

$$(\sum_{t=0}^{r}((p_t - CPC_t)(\frac{uc_a}{tc_a}) - AC) + \frac{1}{I})$$

Web Team

This is the most straightforward team to start with. Let's quickly jot down each of the appropriate variables respective of the web team's platform and see how they fit.

Variable	Value
p_t	$0
CPC_t	$0.15
uc_a	1000
tc_a	1500
AC	$500
I	10
R	1000
T	1 month

Table 3.55: Web Team Representation

We can recall by looking at this that we are working with a company that has yet to release its flagship product and carries no revenue stream with it. They have external funding, but that is hardly enough to consider the complexity of a product. Although anyone who has completed a funding round may note this is not entirely true. Regardless of your stance on this matter, customers are not paying yet and we will not consider non-standard company sales as a portion of the income. The CPC and average unique and total clicks are metrics that are easy enough to gather from the advertising distribution and content manager used. The acquisition cost is a little different than the price paid for a customer arriving to a site, as it is the internal cost per customer paid. This is a combination of fixed and variable costs the company incurs over time t. We took a simple process of gathering this number: we made an educated guess. For this exercise, although nowhere near precise, it can act as a place holder to conduct our further evaluation. The installation calculation is based on a web application, therefore it is a simple count of total web application servers; 10 in our example. As far as the total number of customers, we have taken the timeframe of a single month to aid in the simplification of this particular analysis. We can take the given month and apply the metrics to our equation to see if it fits both the goals we are trying to accomplish and the satisfaction of the Scalability Coefficient as a whole. Using the variable/value matrix from above, we have:

$$\frac{1000}{1500}$$

Reduced, this becomes:

0.667

Although we can be confident this equation satisfies what we are trying to achieve, there are two obvious issues with it in terms of how it applies to the overall Scalability Coefficient. First, it's a small number. Although true, particularly when weighted over only a month's time with 1000 customers, it is nothing to be concerned about at this point. Without full context of the entire equation, we have nothing to weigh the equation against and can therefore ignore it for now. Remember, this is only a tree in the depths of a very large forest. While at the same time, we can easily lose perspective of the size of the tree without looking at the entire forest. The second and more important fact is that the result of the equation is below zero. Certainly this is possible and a solid stepping stone into further dissection; with real numbers, this becomes a much less abstracted process. This approach is a much more intense method than we have used before, but it's another method that can be used. This can be a particularly useful method in the event, which is a modified representation of an already existing equation. When entrenched in a thought experiment to morph it into something more useful, it can be easy to lose sight of the overall goal. With this all in mind, let us take a look at what we have.

We first have the generalized profit gained by serving a single customer. This is represented by subtracting the cost of acquisition from the price the customer paid.

(0 - .15)

There is no price in our example. This will, of course, give us the immediate negative sign. It represents negative profit and its impact. Not a state a business wants to be, but that's the path Intellicorp is traveling and therefore accurate. Let's look at the rest of the dissected equation before we evaluate any connotations this result may have.

1500

This represents the percentage of unique clicks of the total of all clicks through customer-obtaining advertising. Looking at this specifically, we have to ask: how does this number actually compute with respect to the customer? As we have translated it from the original total value computation, it sits as a direct multiplier to the profit achieved for each customer. Although this number does relate to the cost of a customer, it makes less sense as a multiplier. This is fact as we know that the total unique clicks will never be greater than the total clicks (else there are bigger issues that need to be resolved first). We also know this relationship will always reduce the profit for a single customer. How does the total percentage of unique clicks relate to profit? Rather than having it act as a reducer it would make the most sense if we considered the number of unique clicks as it applies to the cost per acquisition. In other words, say it costs $0.15 for the click it took to obtain the user. However, there may have been 10 other clicks between the last acquired customer and the newest one. From this perspective, one could argue that rather than the newest customer costing $0.15, the customer would have cost $1.65. This isn't a perfect case, but the point should be apparent. If we were to take this approach, everything we have considered about clicks pretty much goes away. I am demonstrating two things: review is always necessary, and that a different perspective can shed some better light on a bigger problem you are trying to solve for. Hopefully you are starting to pickup and predict this theme by now. Going back to the revamped equation, if we consider the number of clicks respective of the total customers and how they all apply to the profits, we would end up with something a little closer to the lines of:

$$\left(\sum_{t=0}^{r}((p_t - CPC_t * \frac{tc_a}{t_c}) - AC) + \frac{1}{I}\right)$$

By taking the total number of clicks over the total number of customers (t_r) and applying it to the individual cost, we can obtain the total cost per customer as it applies to the total cost of the organization's advertising campaign. By finding the ratio between clicks paid out and the total number of registered customers, we can apply it to the individual cost per acquisition to determine the total acquisition cost. We can now go back to the regularly scheduled, more atomic calculation of the total profit by a customer to read as:

$$(0 - .15 * \frac{1500}{100}) = -2.25$$

We still find a negative value as we did before and with the same justifications as earlier, but we have a much more reasonable relationship between the costs per individual customer.

500

For the next value we have dissected from the equation, we do nothing more than subtract the overall internal acquisition cost per customer. This number is a calculation that depends on your accounting practices. Ignorant of this, it's an added cost to the cost of acquisition and much like we had earlier. The cost of bringing on a customer is the profit gained, where anything less than zero is the cost; above is the profit (a little 2nd grade math there for you in, as we all forget sometimes).

10

The last portion of this part of the equation is to represent the number of installations. A reversed ratio is what we have decided to use up until this point. This demonstrates the increased complexity as the number of nodes grow. The intent is logical, but the implementation does seem a little flawed now that we have real numbers against it? In this example, we have 10 installations, giving us a value of .10 to add to the coefficient. We have already discussed the logical progression of this, where adding new installations to the product (we used the example of web applications between distributed client applications). Where if we had an example where we distributed 1000 installations, we should have a larger complexity factor to add. However this example would give us .001 to add to the coefficient, which is a reduced value when compared to .10 - not exactly what we're looking for. Reversing this would give us the growth we are looking for, but compared to the rest of the equation, we would be giving an undue heavy weight to installations, which would also be unjust. Another option would be to invert this situation by subtracting the ceiling of the maximum value of the result: 1. This would grant us both the logic we strive for along with the result we need. If we decide to change our equation again, taking consideration into this last iteration, we will then need to determine how much of an impact this will make to the product. The two approaches that are most reasonable would be to add it to the existing equation, or add the percentage of the rest of the equation up into that point. The latter makes less sense as it would imply even small numbers would nearly double the original value, where each additional installation, even to a few orders of magnitude, will add little additional impact. With adding the value to the result, anything less than 10 installations, we will be adding one. The question remains of whether or not it should be a multiplier or not. To keep this short, we can take the same, original reasoning and add the installation result to the Coefficient. This will leave us with the problem of always adding one. A resolution to this is to drop the two earlier ideas and take the base-10 log of the total number of installations. A little curve ball on a 3-0 pitch, perhaps. We can throw out our considerations at this point and take a scaled representation of the number of installations which should suffice for all of the requirements we have. A logarithmic curve of complexity added to the previous Coefficient will satisfy our goal by growing the overall Coefficient. This would in turn transform our working equation to:

$$\log_{10}(I) = \log_{10}(10) = 2.302$$

We have 1000 customers. That number will represent the iterations to gain the sum of the total complexity of the product as it is represented by the number of customers we have for the product.

1000

Putting this all back together, we now have a total equation of:

$$\sum_{t=0}^{r}((((p_t - CPC_t) * \frac{tc_a}{t_c}) - AC) + \log_{10}(I))$$

Calculating everything out with respect to the numbers we already have, we now have an equation that will result in:

$$(((0 - 1.5) * \frac{1500}{1000}) - 500) + \log_{10}(1000) = -495.3422$$

Giving us the reverse of what we want while taking into consideration the goal of the Scalability Coefficient, we can invert the sign of the result. Therefore, we will continue to have negative connotations with the complexity while taking profits into consideration. The larger the profit, the more the complexity of the application becomes worthwhile, so to speak. And with this final change, we can have full confidence in our resulting equation:

$$\sum_{t=0}^{r}((((p_t - CPC_t) * \frac{tc_a}{tc}) - AC) + \log_{10}(I)) * -1$$

We have a little left before we move on to the most important part of this book. The remainder, the second half of the product complexity equation, is derived from (respective of our recently formulated customer equation):

$$(\sum_{t=0}^{r}((((p_t - CPC_t) * \frac{tc_a}{tc}) - AC) + \log_{10}(I)) * -1) + (\sum_{ic=0}^{ic} \frac{w}{c} \div p * \frac{1}{C} * \frac{1}{D_c} * \frac{L_c}{L_k})$$

Which is simply:

$$learning = \sum_{ic=0}^{ic} \frac{w}{c} \div p * \frac{1}{C} * \frac{1}{D_c} * \frac{L_c}{L_k}$$

We can try to keep this analysis a little more concise by using the same approach of applying our real numbers, yet will remain a bit verbose given the size of Intellicorp. Starting with the non-learning, customer focused portion of the equation, we already have the metrics we care about:

Variable	Value
p_t	$0
CPC_t	$0.15
tc_a	1500
AC	$500
I	10
r	1000
T	1 month

Table 3.56: Web Team Representation

A trend we have taken is using values of the direct customer respective of the team for larger calculations such as this one. We could determine how to apply this function, in this case, to the direct customers of each team. Using the search team as an example, we would find a method of applying this function to the web team, as it is one of the search team's primary customers. It would point the burden of specific teams' customers, whom they should be the most focused on. Keeping the paying customers close to the forefront of everyone's mind is an equally valuable proposition. The search team not catering to the bottom line, as the web team must, is not enough justification to ignore the bottom line. Bringing the best value to the customer should be on the top of everyone's mind and this is one way to do it.

Moving on to the second half of the productivity equation, we do not have the ease and ability to decide how and which attributes we want to use. It is respective of the overall learning that will be applied to each project with the appropriate team(s) taken into consideration. To try and make things a little easier on ourselves, we can first try to refresh our memories of what we are looking for.

Variable	Description
w	Time using the language.
C	Number of companies worked for.
p	Number of promotions received.
c	Community.
D	Documentation (as a generalized reference).
D_c	Coverage of the documentation.
L_c	Number of language categories.
L_k	Number of language paradigms.

Table 3.57: Definition of Variables

As we had with the learning for individual contributors earlier, we will again determine the result of this function for each individual. However, as teams and projects will change, we not only want to apply this to individuals but we will need to consider them in their own space as a team, for a particular project or product will involve individuals from independent teams from time to time, rather than an entire team all at once. It applies to a singular language as it applies to a project. The value of the latter half is therefore a sum of sums, or a sum of all people in a project as it applies to the language used. Perhaps the equation would be better written as follows, taken this into consideration.

$$\left(\sum_{e=0}^{e} \left(\sum_{ic=0}^{ic} \frac{w}{c} \div p * \frac{1}{C} * \frac{1}{D_c} * \frac{L_c}{L_k} \right) \right)$$

We have already obtained some of the values. We can reference these to begin with.

Name	T	C	D	c	P	Co	Ca	p
Strider Johnson				1	3			
Arwen Little				15	0			
Erwin Little				15	0			
Chet Smith				2	0			
Grace Hopset				3	1			
Perl Wall				2	0			
Exemelle				2	0			
James Cartwright				1	1			
John Overheimer				4	8			
Percy Greentrain				2	2			
Stan Keyhang				2	0			
Caleb Alan				4	5			
Addie Lane				3	1			
Therese Jean				2	0			
Bill Votex				5	4			
Jason Watcifer				3	1			

Table 3.58: Indvidual Coefficient Matrix, Referenced

Where the column headings are defined as:

L	*Time With Language*
C	*Community*
D	*Documentation*
C	*Companies*
C$_o$	*Coverage*
C$_a$	*Categories*
P	*Paradigms*

Table 3.59: Definition of Variables

It's a big empty playing field, but at least we don't have to go back to the HR department to reconstruct some of the details. However, there are quite a few attributes we have left to evaluate.

Name	T	C	D	c	P	Co	Ca	p
Strider Johnson	3[1], 2[2]	100k, 300k	.75, .9	1	3	.6, .5	1, 2	1, 2
Arwen Little	7[1]	100k	.75	15	0	.6	1	1
Erwin Little	10[1]	100k	.75	15	0	.6	1	1
Chet Smith	4[1]	100k	.75	2	0	.6	1	1
Grace Hopset	3.5[1]	100k	.75	3	1	.6	1	1
Perl Wall	2[1]	100k	.75	2	0	.6	1	1
Exemelle	2[3]	250k	1	2	0	.9	1	1
James Cartwright	.5[3]	250k	1	1	1	.9	1	1
John Overheimer	8[1]	100k	.75	4	8	.6	1	1
Percy Greentrain	0	0	0	2	2	0	0	0
Stan Keyhang	.5[1], 1[4], .5[5]	100k, 50k, 75k	.75, .75, 1	2	0	.6, .6, .9	1, 2, 1	1, 2, 1
Caleb Alan	0	0	0	4	5	0	0	0
Addie Lane	2[1], .5[4], .5[5]	100k, 50k, 75k	.75, .75, 1	3	1	.6, .6, .9	1, 2, 1	1, 2, 1
Therese Jean	2[1], .5[4], .5[5]	100k, 50k, 75k	.75, .75, 1	2	0	.6, .6, .9	1, 2, 1	1, 2, 1
Bill Votex	5[1], 2[4], 2[5]	100k, 50k, 75k	.75, .75, 1	5	4	.6, .6, .9	1, 2, 1	1, 2, 1
Jason Watcifer	0	0	0	3	1	0	0	0

Table 3.60: A really big table (* 1 Perl, 2 C, 3 Java, 4 Ruby, 5 PHP)

The lion's share of these numbers came from our recall of earlier discussions. Some, such as the size of the community and documentation references, were taken from our discussions along with references from the community itself. It's now another application of the same collection, conquering our biggest hurdle. One interesting twist this matrix throws us is the multidimensional aspect of each individual. For those who work on a team that manages multiple languages, such as the reporting team, we have to take each language for each person into consideration. A second interesting aspect of the numbers we have obtained becomes apparent with the last two columns of our matrix. Remember our function:

$$learning = \sum_{ic=0}^{ic} \frac{w}{c} \div p * \frac{1}{C} * \frac{1}{D_c} * \frac{L_c}{L_k}$$

The last multiplier is defined by the number of categories over the number of paradigms. From a philosophical standpoint, this is logical and a path we could continue to follow. It is the magic of our friend, mathematics, that will let us reduce this away completely when we take our business' numbers into consideration. As it turns out, for the five languages the Intellicorp has adopted over the past three years, each of them has the same number of logical paradigms as they do categories. And we also know from our school-age arithmetic that any number divided by itself is 1, where the product of 1 and anything (call it x) is x. Simplicity is our friend in this case, and we are able to reduce the function to:

$$learning = \sum_{e,ic} (\frac{w}{c} \div p * \frac{1}{C} * \frac{1}{D_c})$$

Notice two things we accomplished there, both of which are a little out of the ordinary in terms of how we have re-factored our equations in the past. First, given a logical equation we compiled earlier and have come to trust, we allowed ourselves to change it given the business environment. For this example, it was a simple reduction. Yet it was a reduction after taking the physical numbers into consideration, rather than one done against the equation itself. Remember the equations we are compiling are not those for generic applications, but ones specifically for your business and your decisions; nobody else's but your own. This gives us the freedom to act as we did along with generating the equations in the first place. They are ours to help found our future decisions. Second is respective of the approach in which we re-factored. Rather than taking the numbers and recalculating, we concentrated on the numbers as we were gathering them, taking into consideration the equation as we went along. We used our memory, which is a great exercise to begin. It is your memory that will keep you afloat through your decision making once you understand your overall Coefficient. I not only doubt you will want to re-calculate your Coefficient for every decision you make. The idea is more that once you understand you organization - *really* understand your organization - you can start making good decisions for it; good decisions.

We would normally take this time at the end of a calculative exercise to demonstrate its specific power and what changes will bare different decisions. However, unlike our previous sections, this is the last calculative exercise we will accomplish for this writing. What's next is the true application. We can finally start making decisions.

Section 4
The Breakdown

We have enough information in our hands to start making sound decisions based purely off the physical metrics of your organization. It's you and I, the hired hands of Intellicorp to decide what is best for the organization as a whole. We have become intimate with the team. We now understand each of the internal pieces that make it work. What's most important is that we understand the product and the customers. We probably know these pieces better than the majority of the individuals in the team collectively. This is what any good outside consultant would need to do to make good decisions on behalf of a company. This isn't why we are here, though. This is what *you* need to do. *You* need to understand your organization better than anyone else, leading *you* to better decision making. Will you know everything? Absolutely not. By no means do we know everything about Intellicorp either. However, you have much more time to learn more and evolving what you know into a much more powerful tool. We may not know nor have evaluated everything we could have, but we also have to remember how much we have learned. We can begin drawing conclusions with that knowledge. Conclusions are the catalyst to decisions and when they are backed by immutable facts, rather than assumptions or premonitions, it becomes very hard to make wrong decisions.

Remembering the Past

We have taken a look at the countless moving pieces, and one of the obvious challenges is remembering everything we have done. Of course, this next exercise is a rather intrusive when considering the number of decisions that are made every day. However, repetition is one of the best methods of sustaining a good memory of something, and this would hopefully be the first of the last repetitions you need to become more efficient at making highly complex decisions. Before we move on, there is one last point. We are working with a static company; Intellicorp is frozen in time. Of course this will make our continued analysis much more straightforward, but is not reality. Your business will grow, change, evolve and adapt to the environment it's in, never stopping unless dies or gets swallowed. This means you will have to ensure your Coefficient grows, changes and evolves right along with it. Letting any of your analysis get too stale will bring you into a pattern of decision-making based off the assumption that your organization is the same as it was in the past.

The People

We first took a look at the teams and how their contributions applied to the organization, and how they would define our Scalability Coefficient. The very first consideration we took was to the impact of individuals respective of their past experiences.

We came up with a little equation that defined a learning curve based off of objective attributes of the individuals.

$$learning(w, c, p) = \frac{c}{w} \div \frac{p}{w}$$

Where:

w = *Time Within Field*

c = *Number of Companies Worked For*

p = *Number of Promotions Received*

This is only half of the picture: the half that is represented by the actions people have taken in their past. The other half is your own evaluation based off of the structure of your company and their respective positions within it. This method only works if you have already thought about the positions held within the company and the people you put into them; it assumes you hire with thought instead of premonitions from your crystal ball. In terms Intellicorp, we must assume due diligence has been made. In doing so, we had come up with the following equation:

$$contribution(r) = \frac{\left(\sum_{n}^{n=1} r_n - 1\right) + r}{\sum_{n}^{n=1} r} * -1$$

Where:

r = *Range (or Difference)*

n = *The Number of Subordinate Positions*

The completion of his equation concludes our two-part picture of what defines our strategy, respective of the people that will be effected by the decisions we make.

Internal Components

We also took a deep look into the internal components that made up Intellicorp: the nodes that create the makeup of the internal network, along with the pending queue of tasks that makeup the continued development of those nodes. Our first conclusion through these two considerations was the overall complexity that is generated by the nodes that make the network that must be managed in order to sustain the products. The equation that blossomed from this is as follows:

$$complexity(t, S, D) = t^{((S+D*2)/t)}$$

Where:

S = *Source*

D = *Dependent*

t = *Total nodes*

Who could forget the internal workings of the working task queue for the product? It could be argued that this could just as easily be applied as part of the Product Complexity component and respective evaluation. No matter where it ended up in *your* evaluation, the categorization is nothing more than a function of organization. Where we will soon combine them into our much bigger (and, yes, complex) Scalability Coefficient. It is at this point that the categories will go away anyways, making this level of organization arbitrary. Whether or not you take this approach as well is up to you, as long as you take all the necessary steps to consider the organization in its entirety.

When taking the active bug queue into consideration, we came up with:

$$priority(b, p, m) = \frac{max(p)}{p} * \frac{b}{(m+1) * 30.5}$$

Where:

p = Priority

m = Number of Months Active

b = Number of Bugs Categorized for the Month

This is a high-level review of how the internal components of an organization add to the complexity of it overall, the major players are all here. It is brevity more than anything that has kept us to this high-level. Where the closer your get to your organization will allow you to make more refined and better decisions.

Product Complexity

We had the much longer analysis regarding the complexity of the actual product. In taking the physical product into consideration, we were not only able to consider the pieces that make the product, but also the customers who consume it. A rather intimidating look into the customers and how they relate to the complexity of the product evolved into:

$$\sum_{t=0}^{r} ((((p_t - CPC_t) * \frac{tc_a}{tc}) - AC) + \log_{10}(I)) * -1$$

Where:

pt = Price Paid by a Customer at Time t

CPCt = The Cost Per Click Paid at Time t

rt = Probability of Customer Returning

AC = Acquisition Cost per Customer

T = Time horizon for calculating LTV

And with the physical makeup of the product, the code in our case, we came up with an equation that looked like:

$$\sum_{e,ic}(\frac{w}{c} \div p * \frac{1}{C} * \frac{1}{D_c})$$

Where:

w = Time Using the Language

c = Number of Companies Worked for

p = Number of Promotions Received

D = Documentation, Generalized

Dc = The Documentation's Coverage as a Percentage

Although the tradition has been to keep each equation separate, we took the two and combined them to bring us to an overall product view. A simple summation between the customers and the makeup of the product gave us:

$$(\sum_{t=0}^{r}((((p_t - CPC_t) * \frac{tc_a}{t_c}) - AC) + \log_{10}(I)) * -1) + (\sum_{e,ic}(\frac{w}{c} \div p * \frac{1}{C} * \frac{1}{D_c}))$$

This is important and was brought up for two reasons. First, it broke our convention and that alone is an action worth talking about. Second and more importantly, it was the first step into generating what will become the current organizational Scalability Coefficient for Intellicorp. A summation in this case through the rest of the evaluation of the remaining pieces. It all depends on the relationship each have with one another respective of the goals we wish to obtain. In the case of our product, the two have equal weights to the Coefficient overall, as they happen to play an equal role within it.

What's Next is Last

The last step of building out our Scalability Coefficient is, simply, building out our Scalability Coefficient. When we're done, you will look like the smartest kid in your neighborhood wielding a demonstrative equation. Confusing to the misinformed and ignorant, it can become the driver behind your decisions, as your thoughts will then be engulfed in the inner operations of your company.

This last step is nothing more than applying the necessary glue to put all our pieces together. The tough part is what glue to use for which piece and what the sequence is for the pieces. We must find how part of our Coefficient relates to one another before we can put it together with any effect. Furthermore, we must consider the respective weight of each attribute as well. Remembering up to this point, we have been ignoring the difference of output between each equation. This means that if one is an order of magnitude larger than another, it will have an order of magnitude greater impact on the Scalability Coefficient. Let's say, for example, the Product Complexity equation results in a value of 10, while the individual learning curve results in a value of .001. Any adjustments to the latter will have significantly less of an impact to the Coefficient overall than adjustments to the Product equation. This may or may not make sense and completely depends on your organizational needs. On the other hand, while using the same numbers, we could apply the respective calculations a little differently. For example, and an option we have earlier considered, we can appropriately weight the product of these equations so they each individually and appropriately apply to the Coefficient. Continuing to use the same fictitious two numbers from earlier from this experiment, let's compare the two components with increasing Coefficients both as a sum, as well as an adjusted result for the Product Complexity. Using ten growing numbers based off our originals, each incremented by twice the previous, respective value is represented as:

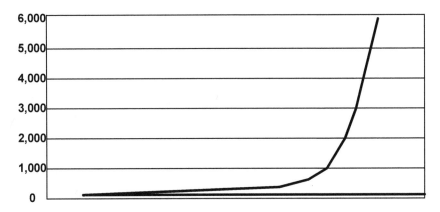

Image 4.1: Exponential Representation

Simple addition gives us a dramatic difference between the complexities of a product with respect to individual learning curves. By adjusting both equations by the natural log of the same numbers, we will find a much tighter relationship between the two factors.

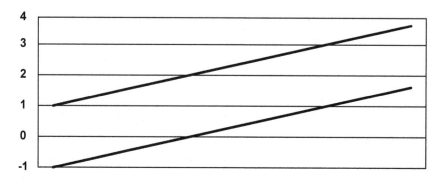

Image 4.2: Linear Representation

This is when our critical thinking has to take foot in our decision making as neither approaches are wrong, necessarily. Further to say that one (or another relationship we haven't considered) will fit better from the perspective of the organization. The two representations of the information ask the simple question: does the increase of the complexity of the product overwhelm the rest of the organization as it grows in complexity, or does it stride in toe with the rest of the organization? I can't answer this question for *you* as that's your job, but we can for Intellicorp. Perhaps it will help with answering yours as well. The ultimate goal of all of this exercise is to find the best representation of how your organization ticks. Are the proportions and growths respective of what happens in reality? In terms of Intellicorp, we are going to err on the side of simplicity again. Although this may not be the perfect representation of our reality, we have to remember the larger point of this writing is to help you think in a new way, not solve all of your problems (although I hope to do both). With this in mind, we will use the sum of each of the components to draw our Scalability Coefficient. This may be a round enough conclusion for you to come with as well, as adding additional complexity to our overall algorithm will more than skew the decisions you make as you get lost in a cloud of mathematics. Accurate decision making can only come from accurate information. Although this may not perfectly apply to Intellicorp, we can still remember what our goal is along the way for you, not our fictitious company we are using to demonstrate the new found power of our calculative decision making engine. This aside, we can finally draw the final Scalability Coefficient for our organization. The very being of our thorough analysis and everything we have been building up and working to. What's next is to make real decisions. To do this, we have the following and final equation to represent our burden:

$$(\frac{c}{w} \div \frac{p}{w} + \frac{(\sum_n^{n=1} r_n - 1) + r}{\sum_n^{n=1} r} * -1) + (t^{((S+D*2)/t)} + \frac{max(p)}{p} * \frac{b}{(m+1)*30.5})) +$$

$$((\sum_{t=0}^{r} ((((p_t - CPC_t) * \frac{tc_a}{tc}) - AC) + \log_{10}(I)) * -1) + (\sum_{e,ic} (\frac{w}{c} \div p * \frac{1}{C} * \frac{1}{D_c})))$$

Together, we have walked a tumultuous adventure to generate perhaps one of the most complex equations you will ever use within your organization. By now, I would hope that you have passed the point of intimidation as you should understand the makeup of every part of this down to the letter - literally. We won't be carrying this around with us into meetings, we will be carrying the concepts and memory of its composition with us. In other words, this equation (which may only a fraction of one that you will come up with), is the definition of the operations and efficiency of your organization.

Decisions, Decisions

The entirety of the work we have accomplished up into this point is for one thing and one thing only: to make sound decisions that is logical and based off of indisputable facts. Not only will this increase the chances of your ability to make good decisions, it will help you back up your decisions when they don't pan out like you had originally had hoped. I will never claim this to be the end-all to any decision you could make - far from the truth, in fact. This isn't the only method you should use either. My guess is you are somewhere in your career where you either want to make, are beginning to make or are already making decisions. To get to any of these places, the decisions you have made in your past must have been sound to some degree. You need to keep using these methods. Maybe it's your gut, maybe it's something else. I don't care how you've made decisions in the past, if they have worked and you have been successful up into now, keep with it. The only thing we can do with our Scalability Coefficient is make the decisions more sound, logical, proven and worthy of an intelligent argument. When you begin to think of the decisions you have made in the past, you may find they have been riddled with assumptions, guesses, feelings and raw emotion. In some extremely rare cases, people have a natural ability to succeed throughout their career with this operation scheme. I would safely bet that isn't you. That's OK, it isn't most of us, including myself. With the lack of this sixth sense, the only thing you have to help you is truth and facts.

The Black Hole of Time

In the eye of declining revenues, feverish product development falling to late schedules and considerations of a new product philosophy, we had a job to do. Our job was less to find an immediate cure, but to find where the time was going as it stood. This is exactly what we have done in many respects. Finding where time goes can be first attacked by finding what people do every day. In building our Coefficient, we have met the teams, discovered how they work together, what they work with, what they are making and how they each contribute to the bottom line. With our newly founded Coefficient and the data that led up to it, we have enough information to see where time sits. Not, necessarily, where it goes; where it is consumed. Near synonyms terms, but will help define our prime directive: to become more efficient.

Buzz Word Compliance

We have our coefficient and to some degree what Intellicorp was looking for: an idea of where time is being spent. We will be able to figure out what exactly Charlie and Intellicorp want. Although we can explain where time is, it's what they want to do with that time that is most important. And, as we led the book with, we will lead into this with a story.

Our heads were held higher, with more confidence as we entered the similar glass-lined room. It may have been the reflective dust floating aimlessly throughout the room, the visible chaos outside the double-lined panes or the sun finally shining into the office; but we felt like we were ready to finally help Intellicorp. The analysis was the daunting, expensive and very subjective matter of our profession. The time is taken with gathering the information and executing plans based off it. The truth will only come to fruition after we have left the trail of intelligence we had gathered along the way.

Charlie shot to the nearest chair as he entered the room, letting his inertia take it back a few feet as he moved his direction key on us - his expectations hit us like lawn darts tossed off a roof by an ambitious five year old. We were on. I was the first to spin my chair, rolling closer to Charlie, failing at an equally graceful chair jockeying maneuver. I was still able to gather enough grace to flip a stack of documented thoughts I had prepared onto the table. I placed my open hands, palms down on the stacks of papers that lay in front of me as I looked up at Charlie, lowering my shoulders just a bit. I then began the explanation of our time to Charlie. It was much more of an intelligence gathering excursions on Charlie's part. The banter back and forth; loaded mostly with questions and answers seemed to come to a steep end after I stated, "Charlie, you want us to make intelligent decisions. To do this, we need intelligence and that's what we've been doing."

I carried on from there, describing the interviews and the thought process we have traversed throughout the time we had given our initial analysis. Conclusion came when we arrived at the task we had been assigned. "You wanted us to find where your company has been spending its time. Although we have this, we need to know what's next. What do you want with the time?"

Charlie leaned back a bit in his chair, resting his forefinger below his lip, spending more time in motion than in thought. "We need to find a way to save money with what we already have."

Ambiguity in direction wasn't necessarily our goal. "I mean, we can try to find out where time is lost and what to do to fix it. Honestly, that's such a multi-ending problem to solve, it may not be the best use of our time here. Ultimately, we have a responsible staff, a goal for the company and ideas of what we need to accomplish in order to get there –" I added.

Charlie jumped in before I could finish. "You're right, to a point. We really only have one goal in terms of our immediate product development. At this point, we have little more than a concept, not a product. We are shoveling money into an engine as if it were coal, building steam, but with the breaks on the entire time. We don't have a product team to itemize the details, but we do have a vision and a platform. Before we will ever be able to see a profit, we are simply going to need more funding to sustain. To get either, we need to combine the two; we need to combine our vision to our platform to create a product and we need to let our technical staff find the best way to do this. I think we've been trying to get there, but we're wading through tar along the way. We need a better use of our time."

More thought and inspiration from Charlie, but laced with the same transparent ambiguity. But his point was clear: the chaos development process they have adopted to this point isn't cutting the mustard. There did need to be a new process, but at the same time, we weren't equipped to find the best fit for the organization. Charlie wasn't finished. "Although we need this combination; our product, it's much less about the end and more of how we get there. Like I said, we need to lure investors with what we have not what we will have. This means we need demonstrable progression. Simply, we don't have the money to work to the end, we need something that sort of works along the way; something we can build on but something we can show all along the way. Show that it's getting better, more importantly."

"Yes, of course." I delayed as I considered his statements.

He was looking for little more than organization and a better process of getting things incrementally out the door and into the customer's hands. Although the definitive goal of most product development organizations, it's seemingly the only one that made sense for

Intellicorp. They didn't have the money to make a fully functional product but they had enough to keep them going long enough to build a prototype - an alpha product. Not one for customers, perhaps, but one for investors to enjoy.

"Two things I think are clear from this. First, there needs to be direction.", I began to summarize. "The teams need to know what to do, how to get there and when they need to get there by; being held accountable along the way. Second, they need a process they can follow to help get them there. One that facilitates the ability to incrementally ship a product while sustaining the goal of a polished product by the end."

Charlie's lips curled upwards as his head nodded in agreement.

"To an extent, we are certainly capable of handling both. But our analysis and experience will truly only help you with one of the two directions: how to formulate the team and process into a situation to attain these goals. The direction, on the other hand, is likely best suited for you and your management team."

Charlie's nod gained tempo as my last statement concluded. "I can't agree more and it's something I'm already working with our product leaders with. But we can only get so far with that, we still need a method in which to travel in the direction we lead."

As I began to shuffle the papers back, pretending they held any true organization to them to begin with, I continued, "Good. We can work with this. Between your help with leading the direction and vision of the company along with our analysis of where the development team is today, I'm confident we can find a suitable process for getting the product to where you want it, how you want it."

"Let's meet then in a week, two at the most to check back on progress from both ends." Charlie said, straightening out his shirt with frantic vertical thrusts as he stood. I stood too fast, pushing the chair out from behind me as my knees straightened, causing all visible heads to turn as it struck the glass lining our existence. As the awkward pause faded, I reached my hand to meet Charlie's with equal nods of our heads as if *either of us knew where to go next. The sun soaked dust swirled behind Charlie as he fled the room, already late for his next meeting. Sliding the chair back underneath me and noticing schedule posted behind the now battered window, we seemed to have the room to ourselves for the next two hours.*

The shrug of your shoulders met my blank look as we tried to relax with a collective breath. In general, we had a basic idea of what needed to happen. First, we needed to hope there was some concept of what the product needed to be, hopefully finding functional release points along the way. Charlie had mentioned putting a lot of the decision power into the hands of the engineering team, which would ease this a bit. Second, and more importantly, we needed to find a good method of arranging the engineering team in a manner that would allow for the efficient growth of the product. Not by necessarily adopting a canned development process, but one that would fit the needs of the organization. One that is different than the chaos that everyone is working in today. Unbalanced teams, working in desperate systems with different technologies all with next to no budget. We can't change the tech, we can't really change the people either. What we can change is how they operate.

Finding Our Way

We have been given this direction for the terms of this writing for one reason: it's highly complex and will let us exercise our pre-existing logic, experience and decision making while enabling us to apply our newly formed Coefficient along the way. With this newfound direction, we have a few things in front of us. First and foremost, the knowledge we have gained of Intellicorp is at our fingertips. We know how the engineering division of the company currently operates and what it is composed of. As we will see, this will be the key to our success. Secondly, we have a method of evaluating different states within the organization to determine the net effect on the operations of the company. Thirdly, we have a goal. Our simple, high-level goal is to find a way to organize the engineering team in an efficient way so they will be able to seamlessly generate a product. This is where the rubber hits the road.

We know how people are operating now. The good news is that's what we've been doing over the past many, many... many pages. As we had hinted on earlier, what's next is we can use the same business logic we have always used to build some options we can then consider. The basic concept of what we are trying to accomplish is finding a way to ratchet through small iterations of a product. In our current organizational incarnation, we have nearly no way of doing this. The organization is built around the premise that single projects will be given to a team, they work on it, and then they move on to the next thing that comes along. We can take these two ways: use it to our advantage or change it. In terms of using it to our advantage, we find ourselves in much more of a scheduling and project dissection predicament than anything. To the point of the latter, we have much more of a logistical challenge to overcome. Likely we will find that a major shift in how the organization operates will result in a cost that is too much for the company overall. But as you have learned while reading, we don't really know that for sure. It's an assumption, and assumptions are they keys to bad decision making. There's little lost of crunching a few numbers and thinking critically before we come to this decision. Therefore, to start, we will take a look at these two approaches and see which may make the most sense, both in the short term and in the long term. Before we do this, it should be pointed out that we will not yet be looking at a product development philosophy directly. At this early point in our analysis, there is no reason to bind ourselves to a thought pattern that is defined by any one development paradigm. Rather, we can attempt to find the most efficient combination of resources, then look to see what pattern it fits; there is no reason to hammer a puzzle piece into the rest of a larger puzzle when it makes more sense to look at the piece first and we can then see where it fits.

Before we start anything, we need to know what the project entails. As Chet had mentioned, a project plan with milestones will be generated for us by the remnants of what's left of the product managers throughout the organization. It is our luck that his word came true, and the responsible teams have given us the following plan:

Task	Duration	Blocked
1. Determine Data Sources (Data)		-
2. Evaluate new partners	20d	
3. Examine quality of data	20d	2
4. Implement data store	15d	3
5. Implement data funnel plugins	15d	4
6. Design Data Source Consumer Models (Search)		-
7. Determine storage platform	15d	
8. Understand underlying data design	5d	
9. Implement core data transfer	15d	4
10. Transfer data	10d	5
11. Research relevance algorithm	20d	
12. Integrate into search platform	20d	
13. Index data	10d	9-10
14. Implement/Extend search API	20d	13
15. Design assignment bot		-
16. Research existing crawler implementations	20d	
17. Determine running pattern of crawler	5d	
18. Design/integrate crawling mechanism	25d	
19. Integrate search API	10d	14
20. Design data structure	15d	
21. Determine linking method	5d	
22. Assign relevant links	20d	21
23. Web design and implementation		-
24. Redline new interface	20d	

25. Design most appropriate implementation	25d	
26. Integrate with assignment bot data results	5d	22
27. Testing		-
28. Data source reliability	10d	3
29. Core data store and content	10d	4,5
30. Indexed data store	10d	14
31. Search API	10d	15
32. Relevance confirmation	10d	12
33. Crawler verification	10d	16
34. Relevant linker verification	10d	24
35. Front-end design verification	10d	25
36. Page layout and user functionality	10d	25

Table 4.3: High-level Product Timeline

Critical Path: 102 days, 20.4 weeks, 5.1 months

Total Project: 425 days, 85 weeks, 21.25 months, 1.77 years

This generic, high-level outline gives us a lot to start with. Not only it is a standard design for a project task list, but one that has come with estimates and logical blocking tasks. It's one that has room to grow and change, which is one of our goals. This is great as any company who has a project outlined for over 1 3/4 years will jerk their knee so hard it will shatter their hip, let alone a company who is tight on both time and money. We know the tasks that will generally get us to the end product regardless, telling us a final first version (v1)'s critical path will hold a duration of 102 work days (5.1 months) and an overall project duration of 415 days (21.25 months) - the end of the line, fully featured product the company wishes to ship to its customers. This is not our goal however. Our goal is to find a way to methodically and incrementally get to this point of development with presentable milestones along the way. Where presentable is not little pieces, but end-to-end integration of all the important components. Not fully featured, but working.

With the two paths we have tentatively laid out at this point, let's start with the more straightforward method: keeping as much the same as possible and changing the project. There is an obvious, off-the-cuff benefit to this; no new training, no big shuffles, and conforming to regularity should help with morale. With or without our equations, these things should all hold true. But one things we don't know is *will* it hold true. Even if it works for the short-term, will it make sense for the long-term?

Starting with the first attempt to determine an efficient method of iteration, we don't need to start with any of the learning we have obtained through our Coefficient, but rather rely on the business logic and decision-making we already have. The first step is to take our original project plan and determine a logical progression path to get from point A (nothing, where we are at now) to point B (a full-featured v1 product) with clear and progressive milestones we can demonstrate along the way. Perhaps the clearest method to this is to start by stripping features and see where that takes us. Regardless of what we do, we know the first milestone will be the most painful to get to. This is mainly due to the fact that starting with nothing, we need something that will demonstrate a full integration, from soup to nuts. We need to find and integrate the data and display it on the site - all things that haven't even been touched. While moving forward, there will be a progression path we can work with and existing integration points we can build on, which will help our goal along the way. To start, let us find out what the first path of least resistance is.

To do this, let's think about all the major points of the project:

- Find new data sources
- Integrate new data sources
- Format and add data to search platform
- Determine and implement indexing method for search platform
- Determine and implement search relevance algorithm for search platform
- Design and implement search API into the search platform
- Design and implement bot crawler to link relevant searches to articles/questions
- Design and implement new supportive UI
- Test

The next step is to determine logical and measurable milestones. Each milestone will represent a checkpoint in the development where we can demonstrate the work to whomever; whether it be the executive team, investors, clients, or inevitably: customers. Let us see what we can do to break this project up into reasonable mini-projects, each with a singular, specific goal. It becomes a question of how much we want to take away first in order to reach a milestone, while balancing the ability to demonstrate something worth value. These two goals are mutually exclusive, to an extent. The value is buried within the finalized v1 release when it is first demonstrated to paying customers. If we can stretch to find as many precise and decisive milestones as possible, we should be able to glue any length of them together into deliverables and prototypical products. After the first milestone, we will have a product to demonstrate; if we don't want to demonstrate the barren wasteland it surely will be, we can wait for the second and so on. A common strategy indeed. Let's get started.

We are going to begin by breaking apart the schedule in order to determine multiple, smaller milestones we can easily accomplish. The first step will be removing the features we don't need for the end-to-end integration to work, leaving the building blocks. Taking apart the list we built earlier, we can decide.

Find New Data Source

Finding the new data source is a requirement; we need this. We have no data without data sources; without data we have nothing to link and therefore no project. However, the intent of the overall project was to have a finalized and completely verified list of all the vendors Intellicorp will source for its content. For our initial milestone however, we only need one vendor. One that will have a nice balance between ease of adoption and integration, while having a relatively substantial impact on the application for initial demonstration purposes. It is with this we can go back to the data team for a new estimate, explaining to them the focus of our new goal and the current milestone we are working towards.

Integrate New Data Sources

Data, as with the previous task, can only do so much until it's stored in a medium that is easily accessible. The net total of time allocated to this task is a respective function of how many data sources are used to generate this underlying platform of content. By only finding one to start with, this task will be reduced for our first milestone as well, which we will present accordingly to the data team.

Format and Add Data to Search Platform

This task is a hard-requirement as well. The question must then be raised of whether or not the task needs to be added to the first milestone. An alternative to adding it at all would be to have the search API connect directly to the funneled foundation of data. There will be some impact on the project of course, by implementing an API that draws data from the data team's data store rather than the dedicated search platform, we have not only undertaken the time and energy to implement the API, but we also know it will all get thrown away in later milestones when it is properly migrated to the search tier. The question then becomes: what is this impact, and how does it weigh on the timing of this milestone to deliver a demonstration with respect to the extension of the overall project. In easy situations, this would be a relatively simple process to undertake. Gain a reliable estimate from the search team of what it would take to source the data team's content rather than their own, and add it to the total duration of the project. The difference between this estimate and the full search integration will be the time saved on this milestone, where the new duration would be added to the project. The savings now weighted with the loss later can be taken into consideration by Charlie to determine if the cost is worth the losses. Although the approach outlined would work, we also know the search team will have a difficult time giving an accurate estimate for work on another's team - the data team. This isn't a fault of theirs, more a matter of not fully understanding the intricate and complex details that is already encapsulated in the mind of the data team. Furthermore, from the reversed perspective, we would also know that the similar difficulty would be for the data team to undertake the task of modifying the search API to source their data set. Although we could gather estimates, if we are going to use these estimates to start the mark towards profitability, shouldn't this decision be a good one founded in a breadth of information we already know? Why yes, yes it should. This is where our work will begin to come together. What is the most efficient decision, regardless of time or duration? We can use our learning of Intellicorp's Scalability Coefficient as it applies to this task to help us make the decision of what to do for this and each subsequent milestones. Let's start by looking at the three options we have already discussed: the search team building out an API based off the data team's content set, the data team building out the search API, and the final option of, neither; building out the API against the dedicated search platform.

We must consider the Coefficient as it stands with respect to the players at hand. For this example, we are taking two of the three components of our derived Coefficient: the people and the components they will work with. In terms of the complexity of the product, although it does apply in this case, is much more a consideration to the end consumer, rather than internal development of the product itself. With this function taken away, we have the remaining two factors to take into consideration. We will start with the first of the two: the people.

We can start by un-archiving the two formulas we have made, decisively combined in our logical manner.

$$\left(\frac{c}{w} \div \frac{p}{w}\right) + \left(\frac{\left(\sum_n^{n=1} r_n - 1\right) + r}{\sum_n^{n=1} r} * -1\right)$$

We move forward by plugging in the numbers for each employee. In terms of the learning curve, these are numbers we have already generated and calculated; we will reuse them. In terms of your own analysis, that may or not be a sound decision. It depends on what has changed. People and experience come and go, and you will have to consider this. We also consider our quest for opposing roles in this condition. Where considering what the impact would be of having the search team work with the data team's competencies and vice versa. In terms of learning alone, we have generated an equation that is ambiguous, as it only takes the facts of the individual's history into consideration; effectively trying to determine how fast they will pick up a new task, no matter the concentration; which is exactly what we are looking for in this case.

Modeling a representation of the search team:

Name	w	c	p	Learning
Exemelle	5	2	0	0
James Cartwright	1.5	1	1	1

Table 3.2: Search Team Attribute Coefficients

And by the data team:

Name	w	c	p	Learning
John Overheimer	17	4	8	.5
Percy Greentrain	6	2	2	1
Stan Keyhang	3	2	0	0

Table 4.4: Data Team Attribute Coefficients

Before we move onto the contributions the individual positions apply, we need to address the standing poison ivy that is represented through missing promotions (p) in the history of some of the individuals we are looking at - Exemelle and Stan specifically. What we have, based on our specific analytical points, depends on your perspective; all with the same result. We either don't have enough information to accurately gauge their level of learning, or they don't hold the ability to learn whatsoever. We can be hopeful that for the sake of our considerations, it's the former over the latter. As we now know the goal of our evaluation is to find the most efficient device, defined by the result coming closer to zero, a learning curve of zero doesn't accurately demonstrate our goal. There are many ways to take care of this, but for our consideration, we will simply have each of these individual's learning curve ratio be represented by the maximum of all in consideration, increased by the average of the group collectively. We then have Percy and James in the running for the highest learning curve, each with a value of 1, and the average of them and John (excluding Stan and Exemelle) being .833. The sum we can then apply to Stan and Exemelle. Because we don't know their learning style or curve, we have to prepare for the worst. Now, we have values of the following:

Represented by the search team:

Name	w	c	p	Learning
Exemelle	5	2	0	1.833
James Cartwright	1.5	1	1	1

Table 4.5: Search Team Expanded Coefficients

And by the data team:

Name	w	c	p	Learning
John Overheimer	17	4	8	.5
Percy Greentrain	6	2	2	1
Stan Keyhang	3	2	0	1.833

Table 4.6: Data Team Expanded Coefficients

We then must find the individual, weighted contribution factors as represented by a function of the sum of the considered positions. We can take from the results we have already gathered in our earlier analysis. For this, we will use the second half of the learning equation as follows.

$$\frac{\left(\sum_n^{n=1} r_n - 1\right) + r}{\sum_n^{n=1} r} * -1$$

We have already analyzed, discussed and implemented this algorithm, while imagining life in the vacuum of a world without a fourth dimension. With our previous implementation, taking consideration only to the development and data teams, we have compiled the following matrices:

Position	r	contribution(r)
SDE I	5	-.1111
SDE II	5	-.2222
SDE III	5	-.3333
SSDE I	20	-.7777
SSDE II	10	-1.000

Table 4.7: SDE Calculated Contributions

Position	r	contribution(r)
Data Analyst I	2	-.1428
Data Analyst II	5	-.5000
Data Analyst III	7	-1.000

Table 4.8: Data Analyst Calculated Contributions

As we apply these to the specific people within our bubble of consideration, we have the following:

Name	Position	contribution(r)
Exemelle	SDE II	-.2222
James Cartwright	SD I	-.1111
John Overheimer	Manager	n/a
Percy Greentrain	DA III	-1.000
Stan Keyhang	SDE I, DA II	-.1111, -.5000

Table 4.9: Individual Calculated Contributions

This brings up two notable and already discussed topics: the impact of management, and the effect of a dueling position such as the one Stan holds. Your interpretation will be best suited for your situation, whereas in ours, we know two things in terms of product development: First, managers don't count. They contribute, but not to the physical development of the product (respective of Intellicorp). Taking Stan's position into account, there are endless ways to determine how to apply him. For our analysis, we will consider each of his positions as separate positions. The justification for this is it is reasonable to believe the rates of learning and contribution are different depending on the task. It could be that Stan just has "a job" with the data team, where his real passion is in development. Thus has an accelerated level of contribution when comparing the act of development to that of data wrangling. And as we have talked about the evaluation of psychological attributes of an individual, which this is, we need to stay away from them; at least within the context of our evaluations. Keeping the values separated is the safest avenue to take for this, which is the reason we have taken it.

With the final calculation of the contribution of individuals, we can conclude with the combination of the two as defined by our larger equation:

$$\left(\frac{c}{w} \div \frac{p}{w}\right) + \left(\frac{\left(\sum_{n}^{n=1} r_n - 1\right) + r}{\sum_{n}^{n=1} r} * -1\right)$$

Name	Learning	Contribution	Total
Exemelle	1.833	-.2222	1.6108
James Cartwright	1	-.1111	.8889
Percy Greentrain	1	-1	0
Stan Keyhang (SD1)	1.833	-.1111	1.7219
Stan Keyhang (DA II)	1.833	-.5	1.333

Table 4.10: Individual Calculated Coefficients

We have marked the first implementation of our Coefficient. The Coefficient that defines the individual and their ability to learn, as well as the contribution they will bring to the project; the lower they're Coefficient, the better. The next step is to move into the components this task will work with. Before we do so, it is worth taking the time to take a step back to determine for yourself if you have a full grasp of the numbers we have calculated and what they mean exactly. This is not a step we will continue to take throughout the duration of this book. It is one that should be taken upon yourself between each transition in order to instill the Scalability Coefficient you have devised in order to understand your team's resulting Coefficient. It's a good time to reflect before moving on, both in terms of your reading and in a real-world application.

In terms of the complexity of the tasks involved, we have the two attributes to consider: overall complexity and priority. With the data we have already ascertained for the overall complexity for the teams we are considering, we have:

Team	Sources	Dependent	Total	Scalability Coefficient
Search	2	3	5	13.13
Data	1	1	2	2.82

Table 4.11: Organizational Network Complexity

Which we can then apply to the following:

$$complexity(t, S, D) = t^{((S+D*2)/t)}$$

And subsequently, the priority:

	P5	P4	P3	P2	P1	Result
Jun	3.9	0	0	0	0	3.9
Jul	4.3	5.3	0	0	0	9.6
Aug	2.1	2.6	0	0	0	4.7
Sep	15.3	28.5	8.1	0	0	51.9
Oct	13.7	24.0	27.3	13.7	0	78.7
Nov	51.9	0	0	0	0	51.9
Dec	16.8	0	0	0	0	16.8
Jan	38.1	23.6	94.6	28.2	19.3	203.8
Feb	56.4	92.2	35.5	54.1	0	238.2
Mar	116.8	107.8	16.6	0	0	241.2
Apr	134.2	91.5	50.6	76.2	0	352.5
May	129.7	123.9	126.5	25.3	38.1	443.5
Jun	203.1	126.9	286.5	50.3	0	666.8
Jul	106.8	95.3	759.4	38.1	0	999.6
Aug	244	381.2	1215.1	305	305	2450.3

Table 4.12: Calculated Priority

Which data we can apply to our priority equation:

$$priority(b, p, m) = \frac{max(p)}{p} * \frac{b}{(m + 1) * 30.5})$$

We will soon be taking each of these attributes together, but before we do, we need to put a nail into the coffin of the exponential, one-sided priority evaluation. There is an awkward relationship between bugs and critical analysis in the first place. While the number of bugs does demonstrate the complexity of a product, the lack thereof does not. Since the bug queue is used by all the teams, it only applies to the search team's product. Up until now, we have been ignoring the practical applications and results. However, the data is valuable now. Its value is only weighted with consideration to the points we have risen throughout. It is a one-sided perspective. As long as the only reason for taking bugs into consideration is to evaluate complexity, (which is a highly argued topic in its own right) rather than performance or other personal attributes, there is value to keeping the data set. It's a valuable gauge into the window of the product's complexity and we still have the ultimate power to define how loose or tight that value is represented. It's exponential. We can figure that out with a little math. The route we will take is to scale down the priority with some ambiguous weighting against the logarithmic result. The net effect of this will allow us to take the priority into consideration while having its impact be lessened to counter the effect of any negative connotations that may take place. We will do this once we start combining our results with one another, as the relative weighting we need will be the most apparent then. Once we take a full view of the forest, can we determine the true size of the forest?

Between the individual contributions alongside the product contributions, we have everything we need. It's time to put them together. To start, let's look at our options. Remember, we're working to determine what would be the most beneficial to SC, Inc. in terms of getting the data from the data team into the search engine. The three logical options we're considering are:

- Having the search team build an API directly against the data team's data set.
- Having the data team build an API directly against their own data set.
- Importing the data into the search tier, extending the existing search API.

Let's start with the first. In all our examples, we will take consideration into learning:

$$\left(\frac{c}{w} \div \frac{p}{w}\right) + \left(\frac{\left(\sum_{n}^{n=1} r_n - 1\right) + r}{\sum_{n}^{n=1} r} * -1\right)$$

Complexity:

$$complexity(t, S, D) = t^{((S+D*2)/t)}$$

Priority:

$$priority(b, p, m) = \frac{max(p)}{p} * \frac{b}{(m+1) * 30.5}$$

The first situation will mix into cross-team collaboration and will need to consider how the individual learning will apply to each of the teams. For example, the learning curve for members of the search team with respect to the search application is significantly lower as they have already jumped the curve. Whereas the search team working with the data team's infrastructure is much more significant, as the learning will have to be absorbed in the task itself. To combat this, we will simply consider a negation of the learning curve for teams within their own product. When we consider the search team working with the search application, there is no longer a learning curve; thus no need to consider learning at all, just the product-specific attributes. Furthermore, when considering learning as it applies to the complexity of the product, we must apply it as a function of how it works against the complexity of the product, not just as a sum of the two. It's not a linear function of how people learn, but how they learn particular tasks and how they learn the product, not now they learn in general. Now all things considered, the overall Scalability Coefficient we will consider is the product of learning of the sum of the complexity and priority, or:

$$ScalabilityCoefficient = learning * (complexity + priority)$$

We are first looking into the search team's API built directly against the data team's data set. What we can infer from this is:

- The search team will build the API, needing to learn the data team's infrastructure.
- The data team will build the importing, tools, etc. needed to support the infrastructure and host the data.

Now as the most recent month is the cumulative total of the respective priority, we will use it to apply to the priority in the function. We must then consider the relative weighting for the priority. The last point we needed to have is the composition of the Coefficient, along with the knowledge of all things surrounding it, which we finally have. Priority aside, we know that learning and complexity are relative factors which will be an order of magnitude smaller than the last month of our priority Coefficient (2450.37 versus 22.58, the maximum product of learning and complexity). We also know, from our earlier analysis, that we need to heavily adjust the priority, as it is only applicable to work with the data team and doesn't span across to the other products. It's unfair to increase the Coefficient as it applies to the data team and not the others due to a lack of metrics, but it still has some weight and should be applied. Also, know that arbitrary weights are just that - arbitrary. Being that priority is an adjustment to complexity, and one that should be reduced to something somewhat insignificant, we will adjust the complexity to a fraction of the minimum complexity Coefficient: 2.82 (data team). Let's say, half:

$$2450.37 * x = \frac{2.82}{2} and x = 0.00058$$

As we move back to the two tasks we are evaluating, have all the information we need to make quick, intelligent decisions based purely off the facts of our business. We must first consider the search team building the API from the raw source provided by the data team, forcing the search team to learn the data team's infrastructure. To accomplish this, we will consider the respective Coefficients for either team, with respect to learning where it is applicable. Thus, we have the sum of two Coefficients that will illustrate how either team will adapt. Taking what we have just discussed, it will break down as such:

$$Coefficient_{search} = \sum_{i=1}^{n}(learning_{search}^{n} * (priority_{data} + complexity_{data}))$$

$$Coefficient_{data} = priority_{data} + complexity_{data}$$

$$TaskCoefficient = Coefficient_{data} + Coefficient_{search}$$

We must remember that we must consider the learning as it applies to the individual across the complexity of the product they are learning; where if there is no product to learn, there is no learning and therefore the sum is not needed. Using our previously calculated values, let's find the task's Coefficient:

$$TaskCoefficient = ((1.61*(0+2.82))+(.889*(0+2.82)))+2.82 = 9.87$$

And to the first alternate configuration of the same task, we are having the data team build an API directly against their own data set. This task is a little interesting as it doesn't directly include the search team. However, the data team must still facilitate an interface that will not only be somewhat compatible with the existing API, but will need to be compatible with the future API, otherwise risking the potential of being redone. Even though the search team doesn't have to be involved directly, the understanding of the search tier does; we will take this into consideration.

$$Coefficient_{data} = \sum_{i=1}^{n}(l_{data}^{n} * (p_{search} + c_{search})) + (p_{data} + c_{data})$$

$$((0.001*((0.00058*2450.37)+13.13))+(1.7219*((0.00058*2450.37)+13.13)))+2.82 = 27.8902876$$

With this alternate scheme, we are keeping everything within the standard method of completing the task: working with the data team to import the data into the search tier, and extending the existing search API to conduct the searches. Interestingly, in this form, we will find a result in the same way as we had with our original configuration. The net attributes that comprise the Coefficient are the same. The search team must learn the data design and extend an existing API; while the data team has to work and import data into a known, internal data architecture. Copying what we have already calculated for this similar task, we have:

$$TaskCoefficient = ((1.61*(0+2.82)) + (.889*(0+2.82))) + 2.82 = 9.87$$

To summarize the three task's Coefficients:

- Having the search team build an API directly against the data team's data resolves a Coefficient of 9.87.
- Having the data team build an API directly against their own data set resolves a Coefficient of 27.89.
- Importing the data into the search tier, extending the existing search API resolves a Coefficient of 9.87.

You should be confident enough at this point in the evaluation of the Coefficients we have built to believe beyond a reasonable doubt that having the data team build an API against their own data set is simply not in the cards in terms of the options that are available. However, this is a case of education and reflection, and one last justification is maybe worth our time. What it comes down to is the general complexity of the two alternate systems: the search tier and the data tier. The search tier is the central hub of the entire architecture of the company, whereas the data architecture is nothing more than a temporary storage center for information. We cannot discount the data architecture too much, as it comes with its own complexity of course. But the application of learning is a bigger hill to climb with respect to the search application than it is with the data application.

The two remaining tasks have beheld the same Coefficient. With all we have discovered and learned up into this point, one thing we haven't considered is that dueling results build to a lack of conclusions. The Coefficients don't tell us much above the attributes we have used to compile the them. The Coefficients are equally optimal. But, in reality, they are not equal. This isn't a negative proof of the concept as a whole, it's much more an example of why this conceptual thought experiment isn't a replacement to what you already know in business. In reality, this is an unlikely and specific case, but similar concessions will have to be made with similar situations. Given a different organizational structure, with three similar tasks. Rather than having one third of them be three times larger than the rest and the other two be exactly the same, all three may have been within a small percentage of one another. There is a small enough of a margin where you would have to take your standing business logic into consideration to further your decision. Remember, in these cases, there is no loss into making it this far while having the results circle the drain. Any decision you come up with now will still be backed by indisputable facts, based off of attainable, unarguable and defined metrics. It's a foundation built for your business logic rather than simply experience. Your experience is now the subfloor to the foundation of reality shouldering your experience. Do you want a house built with a foundation? I prefer a foundation.

We should refocus our attention back to the two remaining tasks, we need to decide which is the best for the situation; remembering the goal of this exercise is to find the quickest road to getting a demonstrable product out of the door. In terms of work, let's compare the two remaining tasks to take care of this. The only real difference between the two are whether or not the trouble will be taken to import the data into the search index as is normally done. With taking the long-term into consideration, this approach certainly comes with its drawbacks. First, the data will eventually have to be ported into the search index, no matter which task we take. It then becomes a question of whether or not we do it now or later. In either case, having the search team build out the API is equally optimal; it's all a question of the critical-path schedule to the first releasable product. Second, there is further integration after any implementation from the search team, and again with the integration from the yet-designed "assignment bot". With the web integration in particular, we can immediately summarize a few things, knowing what we know and what we have learned up to this point. First, the web team will have to learn a *new* API, where they have already learned the *existing* API. In theory, this can be avoided with an intelligent design (create the new API to mimic the existing API in terms of generalized interface consumption). If we can assume only reasonable, logical designs will unfold, we can mitigate this learning curve as best as possible. The net result is simply where the data is stored. With this in mind, we know the underlying storage designs, implementations and overall quality will be different depending on who hosts the data out of the box. This means very little to anyone outside of either team (specifically the client, the web team). However, this means a lot to the entire project. Keeping the searchable API on the data teams implementation will effectively force the scrapping this entire portion of code implementation when the data is properly imported into the search tier. This tradeoff comes at a significant cost, as the majority of the time spent on this task will become a sunk cost once the post-beta/version one of the product reaches completion. Knowing both tracks are equally optimal and its effect won't spider out to different teams and future tasks, it becomes a cost-benefit analysis. Is the time saved now worth the same time lost and doubled in future tasks? A dueling estimate can give us that answer, and with all other considerable attributes simplifying out of the equation, that's what it comes down to: is there a significant time savings in not importing the data into the standard search corpus, allowing us to get a demonstrable product to market quicker? At the end of the day, from everything we have talked about with this task, we know that the answer to this is simply: not really. Custom data cleansing and learning data implementation is the tradeoff for the data team building out their standard suite of filters to export into the search tier. Although there is time savings, it's not significant enough to take the small shortcut now, knowing that we will have to eventually double-back and do it again. Take the slightly longer path now, saving time to get to the end of the road; all other things considered.

This was a long path to determine what may have been blatantly obvious to you all along. Before we move on I want you to consider the length of this exercise is relative at this point. The actual hard work is behind us - determining the relationships between the attributes that comprise the Coefficient. Furthermore, this is our first full compilation of everything we have learned up into this point and so I wanted to take a little more time with it. Regardless, even though the most difficult and truly time consuming process is behind us, it's the application of our findings that lead us to the best possible decisions. It's indisputable, factual, and reality which takes your due diligence to complete.

Critical Business Analysis

With any implementation comes its practical application. We must review our organization critically to apply our newfound Scalability Coefficient. Let us take a look into our organization's project to learn how all of our hard work ties into a practical application.

Determine and Implement Indexing Method for Search Platform

This task is a simple and depends directly on the work we have just completed. Ultimately, the decision of which indexing method to use is a function of where the base of the data would reside, which we decided in the previous task: under the search team's standard umbrella.

This does bring up two strategic points, however. The first would be the analysis to determine whether or not to use a new indexing scheme. Should the search team find a new underlying index in order to un-archive its new content, over what it has been using in the past? Secondly, how much consideration should be made to the entire project? The best strategy is to take a step back and view the entire forest rather than singling out specific trees. These two points are dependent on one another as well. The only modification to the project will be in the event of a new indexing scheme. We would only consider a new indexing scheme if we chose to build the API on the existing search platform. A tangled web. So being we would only consider a new indexing scheme if we were using the search API, this seems to unfold for us pretty simply; even within the tangles. Since we know the search team will be hosting the data and the API, and that this decision opens the consideration for the new indexing platform, now is the best time to consider it.

We are going to take a much smoother, quicker and logical approach to this particular analysis. For one reason, it is to demonstrate what we can do to with what we already know, another in an attempt to keep things moving.

With anything new comes learning, of which we pretty well understand in terms of the search team. The complexity, as it applies to this task, is a little different than what we have seen in the past; it's the reverse and crosses the team into the data-sphere. For the last task we analyzed for example, we would have looked into the Coefficient to help us determine the most optimal method of continuing, but we already know the answer: we either do it or we don't. In conducting the research and implementation will give us a Coefficient and not doing it will not. No Coefficient is the most optimal. This really only makes sense with respect to the task at hand. Taking what is seemingly the most optimal route, not looking into a new indexing scheme, may or may not need to happen. Yet, it most certainly does not need to happen *now*. Unlike deciding where the API should be formed from, work and time will not be lost by working on this later. For our immediate goal of driving a relatively solid product out of the door, we can continue to use the indexing methods that are already in place, saving us the immediate time while putting the task on the back burner for later consideration. The most optimal solution now becomes the best route to take, even with respect to the schedule goal we are under. With that, the current answer is that we should use the indexing method the search team already uses and understands.

Determine and Implement Search Relevance Algorithm for Search Platform

We can quickly discount this task, in terms of our immediate goal. A working prototype can lack in advanced functionality as long as it works - at least as it has been defined to us. In other words, when it comes to new, advanced technology being added to a project - such as a new search relevance algorithm - we can remove it from the project plan if our immediate concern is getting the product out the door. Simply, "We Can Do It Later™".

Although we will do it later, we can still walk through the thought process of this task in the light of pure educational purposes. The view into this is quite similar to the new indexing platform. To draw any conclusion, we will take a somewhat different road in order to demonstrate how different trains of thinking with respect to our known Coefficients can take us to the same conclusions. We will assume we are at the point in the project where we are no longer considering *when* to work on the new algorithm, but *how*.

In terms of a new search relevance algorithm, we have a problem that's rooted in computer science research and theory. There are two things taken from this: there is no specific organizational group within Engineering that has any specific hubris on the given topic, and even though the knowledge of relevancy isn't honed in the company, the area of expertise is. From each of these points, we have a singular Coefficient determination to make: it's much less about *how*, much more about *who*.

If we think of it in these terms, we have at least three possibilities:

- Internally by the search team (as search is their expertise).
- Internally by another team as they would have domain knowledge by working for the company).
- Externally by a team who's knowledge is honed in search relevancy or CS theory and research.

To come to any conclusion, we won't take this as far down our Coefficient path, but we will take it as far as we can with the thought process and implementation. I say this because something here has happened we need to discuss, but really have no need of applying. This is the addition of a new topic of complexity, learning and involvement with the company: a theory problem that has yet to be adopted with consideration for an external, third-party.

We still need to consider the attributes that have carried us this far: our Coefficient as a product of learning, and its complexity. We know the learning and complexity of their product. Yet, in terms of the third-party specialists, we know nothing about them; or about the complexity of the algorithm itself. Budgets and schedules aside, determining the most efficient is determining the lesser of two evils: a third-party researching and implementing a new algorithm in an unknown application with the help of the search team, or the search team doing the research in no man's land to implement an algorithm in an application they know better than anyone else. For us, in our case and our reality, none of this matters. So let's assume the two initial variables that could swing any decisions before they're made are non-issues: budgets and time. In other words, to move with the exercise of how to handle this new situation, we will assume an infinite budget and any adjustment to our schedule will be met with open arms. This is not the reality of the situation. In reality, we're sticking with the relevance algorithm that's already implemented for the sake of the business' real constraints. There isn't anything saying we can't continue to learn.

Spinning our approach into a thought experiment, we can take the attributes we have learned and ignoring the numbers. You have graduated, congratulations. We can start first with the teams we know, the search and data teams. First, the search team. What we know is that we need a search relevance algorithm. The search team is the most obvious front-runner for this this task for three major reasons. First, they know the business, the rules, the existing platforms and the code. In terms of learning, from this perspective, they are already caught up. From the perspective of our Coefficients, this is a major contributor to our decision-making. They have the background and experience with the current algorithm: how it has evolved, why it has evolved, lessons learned, the technology behind it - everything. This also includes the complexities that are formed within the application and outward-facing affected factors. Remembering these are two of the major players in our equation, having these factors minimized is a big benefit to the search team's candidacy for the project. There is one thing they don't have expertise that could throw everything they do have out the window: they are domain experts, not experts in the specific field of search relevance. As with everything new, as we have learned and with respect to the direction we are taking with this analysis, there are two factors to first consider: learning and complexity. There is a lot to become familiar with in terms of learning. This project is an exercise of academics over practical business implementations, which is a world away from what the search team has grown accustom to. There are the endless paths that will need to be taken to gather a full understanding of the research and findings in the field of search relevance, all of which will take a significant amount of education. On the team's side is a background in search relevance. They may not hold the deepest experience in the industry, but some that spans a couple of years for a portion of the team. This won't topple the daunting task ahead of them, but it will aid in their understanding of the applications, studies and methods they will come across along the way. The factors of advanced mathematics, computer science techniques, and endless dead ends all escape the search team to a degree larger than what they have going for them. Now let us step outside of the Coefficient and into the world of project management and our business decision mind. Let us consider the ability to actually get this project done. First things first, everything will start at the point of requirements. How perfect are we willing to be for the money we have? We can play outside of the real world at this point to the point where we can pretend we have a blank check. Blank check or not, we can't be stupid about it. Waste not want not. For this exercise, we will assume the requirement is simple: we want the best. Where the best is something that hasn't been done before. With anything that hasn't been done before, it's an expensive and lengthy process. These two factors do not bode well for the search team, as both the overall expense and length will be amplified with the amplified Coefficient that has come from not understanding the specific field of search relevance. In terms of this project and its extended schedule, it also becomes part of the critical path. There's only one search team, and with them allocated on this long and potentially exhaustive trek, little to no project or daily work could be completed simultaneously. In terms of cost, we have written off the cost of this project by allocating an infinite stream of cash flow to it. Like we have said before, we can't be stupid about it. We have to consider how central the search team is to the rest of the organization. Blocking the search team on this task not only puts off the schedules for future work they have, but for current work as well. Their current work is primarily dictated by the requirements of external projects; anything that stops them now will have a net effect on any other project that requires their expertise. It becomes a function of priority at that point. Some potential mitigation tactics could be: let the team swap between research of a new algorithm, and/or train another team to work on the search application on their own time. Both are viable, but both are expensive in their own right. Distractions cost in terms of the loss of direct concentration but also in the continued extension of an already tight schedule. On the other hand, we have the entire concept of learning and complexity that will have to be transitioned into another development team, which we know holds the highest bar of each of these activities within the organization. Giving another team the ability to learn now, at a cost, will have long-lasting and beneficial effects which are a direct effect of cross-training. There is a cost and with that cost will come a spidered effect on the rest of the organization, whether or not another team is given the chance to learn more about the search team; now or later. Let us consider a scenario where the search team is already the definitive expert in search relevance and holds the highest degrees in advanced mathematics and computer science. We would still have a wild scheduling and cost exhaustive process to consider. Taking the net effect on the development organization's schedule as a whole, the holes in the schedule this will create in the road to what can hopefully become eventual success are vivid as the sun at high-noon on the clearest of days. Before we move on to the next group, let's summarize what we know. We have a search team who is fully versed in the business, the search application and the existing relevance algorithm. We know this is good to a point, but only a small portion will come to fruition as they undertake a project to start from the ground-up to change everything. Furthermore, they will be diving into a field that is not only beyond their area of expertise but potentially beyond their current capacity. All of this aside, any project the search team takes on will have a lasting ripple effect on their future and the future of the organization. We know this can be mitigated, yet it too will come with a price tag; perhaps one that will shrink over time (and eventually give a return), but a price tag nonetheless. In other words, the search team knows a lot about what they've done, but little about where they need to go. And a detour now will close all the cross streets until they get back, when they have to manage the traffic jam that piles up in their absence. Maybe our best internal option, but it can certainly come with some heavy weights.

We can consider the data team next, which should be a pretty swift experiment. In terms of our Coefficient, the immediate benefit is the experience with the organization. As was with the search team, the existing foundation of the business is an exceeding benefit. With history will come efficiency. The parallels between the data team and the search team end there, however. The data team holds little benefit outside of this rather minute attribute in terms of potential work on the new algorithm. Their experience with similar algorithms is nil, their background with the search appliance is non-existent, and their overall experience with advanced programming in large-scale applications is missing as well. All things considered, the data team really has little to offer. In terms of their task's Coefficient, they have greater obstacles for learning and understanding the search engine's complexity; the most complex network within the organization. Not all is lost, of course. One of the hindrances with the search team is their general availability. Working on one project will block them from working on anything else. Remembering the search team, without intervention and in the current organizational state, they are the critical path of most development throughout the entire company. The same task with any other team would remove this barrier all together. Of course, tasking any team with an entire project will certainly interrupt their future schedule and timelines. The data team, on the other hand, is not the central piece of the organization as the data team and their work isn't in the critical path of the rest of the larger project; the most important development project in the organization (which is important to remember as without the finishing of this project, we can assume the company will fail). Even by removing the critical path impedance, the data team is still a very unlikely candidate. We should remember that with the impact of learning and product complexity, the net effect of the time spent and efficiencies lost by utilizing the data team – respective of the time gained by multitasking the project – are still much on the negative side, and likely not of any great interest to the project. Not even to the point of verifying this assumption through a re-examination of the literal Coefficient. Simply, there's too much to learn in too little time.

The analysis of the data team hides another situation we could take the time to quickly evaluate. There is another development team in the organization that fits snugly in the middle of the data and search teams. The web team, like the data team, is an organization that can allow for multiplexing the search relevance tasks, bringing large efficiency gains purely in the schedule. As with the data team, this will again effect the web team's underlying and exterior schedule. But again, that only becomes an issue when it begins to block a task for the rest of the project. What the web team can bring, allowing for them to take the lead in the internal race of whom should work on the task is their understanding of not only the business, but the search application and programming in general. They may not understand the search architecture and implementation and relevance as well as the search team. They do, however, have experience with the integration between the web and search tiers, which is a portion of the overall search network that is already understood. This alone will give a reduction to the Coefficient when compared to the data team. A reduced coefficient is a signal to gained efficiencies, time and money; all the things we want. This alone is not enough to write off the data team. However, it is enough to bring a heavier pen when considering to write them off. Clearly, they are a member of the top two in consideration, so let's think a little more critically. We can consider them with respect to the search team as they are the most equal. The most efficient way of doing this is minimizing our analysis by ignoring the common attributes between the two. The fact they both understand the business equally means we can ignore this attribute all together as the Coefficient therein will be the same. This still leaves us with the largest of our Coefficient thus far, the complexity and learning with respect to the search platform and the new algorithm the team will be working on. In terms of the complexity, and the platform itself, we know the search team will have the upper hand. The question is then how much of an impact does this make. Although the search team knows their platform better than anyone else, the web team knows more than enough to get them into trouble themselves. The web team has been integrated with the search API since its inception, which doesn't fill the entire gap, but exposes them to the abstracted infrastructure. All things considered, the search team is leaps and bounds ahead in the understanding of the entire complexity matrix we have drawn. Yet this truly only applies to the integration with the application itself and the resources it takes to run. When it comes to a new search algorithm, we have to consider the discount we need to give the complexity, as its impact on the entire project is minimal. At a high level, finding an implementation of a suitable search algorithm has little to do with the servers that power the search platform, the teams that integrate with it or the number of bugs that are against the application. At the end of the day, this is a new research and development task, not a change to the immediate platform. All of these attributes will come full circle and matter once again once it comes to integration, but the larger task of research and development can very well happen outside of the application entirely. We could consider splitting this task down into further sub-tasks: finding the best algorithm to use and implementing it. The first can happen regardless of the complexity of the search network, and the latter will. The task of integrating the new algorithm will be substantially less of an impact to the organization as a whole, where implementation of a known and defined design is orders of magnitude less consuming than implementing the unknown. The web team suddenly comes neck and neck with the search team in terms of finding a new algorithm with this revelation. In terms of integration and implementation, we can understand the search team is in the lead; the integration will be heavily swayed by the complexity of the platform - something well better understood by the search team. Next to consider is the learning that will need to be applied to either the task as a whole or the two sub-tasks we have generated since. In terms of the algorithm itself the search and web teams are basically neck and neck. The search team does have some experience with indexing and searching, as they have been applying this since the original incarnation of the search tier.

However, in terms of advanced searching and sorting applications, they are still quite inexperienced. We know this as we now understand the technology they use. They have adopted Lucine as their core search and indexing application, which does a number of things really well, including abstracting the tough logic of index and search out of the game altogether. Certainly, the team could opt to change the Lucine engine but we also know they have not. In terms of learning, this keeps the web team on relatively even playing ground with the search team - perhaps a bit behind, but not to the point where we should consider it too heavily. Although the search team may not have implemented the existing algorithm, they have worked with it over time. This won't give them perfect information; they know what behavior to expect, where it shines and where it fails. On the same note, it's the same algorithm that dictates the output of the search platform's API, which is consumed by the web team. Therefore, although they're not as neck deep into the issues as the search team is, they have experience through the expectations from the results. Now, this same application does sway a bit when we consider the second sub-task we discussed earlier: the integration of the new algorithm. It's separated from the research and development of it. The search team seems like the clear winner from this perspective. They may not have a perfect understanding of the existing algorithm they never designed, but they do have a clear understanding of the mechanics in front of the algorithm. They are working in a customized instance of Lucine, which tells us one (many; considering one for now) important things: they understand the underlying architecture, Lucine. This is a gap of learning that will put them ahead of the web team once again from this sub-task's perspective. Not only is an understanding of the architecture important; completely replacing the Lucine indexing and search solution will take a deep understanding of Lucine in order to adhere and take advantage of the API available. What's more is the understanding of the language itself will be important. Java, the dominant programming language, well known by the search team, and what Lucine is developed in, is one that is still foreign to the general whole of the web team. Perhaps some of the individuals on the team have past experience with the language, either professionally or personally. In terms of their work with Intellicorp, they do not. Granted, we normally look beyond the scope of the current organization when it comes to learning, knowing the web team doesn't work with Java (nor any other strictly-typed, highly abstract language) every day. The learning that would have to be applied for them to catch up to the search team is likely to be substantial enough to keep them in a steady second place for the integration sub-task.

We will take a step back and recollect all that we have considered with respect to each of the situations after we evaluate our third option, a completely separate third-party organization. There are a lot of options when we start thinking in these terms. We could find a partner company to work with the organization, a specialized contracting firm or even solicit a local university to gain some of their deep research and development resources. Naturally, the differences between each of these options can be quite wide. However, the similarities can be quite close as well, particularly in terms of the Scalability Coefficient. Let us first take consideration into the similarities before we pick apart the differences, as these will mostly come down to the bottom-line than anything. For our continuing examples, we will assume each of the options in this perspective (partner, contractors, and working with a university) all have a generally equal skill-set and would each be able to accomplish the job. If we assume this, we can compare the tangible attributes and differences between this third party option with respect to conducing the project internally.

From the perspective of a reduced Coefficient score, we can look at a few immediate attributes. The most obvious of these is the learning. You gain the ability of domain expertise working with a third party. Perhaps one of the largest Coefficient-bloating properties from each of the internal teams is the fact that they have no idea where to start. The reinvention of an advanced search and relevance algorithm is not a task just anyone can undertake. It's a riddling experiment with computer science, invention, creativity and a deep understanding of what can be done, along with what has already been done. It's an industry all of its own. You need specialists, which is a luxury most smaller companies don't have, including Intellicorp. As we already know all too well at this point, learning is a major contributor to the evaluation of our Coefficient and the reduction of is what we want. Bringing domain experts in will reduce the bloated learning portion of the equation to something next to zero, exactly where we prefer it to be. Of course, the evaluation is two-fold: research and implementation. With the domain expertise comes a potential lack of knowledge of the existing system. There are methods to combat this that we can take a look into as well. First, we can let the contracted help decide on the best method of implementation. From a design standpoint, away from the Coefficient, this is a good idea. A constraint such as the platform of which to implement the algorithm is one that may constrain the creativity required to develop a new process of search and relevance. In doing so, although the new search design will be one bringing its full potential, we would end up with a new learning curve to take into consideration when the new platform is brought back into Intellicorp. What would likely become of this is the underlying destruction of all the knowledge and expertise the search and web team has built up until now. Although the net effect of having the third-party team work on the research and implementation with minimal constraints will reduce the Coefficient for the project, the ripple effect of losing the domain knowledge within Intellicorp will not only grow the Coefficient for the term of the project, but will grow for future projects until the respective team's learning tapers back later. An obvious situation arises that will present it with most decisions you make: which decision will be the most efficient? As we have demonstrated here, the simple question births a web of potential paths that need to be followed. In this case, we must ask ourselves: what is the most efficient for the project, and what is the most efficient for the company in the long run? Saving time now will lose time later, but will the time (and money) lost in the future be less than that of the time gained now? What are the gross effects of the time lost? For example, with the education of a new system, not only will you lose the general efficiency brought on through learning, but there will be a ripple effects that span beyond the learning such as bugs introduced in the new system. Breaking something and fixing it later is a proven and logical method of learning, but the effect will reach into other teams in the organization. What we are getting at is a relative cause and effect. The deflation of one side of the overall Coefficient will bring a bulge in another. The differences can be yielded through some quick calculations. Let's consider some alternative paths to see if we can get an immediate adjustment.

An alternate to having the contracted team work with a blank slate is to pre-define some of the specifications they must adhere to beforehand. The intent of this could have some drawbacks, depending in part on the knowledge held by the contracted team. If, for example, it is the responsibility of the contracted team to design a new algorithm and implement it into the Lucine platform, we quickly minimize the learning portion of the Coefficient in terms of the search team. The future learning will still be obvious when working with the new algorithm, though the learning wont affect *every* project from the point of the contractor's leaving until the learning has subsided. The effective growth of future Coefficients will only relate to projects which work directly or indirectly with the new algorithm, assuming the integration with Lucine is transparent enough to keep the search and related teams at their current educational bar. With every reaction, there is a reaction, specifically in terms of the contractors working on the integration of the algorithm into the software base. In the event the contracted team has a rich knowledge of Java and Lucine they will still have to learn SC, Inc.'s modified implementation of Lucine. Any modification off the critical path of the original download is something any other team won't be able to recognize, and will therefore have to learn. If nothing else, this learning is put at bay with two factors. First, it is localized to this one and only project. Secondly, the advancement of the platform, as we can remember, is minimal. What this means is although the learning will be a factor, it should be relatively small. As we can remember, the experience of one's past will affect their learning in the future. For a team with experience with the core technologies, learning new aspects are easier than most. The smaller the number of alterations, the smaller the impact of learning. All things considered, the overall short and long-term learning can be observed as less than letting the contracted team work with an open slate. However, the effect is still significant, as it becomes broadened to both the short and long-term. Likely, this level of effect is completely unavoidable when something new is built out of the core of any organization. There is no way for collaboration of unseen teams to conglomerate without some level of education to glue the two together.

A third potential option is to solicit the contractors for the research, having them work with the search team on the implementation. This is a mix of the two previous situations. Removing the implementation requirement from the contracted team again lets them work with a completely blank slate. This doesn't completely erase the need for education, learning, and a need for an effect on the Coefficient of the current and future projects, but will potentially reduce it. By having the two work together as closely as possible, the contractors will not have the immediate need to learn the search team's implementation alterations to the Lucine platform, nor does it necessitate much background knowledge in Java or Lucine by the contractors. Furthermore, this will allow for the search team to completely build the implementation from ground-up on their own. When something is designed from soup to nuts, it reduces the learning to a slight simmer. The domain knowledge is built by the person who will carry it, which suggests the overall learning won't be such a factor with future projects. In the same tone, through the integration paralleled with the practical implementation of the research set forth by the contracting team, they will reduce the

Coefficient in terms of the current project as well. In other words, learning will be a factor, there is no avoiding this. Any learning is a loss of efficiency. The point is that instead of a slide-show or other tutorial-based method of education, the contracted team will work with the search team along the road of the practical application and integration into the existing search platform. With the confidence and expertise of the contractors by their side, the search team will gain a substantial benefit of ensuring the proper integration, along with the amplified learning given the method of which it will take place.

Taking a step back with the three loosely analyzed situations, each quickly exposes what may be our best approach. Before we review what we have, I want to point out a major point we are trying to make in this portion of the analysis. What we have been able to do is take everything we know about the Coefficient and apply it without calculation. This is the greater point of this exercise in its complete entirety. To help make the best decisions is simply knowing how, and by what factor, each contributing attribute affects the project at hand and future projects to come. No pen and pencil needed for this evaluation, no recollection of the massive equation we built earlier. It only took a memory of what was put into it and how it affected the Coefficient. Reduction in efficiency can be seen through a much cleaner window when you know how it applies to your organization.

We need to review the different situations before we can make a clear and concise decision. In the first situation of having the contracted team work through the entirety of the research and implementation without predefined technology requirements, we gain the benefit of increased creativity and flexibility. It also brought with it the burden of education. Where the burden is the effect of having a black-box piece of software power the entire backbone of an organization with nothing more than a walk-through training exercise provided by the implementers upon its inception. This is very assumptive, of course, and we can assume the contracts will protect Intellicorp a bit better than this. The point is that someone else's software will take a long time to learn, particularly when it drives the majority of the organization's platform, and when it's intended to rewrite the core knowledge of the team at hand. The impact on both the short and long-term Coefficients, in terms of learning, will be dramatic. The second situation will reduce this, but will have drawbacks of its own. It will bring a much reduced learning Coefficient, as the integration will be required to be with the already built platform which the search team manages. This reduces the long-term growth of the Coefficient in terms of projects that aren't affected by the new algorithm, but it still brings with it a growth of learning on behalf of the contracted team as they will be forced to learn the new application. The long-term reduction will outweigh the short-term, and this can be further explored (or disproven as the case may be) with further analysis and calculation. If this logical assumption (assumptions are OK when they're educated assumptions) is true, it becomes a better situation for the team as a whole than the first. The last option is the best as we can recollect. The alteration to the approach is to bring the best of the first two together, while doing something to reduce any bloating to the Coefficient. We can give the contractors creative freedom by asking them to work on the research, having them work closely with the search team while the search team physically design and implement the solution in terms of software. This allows both teams to work with their core competency, while leveling out the learning of the new algorithm by having the search team apply it as it is taught by the contracted firm or team. This gives us the dramatic reduction in the overall short and long-term Coefficient by removing the necessity to have the contractors learn the existing search platform, while allowing the search team to fully understand the research through implementation. Reducing the long-term Coefficients by the sole fact that we have granted the ability to compress the learning into the current project, rather than extend it out into the indefinite future. Although it's not crystal clear without drudging out the calculators again, it's pretty certain the last of the three options is the last of them based off the gained efficiencies that come with it.

In terms of the research and implementation of a new search algorithm, we have traveled through a number of options. For each of the possibilities, whether it be conducting the research and implementation fully in house, outsourced, or somewhere in between, we now know what the most efficient will be. To come to the raw conclusion of which path is best for the company, we have to remember that the determination of the Scalability Coefficient is nothing more than a few pieces within the scope of a much larger puzzle. Because we can prove a decision we make is of the utmost efficiencies and the benefits inherited therein, it may not be the best approach for the business at the time. This project, for example, we have already determined is not necessary for the current iteration. In terms of Intellicorp's current needs, we don't necessarily need a new search algorithm to get a working beta out of the door. It can be argued that the build-out of a unique search algorithm will create a higher barrier to entry for its current and future competitors. We must still consider the many other attributes of our already successful decision-making arsenal such as budgets, time available, resources available, etc. In our case, as we have demonstrated, we have an efficient path we can take. The most efficient method overall would be to work completely internally on the project, soliciting talent from both the web team and search team in order to build the new product, while taking considerations into the other projects going on in parallel. However, we would have to also consider that in going the most efficient route, we will be losing the massive skill we could bring on with a third party in making an even more intelligent and groundbreaking algorithm. Of course with the solicitation of domain experts comes a price. Gained efficiencies - as the contracted team would - in addition to the current team, allowing the internal teams to work on other projects while the research is being accomplished. Then again, some time is lost as the search team works with the contracted team to put the pieces back together. In other words, you cannot lose yourself in the power of the Coefficient, but rather endure the fact that it is a strong portion of a larger decision you still have to make. In our case, it's one we won't make. It doesn't fit the goals, the time, nor the budget we have as defined by Intellicorp, and therefore will table the decision until the right circumstances show themselves - if they ever do. This is OK, as long as the decision is made in full, with a framework of mindful thought in the light of the best decision for the business; it's ultimately the right one.

Remaining Project Tasks

We have traveled through the majority of our project planning, and there is still quite a bit left. Namely, how to approach the design and implementation of the search API into the search platform; the bot crawler to link relevant searches to the articles and questions; and the design and implementation of a supportive UI. As a decision maker and planner for your organization, the work doesn't stop here. It must continue to the end in order to come to the best, fullest, most intelligent overall decision you can come to. In terms of this writing, we won't. Our ultimate goal of this chapter is to illustrate the different methods in which to apply the Scalability Coefficient, with respect to your organizational needs and the attributes and elements that will affect your decision. The reiteration of the same principles becomes mundane and rather against the point altogether of this entire writing. I won't leave you completely in the dark with the remaining tasks, but we will circle through them at a much faster rate. The intent here is another demonstration into how to apply the Scalability Coefficient with a much quicker mind. Not everyone has the luxury of taking time to think about every decision they make. Some have to be as rapid as the company. This is completely possible when you fully understand your organization, the attributes therein, and the cause and effect each of them have on one anther.

In terms of the design of the new search API, we have two questions; firstly we need to ask before we continue to the second: do we even need it? Absolutely. It is the API into the new components of the linking bot, which will provide data to the web team with the relevant data. Without it, little else matters. Being that nature of the new API is directly tied to the development of the bot itself, we can immediately draw the line between the two which suggests two things: the API and the bot should be built serially, and they should both be built by the same team. These are suggested simply because the team who builds the bot will be the best trained, and knowledgeable enough to quickly design the API. The ordering of these two tasks are suggestive in that the design of the bot and underlying data store will be suggestive to how the API operates, particularly since it will be internally consumed. This will affect the build out of the supporting web UI in that the development of this portion of the project will require a "working" API, but this is something that can easily be mocked throughout the development of the related products, assuming the teams can work together close enough to draw the mock API close enough to what will become the finalized API. Reversing the approach will allow for the UI to consume a non-mock API, yet will suffer the same consequences of design changes. Assuming the most effective method of development is to design the API with respect to the bot instead of the inverse, and assuming the sunk-costs will be the same; the secondary approach can be dropped for efficiency. We can quickly draw that we have two teams that can work on these projects: the web team and the search team. It should be relatively obvious that the web team is best suited to work on the web UI component, which by default leaves the search team on the remaining two components. In the event any of the components are completed before the alternate team has completed, we can offset a portion of the team to the other team to help expedite its completion.

What comes of this is the following:

- The web team will work on the design and implementation of the supporting UI, integrating the application to the new bot API.
- The search team will work on the design and implementation of both the bot and its supporting API, in that order.
- The search team will work on the design and implementation of both the bot and its supporting API, in that order.

You can see what has happened here. We have been able to come to conclusions of what needs to happen in very short time. Little justification was given for a reason: it's subliminal decision-making based off solid education of the attributes at play. This is how we have to react in the real business world. Quick decisions are made every day. Of course, like most decisions, there will be a point where they will be second guessed. When this eventually does happen, we can refer back to the deeper thought process we skimmed over and refer to at that time. For example, in terms of the web team working on the web UI. This is justified simply because they understand the existing technology, network and associative effects. The complexity of the web tier with respect to the team is unaffected by a non-transition of teams, therefore becoming the most efficient decision, as well as lowering cost and time to deliver. This will be the least scrutinized decision. However, using the search team to build out both the bot and the API can seemingly become a quick red-flag. It can equally be justified, however. Both the web teams and the search teams are talented enough to build a new system such as this. The web team, to counter, has a larger team which will allow more resources to allocate to the design and development of both tasks. We also know the web team will be the best suited for the web UI component. Though is the overall efficiency of not transferring teams less than the gained efficiencies from having them do so?

First, the search team has experience building a network of APIs as has been proven via the API already used by the core search product. The web team has the most experience with *consuming* the API. In terms of the network complexity of both relative products along with the learning therein, we have found further gained efficiencies. Neither team has experience with the design of an automated robot (knowing their history both at the company and prior), which means it will come down to the lowest learning coefficient of either team. Which of the two teams will likely learn the intricate details of the design of a good bot the quickest? Referencing back to earlier readings, the web team will be the leader of this, as their overall learning coefficient is lower than the sum of the search team. We have to remember this will subsequently be affected by the design and delivery of the data store as well. Both of these sub-components fall within the forte of the search team for what has now become obvious reasons. We would have to apply the learning coefficient both to the bot and the data store design and development for the web team, yet only the former for the search team (perhaps with an adjusted Coefficient for the latter as it is new as well). We can easily determine the sum of both Coefficients with respect to the web team. With the web UI component taken into consideration in conjunction with the search team's lack of knowledge in terms of the web tier, knowledge of data storage and retrieval demonstrates the solidity of the decisions we have made up until this point. Now, the serial design can also be brought into question. It is easy to point out there are three major components with two available teams, but there are other options. We could have the data team work on the underlying data storage and retrieval, allowing the web team to work on the API and the web component while the search team works on the crawler. This is just one example of many. With this case, however, we have a growing network of communication. With any increase of any network we add complexity. The adding of complexity reduces efficiency, which is something we're trying to avoid. We would be moving the design and implementation of the API away from the data and the bot, the bot away from the data and API, and each other combination therein. This is yet another growing network to take into consideration. And to further consider the education on behalf of the data team that would necessitate the integration between the data store and the bot, summed with the education the search team would have to entertain to integrate the bot into the data.

The entire point of the thought behind the last three remaining tasks is the last perspective we will take: how to make quick decisions by skimming the top of a rich foundation of information we have already compiled. Even simpler, it's possible to make quick, rational, solid decisions when you know what you're talking about. There are some things we have side-skirted, certainly; specific budgets, timelines and other extremely important decision-making properties. Yet, we are working on a tool for our decision-making belt, not the entire belt. This exercise is a clear completion to the remaining tasks we had to work out when drawing the catalyst for the final project plan for this journey.

What's Last is Actually Last

We have taken a long journey together. We have taken a journey that has struggled through non-traditional mathematics to help us make decisions. This has been a different approach, but one that has hopefully opened your mind to the larger points that I have drawn for you. Concentration is the back-bone of everything we have developed. This methodology lets us design a structure of decision-making that is designed and customized from the ground up. By concentrating on the smaller things first, to build the foundation, we are allowed to change the structure easily and dynamically as our environment changes. It's not about the math; it never was. It's not about the high-level thinking. It's about knowing what you're talking about. Understanding your business is one thing and you can be 100% successful at. Understanding how your business works is the level of understanding we are trying to reach here. Not only understanding how it works, but why it works that way. What actions cause what effects and why. Where can we learn, where can we grow, what and why are things the way they are? A similarity can be drawn to the inhabitants of the Melanesian Islands throughout the span of World War II. Japanese and allied forces airdropped supplies to the island to take temporary asylum on the island to assist in their respective military strategies, thus altering the lives of the previously unknowing, native citizens. When the war concluded, the remaining Melanesians began to build airplanes of straw and cut runways in the jungle, hoping to attract the God-like military activity back to the island. This didn't work. As the islanders never really understood what was going on in the first place. They simply sat back and enjoyed the fruits of war with the divine birds in the sky dropping gifts to them. To the contrary, an exploration of the planes and the people that were arriving in droves to the island may have exposed the grim reality that what they were enjoying was a more technologically advanced civilization that had been able to manufacture machines that could take advantage of the atmospheric pressures and aerodynamics to lift and propel heavy objects through the sky. In other words, if the island inhabitants would have known the details of the situation they were presented with, they would have been able to make sounder decisions of what to do with their time after the war had ended. Much like the decisions we have been able to conclude up into this point, the more you know the better off you are. Assumptions can sometimes work, but it's highly unlikely and not worth building your career on. It is the education of your surroundings that will allow you to change the environment you are in. If nothing else, I want you to take with you one thing as you close this last chapter: know what you're talking about. It's that simple.

It is easy to break down the points into a simple statement, though it has also been proven that making better decisions is founded on a highly complex matrix of attributes, each affecting one another in different ways. Each point we have reviewed, each equation we have drawn are all beacons to the larger scope of the situation you are working with. Applied in business or elsewhere, it can easily be drawn that even the simplest things are not simple at all. It's a burden if you believe this to be false. When you get to know and understand the complex details that comprise your environment, your decisions are simpler, as you're no longer filling in the gaps of your simplified decision-making with the sprinkling of assumptions. There's no need to assume when you have the knowledge and when you know what you're talking about, it is then that you can actually talk about it assertively and logically to draw solid decisions.

It is with this that I leave you to tend to your business. Take with you not the equations, numbers or applied math we used to make the decisions, but the process. Throw the math out altogether for all I care, the core of the point was never embedded in the equations. You will have still learned from the concept, although to a lesser extent. What you need is a thirst for knowing your surroundings and nothing more. Satisfy this thirst with education first, then make the decisions you need to make. It's all a matter of reducing your assumptions with structured methods in order to streamline the complexity of your organization to logically step through a decision-making process. Nothing more, nothing less.

Know what you're talking about.

About the Author

Trevor Hall is the Senior Architect and Operations Manager at Golden Guru, where he provides leadership for the design, development, and technical operations of the technology they work on. He is an active entrepreneur having founded LootTap, LLC in 2010 (http://www.loottap.com) and most recently appointed to head the Seattle-based startup WealthVisor (http://www.wealthvisor.com) as President and CEO in 2013. He holds his undergraduate in Management Information Systems and Decision Sciences from Washington State University and happily resides in Poulsbo, Washington with his family.